Rubies in the Rubble is a work of nonfiction.
Some names and identifying details have been changed.

The author has used her best efforts to present the historical events in this book using her memories and public records including broadcasts from NewsChannel 5.
She disclaims any warranties for a particular purpose.

Because of the dynamic nature of the Internet, any web addresses or links contained in this book may have changed since publication and no longer valid.

Printed and bound in the United States of America

Available through amazon.com and bookstores

Paperback - ISBN: 987-1-0879-8541-1
eBook - ISBN: 978-1-0879-8645-6

Cover art by Georgianna Anita Bice and students at Matakana Primary School, New Zealand

There are only two ways to live your life.
One is as though nothing is a miracle.
The other is as though everything is a miracle.[1]
~ Albert Einstein

A woman's life can really be a succession of lives,
each revolving around some emotionally compelling situation or challenge,
and each marked off by some intense experience.[2]
~ Wallis Duchess Of Windsor (1896-1986)

It is nothing short of a miracle that modern methods of instruction
have not yet entirely strangled the holy curiosity of inquiry.[3]
~ Albert Einstein

To all those who have supported my transformation:

My mom, who taught me that I could trust myself and achieve whatever my heart desired,

My brother, Bobby, who was a surrogate father to me,

My sister, Phyllis, my constant companion and ally,

All the students and teachers who helped mold me into a highly sculptured teacher,

Amy Frogge, whose friendship and courage sustained me during my hardest days on the Metro Nashville School Board.

To the loves of my life:
Lori Waddell Bice and Phaedra Dianne Barton, my two most precious daughters, who enrich my daily life and serve as a lighthouse for love and spiritual guidance,
And finally,
Dan Speering, my sweet husband of 25 years, whose love and support anchor me through life's highs and lows, always with kindness and spiritual fortitude.

Contents

—

PART II

PART III

Author's Note

THIS BOOK IS ABOUT OVERCOMING TRAUMA AND ADVERSITY. Widely known by therapists and educators, complex trauma can negatively affect children's ability to learn; they may have difficulty thinking clearly or problem-solving. Shame is often associated with chronic stress, which only exacerbates difficulty in learning. When children grow up under constant conditions of abject poverty, violence, or abuse, it takes all of their internal resources to navigate survival. As you read this book, you may be able to recognize children like me in classrooms, under your care, within your family, or in your relationships. My desire is that those who have suffered severe stress can use the strategies expressed within to help propel others to a more positive educational experience and successfully navigate life as a result of reading my story.

As a student, I needed loving, patient teachers who could see my potential and have faith in my emerging abilities. As a teacher, it was necessary to look beyond students' present behaviors to experience their true essence and discover their learning potential.

Some readers may notice similarities in characteristics or behaviors of individuals or events. The following names, listed in alphabetical order, have been changed: Alice, P. H. Associates, Steve Baker, Belinda Cox, Kathy Cowan, Sue Gallagher, Michael Henderson, Pat Hughes, Henry Jackson, Chris Jameson, Sam Lake, Mr. Lewis, Mark, Jim Nordstrom, Ms. Richard, Jim Roberts, Rochon, Mrs. Spurlock, Mr. Whitman, and William.

Introduction

September 2021

I HATED MY FATHER FOR 39 YEARS. The events of World War II changed Dad and consequently affected the lives of his five children. My profound hatred was caused by his authoritarian, controlling attitude and abusive behavior toward my mother, siblings, and me. It wasn't until after his death when I discovered love letters he'd written to my mother that I began to get a glimpse of who Dad was before the war.

Dad was a bully; he made me feel small and insignificant. Although most fathers teach their young daughters to demand respect, Dad didn't respect himself, so he wasn't able to bequeath respect to me. Even after his death, other authority figures with similar characteristics came into my life. Their domineering attitudes and narcissistic behaviors fueled my determination to fight for the underdog.

Dad never shifted his worldview to match his world experiences. Growing up in Gallatin Tennessee, my father appreciated aspects of a simple life; however, over time he found life to be way too complex. Dad never learned to reconcile the overwhelming complexities of physical abuse, war, unfaithfulness, and loss. Being out of harmony with himself was the fabric of why he was unable to be the loving father his family needed. Although he yearned for simplicity, complexity thrust him into disequilibrium, which tortured him throughout his life. As a result, he lost himself.

I've written this book because of my negative experiences with authority figures like my father and school system administrators who misused their power, thus negatively affecting teachers, children, and employees. Being aware of these profiles, school boards can concentrate on choosing transformational rather than cookie-cutter traditional leaders focused on building their resumes. Traditional leaders place their attention on the business aspect of the organization whereas continuously improving leaders ensure that employees and students are growing in all areas including professional development, learning, autonomy, and health. When teachers, administrators, and children feel respected and supported, motivation and joyous learning are the outcomes.

There are five overarching themes in this book:

(1) Setting Boundaries with Bullies

As a result of World War II, my father became an angry bully when he returned to his loving family. I continued to encounter bullies throughout my life, even as the Vice-Chair of the Metro Nashville School Board (MNPS). Learning to stand up to bullies has been a life lesson resulting in both positive and negative consequences. However, bringing courage to those negative experiences heightened my conviction and allowed me to stand firm in how to best serve students.

Working with people who exhibited characteristics similar to my father provided more opportunities to practice dealing with oppressors. I learned to go around them, leave the situation, and finally stand up and say, "No!" The dynamics from my childhood became a metaphor for the agitation of what was to come working with a superintendent in MNPS. I've spent a lifetime standing up for the underdog: for my mom, indigent children in Nashville, and teachers like myself. The events of this book reveal my transformation through the struggle and emotional expense of dealing with a flamboyant cluster of personalities.

(2) Developing Self-respect

Oftentimes mistakes are made through the voids of our lives. For the biggest part of my life, I lacked self-respect and confidence. These voids threatened to destroy me. Even though Dad made me feel small and insignificant, I learned the power of conviction and strength. From this place, I found my greatest growth through my most difficult situations. As a school board member, I helped hire a director of schools who consequently mirrored my dad's personality flaws. I found myself in the path of the superintendent's rage for holding him accountable to the children and taxpayers of Nashville. His anger didn't escape my concern or authority; it was all too familiar considering my experiences with my father. My struggle played out in bright lights in public view.

(3) Trusting Inner Guidance

There is a force that has led me through life. I call this force God, Inner Guidance, Holy Spirit, and Universal Energy. The birth of wisdom emerges from difficult times. The obstacles to my learning, my profession, and my marriage, were the very blessings that created the evolution of my soul and brought me, at last, to self-respect. Much to my surprise, I didn't have to plan my life. My perfect life has been a cacophony of doors opening and closing. All I had to do was to check in to see which path felt right. Following my inner passion led to exquisite outcomes.

(4) Transforming Negative Experiences

Although I hated my father for the biggest part of my life, I came to realize that it was his presence that led me to become an educator. I wanted to help children who had experienced similar childhood trauma. Through my teaching career, my life unfolded into support for students and teachers, and my existence became meaningful in a new way.

(5) Experiencing Peace

Although Dad served in the most brutal war in history, I see how my life reflected my own world war. Sometimes at war with my dad, sometimes at war with myself, often at war with authority figures, my path to redemption came as a result of my internal and external conflicts.

I've suffered many failures in my life and spent most of my years hiding from the truth. I feared the ignominy of being exposed for my childhood upbringing and my failures. Writing this book has provided the opportunity for reflection as I've faced my past and begun to find the mysteries in my evolution.

As I relived my life through the writing of this book, forgiveness has proven to be a struggle and an ongoing process. With a laser focus on Divine and self-love, I've been able to reach peace. Through my life experiences, teaching career, and the training of countless educators and students, my life has become meaningful in a new way; I became a voice for the voiceless and realized my life had come full circle through discovering rubies in the rubble.

Part I

The worst feeling in the world is knowing you did the best you could and it still wasn't good enough.[4]
~ Anonymous

Chapter 1:

Flawed

"WHAT'S WRONG WITH YOU? Are you stupid?"

My father's perpetual mantra penetrated my ears and pierced my heart. Every word reverberated with powerful energy as his voice boomed, his eyes dark and angry. At the tender age of four, I suspect I didn't understand the deep meaning of his words but his intonation was clear. As I grew older, I remember the embarrassment I felt as my face grew hot and flushed. I felt paralyzed, finding it difficult to move my body or even to breathe. Time stood still. *Dang! What have I done now?* I could only hear the pounding of my heart beating like a drum. *Why was he so displeased with me?* At four years old, I had no clue!

Although my father was quick to repeat his banter about my intelligence, he often commented proudly referencing my sister who was two years younger.

"That Phyllis! She can even remember when Grandpa Neal was born."

Even though it was a joke, Dad's words were filled with pride, dignity, and respect - emotions I ached to feel. Just to hear him say one kind word to me would be a cherished moment. I often heard Dad brag to others about Phyllis' intelligence. "Phyllis made the highest score in the history of Howard Elementary in first grade."

Aunts and uncles commented on her beauty. "Phyllis is so cute!" I found myself looking in the mirror, studying images of myself. *What happened to me? Why aren't I pretty like my sister?*

I loved special times with my mother when she read fairy tales to me. I especially connected with the story of *The Ugly Duckling.*[5] *That was me! But would I ever become a beautiful swan? I doubted it!* I longed to hear some sort of accolade from my dad, but he and others seemed oblivious to my existence. When I heard Dad brag to others about Phyllis' intelligence, my tenuous self-respect dwindled as I felt "not enough" - not smart enough, not pretty enough - just not enough.

As far back as I can remember, my parents engaged in hellacious fights. Dad was loud and obnoxious. Mama would listen to him rant and rave, and then she would scream, "Smith, I can't take it anymore!" It was not uncommon to see Dad backhand Mother across the face. No place or time was off-limits when my father would fly off the handle - dinnertime or bedtime, day or night, in the car or at home. When Dad wailed, I sank into my being - cold, closed, and confused.

Nestled in my bed one night in 1953 at five years of age, I awoke to the horrendous sounds of yelling and screaming. I ran into the living room and found Mother pinned to the floor with Daddy on top of her. I don't remember what words were spoken, but they were strong, loud, and emphatic. Mom was crying desperately; Dad had a Goliath hold on her as he spit pungent words. I have no idea what they were fighting about. Fueled by some internal passion, I approached my father from behind, grabbed him around the neck, and tried to drag him off my mama. Although my small stature was lacking in strength, my very presence interrupted the bedlam. Dad gaped at me with fire in his eyes, but my surprise seemed to render him speechless. I don't remember what happened after that, but I returned to bed feeling powerful, as though I'd saved Mama from the tyrant.

When Dad bullied me, I went inward. I became quiet, ashamed, and withdrawn; but when he bullied my mother, cogs of conflict burned away any of my sensibilities. Strong pulses of adrenaline activated a surge of energy throughout my body. I was ready to fight without any consideration of consequences.

My siblings and I lived in a state of constant terror. Although my father had a small frame, his presence somehow swallowed the room. Never knowing what would set him off, we were hypervigilant, always on guard when he entered our space. His voice was forceful and absolute. I hated my father and was quick to tell him so. By the time I was six years old, my father and I had weekly, if not daily, altercations. The shy, withdrawn child came out of her shell. Not only did I fight for my mother, but I also fought for myself. Our encounters involved my father grabbing me by my long, curly hair, and flinging me around like a sack of potatoes. I'd hit the wall, bounce back as I shrieked words of malice at him, and then he'd throw me against the wall again. Dad seemed eager to fight, to show me he was superior and tough. "I may not always be right, but I'm never wrong," he insisted. If I cried, he told me to dry up those tears or he'd give me something to cry about. If I looked at the floor, he snapped, "Look at me when I'm talking to you!" In contrast, Phyllis was quiet to the point of invisibility. Sometimes I forgot she was even in the house. Even though Dad's fury was not focused on her, she suffered from witnessing his condemnation of me. Traumatic fights with Dad ended with my mother lying in bed with me to help me calm down.

As Mom held and consoled me, each time she warned,

"Jill, he's going to kill you! You've got to stop talking back to him!"

But I'd beg her, "Get us out of here! I hate him!"

With clear eyes and a voice as soft as cotton, Mother gently explained, "I can't make a living for you kids. We have to stay with him. Dad wasn't always like this. The war changed him." I didn't understand the meaning of her words until much later in life.

Before I was born in 1948, my father retired from the U. S. Army with more than 21 years of active service. Although he was a brilliant officer, as indicated by his military records, he lacked parenting skills. He ran our home like a military base, setting unreasonable expectations for his five children. Dad attempted to train his children to do exactly and only what he instructed us to do - with no questions, no thought - just blind obedience. "When I say 'Jump,' I expect you to ask, 'How high?' on your way up."

Each night after Mother prepared dinner, cleaned the kitchen, and started laundry, Daddy laid around, drank beer, and watched TV. I believe Dad was an alcoholic long before the term was coined in 1935. When my sister and I had company, we'd notice Dad coming into the kitchen, popping open a beer as he squatted behind the kitchen counter to kill the beer. In one tilt of the can, he chugged the entire beer. Then he would go back to his bedroom, and we saw no more of him until he was ready for his next beer. On a good note, we were happy for him to drink beer because when he drank whiskey or wine, the demons were unleashed.

One hot, humid summer evening, Mom and Dad were fighting after he'd been drinking whiskey. Phyllis and I were together in her bedroom playing guitars and singing when Dad came in and announced, "You better go find your Mama." Mother was outside hiding from him. We went out looking for her. When she heard our voices, she shared her hiding place behind a car. Dad followed us out the door and fell down the steps. He hit his head and was bleeding. Mother came out of hiding and bandaged his head, but there was no more singing in our home that evening.

I was not the only kid in the family to suffer Daddy's wrath. My older siblings, Betty and Bobby, were also involved in hundreds of arguments and confrontations with him. Years before I was born in 1948, my mom and older siblings lived horrendous lives in the shadows of my father. I knew little about these times, as Betty was 11 years older than I; Bobby was eight years my senior. I came to learn about their experiences with Dad's agitation over time.

For some unknown reason, my father was full of venom and held his family hostage to his anger. We never knew when the blue-eyed monster would appear. The most insignificant thing could send him into a rage. At dinner one night, seven-year-old Bobby reached across the table and helped himself to two biscuits. Dad hauled off and slapped him in the face, scolding, "Don't take two biscuits. Take one. Eat it. If you want another, get the second one after you've finished the first." Dad's thunderous voice wreaked havoc on the family, subverting any peace and respectability in our home.

One story stands out in my mind as though I'd been there to witness it. Bobby told me about it many years later; it only lives in my memory due to its absurdity. It occurred when Betty was 10 and Bobby was eight, after Dad eventually made his way back to the family after WWII.

Betty began to suck her thumb in order to soothe her stress and anxiety. In an attempt to make her stop, Dad painted her small appendage with a purple, awful-tasting ointment. Although Betty tried to hide her continuous thumb-sucking from her father, she continued the pattern. The horrid tasting ointment hadn't deterred Betty's need to draw comfort from her thumb; therefore, Dad purchased a small steel cage that encased her short appendage. Betty eventually figured out how to maneuver her thumb out of the enclosure so she could continue to get her thumb back in her mouth. One night at the dinner table, Dad noticed Betty's thumb in her mouth with the cage dangling beside it. My father rose out of his habitual and peculiar squatting position on a small stool, reached across the table, and slapped Betty across the face, breaking her glasses. Amid the commotion, Bobby was knocked to the floor in collateral damage. Betty never sucked her thumb again. I visualize food flying in the air, my brother lying on the floor, and Betty sobbing, "You broke my glasses!" All the while, Mom fearfully cleaning up the mess in silence.

Another story shared by my brother that characterizes my father's dark side has lodged in my memory. Before I was born, Betty and Bobby were asleep in their beds while Mom and Dad entertained guests in their home in North Carolina. Perhaps there had been a lot of drinking. Betty woke up to find Dad loud, drunk, and angry. While Mother attempted to quiet him, he slugged her in the mouth, knocking out her two front teeth. Betty had no idea what had precipitated the brawl, but the next morning she woke Bobby up with the news. "Bobby, Bobby, Wake up! Mama got hurt last night. She's missing her two front teeth."

Through the years, I recall hearing Dad make fun of her, calling her "snaggle puss." Even though Dad bought a partial plate to replace Mother's front teeth, in later years she confided in me that she wouldn't wear it because she wanted Dad to remember what he had done to her.

Although there is an eight to 11 year age difference between my older siblings and me, we grew up in similar ways at different times. I can imagine my father speaking to his older children in the same manner he later spoke to me. Roaring commands. Preaching that children are to be seen and not heard.

Bobby recalls how Dad spoke to him as a young boy. Dad asked eight-year-old Bobby a question that he didn't understand. Young Bobby searched his mind, wondering what answer would please Dad. As Bobby pondered his options,

Dad asked: "What's your head for?"

Bobby: "For my mouth and my ears and my eyes."

Dad interrupted before Bobby could get the words out of his mouth.

"Naw!" (louder) "What do you use your head for?"

Bobby wanted to keep his teeth so he proceeded with caution. "I don't know."

Dad: "You use it to think! You got a brain in there?"

Bobby: "Yes sir."

Dad: "Then use it!"

Bobby doesn't remember the answer Dad was seeking, but he never forgot the interaction.

Dad had a short fuse. I bucked under any constraints he put on me or my mother. My nightly battles with Dad continued, as I wouldn't keep my mouth shut. Mom warned again, "Jill, he's going to kill you. You must stop talking back to him."

I guess I didn't take her seriously. Perhaps in an effort to save my life, Mother divulged a story she hoped would make me realize the perilous outcomes I could face by talking back to my father. Mother began her account by saying Bobby never talked back to Dad even though Bobby had experienced Dad's rage much more than I. To make her point, she told the story of the worst beating Bobby ever encountered. Many years later at a family Christmas gathering after Dad died, Bobby and Betty began to tell stories about the old man. The same story became more vivid as Bobby jokingly said, "Betty was always getting me in trouble!"

Dad brought a new adding machine home. Betty at age 10, and Bobby nearly eight, were instructed not to touch the machine; however, while Dad was away, their curiosity got the best of them, and they began to investigate the new apparatus. After some initial experimentation, Betty hammered the keys while

Bobby pulled the lever. Betty's thumb got caught in the ink roller. She began to wail, "I can't get my thumb out! Take me to the doctor!"

No adults were home. Mom and Dad ran a gas station/convenience store a mile away. Betty carried the adding machine next door to the neighbor's house to seek help. The neighbor called Mother and Dad at the store.

Dad, smelling of whiskey, went to the neighbor's house to remove Betty's thumb from the grip of the adding machine. Afterward, he burst into our home to find frightened Bobby standing across the room. Dad's eyes were dark and angry. His pace was fast and eager. My father knocked eight-year-old Bobby to the floor with his fist. He sat on Bobby's chest, pinned his arms under his knees, and slugged my 40-pound brother in the face until he was swollen and bruised. When Mother came home that evening to find Bobby's face inflated as big as a basketball, with two big black eyes swollen shut, she screamed at my father, "Oh my God! Look what you've done to this child! How could you do this?" Mother kept Bobby home from school for a month until he healed enough to go out in public again. Dad never apologized or showed remorse.

I often wonder, *why Mother stayed with Dad. Why didn't she protect her kids? Why didn't she call the police? Why was my father such a monster?* Anger seemed to overtake him, and he lost his humanity. I can't understand how Dad could have beaten my brother. He could have killed him! I had a lot of questions. It would be many years before those questions were answered.

I might have been 10 myself when Mom first told me the story. If she was trying to scare me into being more submissive to Dad, it didn't work. I loved my brother. He was more of a father to me than my dad had ever been. My heart broke knowing this story. It was hard to imagine that Bobby never talked back to the bully; however, I couldn't bring myself to stop shooting hateful remarks to Dad's face for years to come during weekly encounters. Knowing about Bobby's face beating only made me more determined to tell Dad what I really thought. I hated him so much; fear of him escaped me. As I look back today I wonder, *How did I escape one of those severe beatings, like Bobby? Had Dad mellowed?*

Chapter 2:

Family

MY FATHER WAS THE ELDEST of 11 children born to Jesse and Ova Ann (Ovie) Neal from Jackson County, Tennessee. My grandfather, Pa Neal, was born in 1880; my grandmother, Ovie, was born in 1886. It was said that Ma Neal gave birth in the morning and by the afternoon, she was out plowing the fields again. She passed that work ethic through generations to come. Ovie was a slender but hardy woman. She gave birth to her youngest child two months shy of her 46th birthday.

For over 30 years my grandfather spelled his name, *Neill*. However, in the early 1900s, my grandfather visited a doctor with the same last name, except he spelled it, *Neal*. The country doctor asked my grandfather, "What's wrong with you? Don't you know how to spell your own name?" This comment embarrassed my grandfather. Although he could read and write, he only had a third-grade education. Pa Neal immediately began to spell his last name as the doctor suggested. Some of Pa's children were already grown and married by that time, but eventually, they all adopted the *Neal* spelling.

Occasionally, when I was sick and unable to attend school, I'd spend time with my paternal grandparents. Pa and Ma Neal lived in a small, two-bedroom clapboard house with running water. Grandma washed clothes in an antique manual washing machine. She scrubbed the clothing on a washboard and then hand-fed each article of clothing from the tub through a wringer to dispose of excess water before the clothes were hung outside on a line. A couple of beehives sat beside the clothesline. Pa Neal looked scary in his bee attire. His beekeeper jacket had a big hood and round veil. The jacket and pants were secured by elastic around the wrist and ankles, and his goatskin gloves were sturdy and oversized. He encouraged me to come closer to see the queen bee,

My Grandparents:
Jesse and Ovie Neal

but since I didn't have protective clothing, I refused his invitation.

Ma Neal was half Choctaw from the Chickasaw Tribe. Although I never met my great-grandmother, Lydia McKinney was a full-blooded Choctaw/Chickasaw Native American. Ovie spent her days cooking and reading the Bible. Pa Neal made fun of her constant engagement with the Bible, but she didn't seem to mind. Words just rolled off her back. She was a distinguished-looking woman with high cheekbones and hair neatly wrapped in a bun. As a kid, I loved watching her take down her hair from a bun and, in amazement, seeing her long brown hair, streaked with gray, fall to her waist. She dressed simply, was kind to me, and I never heard her raise her voice or say an unkind word. When she and Pa Neal took a nap after lunch, I was offered a spot between them to rest.

Eating meals with Pa and Ma Neal included homemade biscuits made with lard. There was always a vegetable from her canning stock. For dessert, we mixed a little bit of butter and brown sugar in a saucer, accompanied by a spot of coffee. When the consistency was just right, we scooped the sweets into a hot open biscuit. I loved spending time with my grandparents.

I remember when Pa made a rocking chair from a hickory tree. He wove thin slices of the wood together to make a lattice for the back of the chair and another for the seat. Every measurement was perfect. The chair was conditioned for his body and was extremely comfortable. At 65, he carried the chair on his back to my father's business. Now when he came to visit, he would have a place to sit. The rocking chair was eventually passed down to me. I don't think anyone else in the family wanted it. It wasn't a thing of beauty, but to me, it was a piece of art. I treasured that rocking chair and eventually painted it white. When my grandson, Mason, was born, I gave it to my daughter, Phaedra, to rock her newborn baby. The rocking chair was passed down through five generations.

Dad signed his name Robert Lewis Smith, Sr., but his parents and siblings called him "Tom." As a child, I didn't understand the variance. Learning why Dad changed his name shed insight into my Dad's complicated life. When my father was 20 years old, he couldn't wait until the legal age of 21 to enlist in the Army. Nine years earlier, in May 1917, Congress had passed the Selective Service Act, which established local, district, and state boards' responsibility to register men between the ages of 21-30 for military service. Dad was too young to enlist without his father's permission; therefore, Dad changed his name and date of birth to flee the clutches of his domineering, often abusive, father. Birth certificates were nonexistent in the early 1900s. Family bibles were used to memorialize births and deaths. It was hard for me to imagine Pa Neal as cruel, but as I continued to listen to the family stories, I began to accept the unimaginable.

Because I couldn't comprehend how intense Dad's pain must have been to go to such efforts to leave home, I talked with Cordell, Dad's younger brother. Cordell was ten years younger than my father. With the large age discrepancy, Cordell didn't remember a lot about Dad's relationship with my grandfather, but he relayed that Pa Neal beat the boys. Pa continued to beat Cordell until one day Cordell slugged Pa Neal. As my grandfather fell to the ground, Cordell warned, "That will be the last time you ever hit me, old man." And it was.

My mother, Eunice Viola Redmon, was born on a small farm in Concord, North Carolina in 1914. Mom's family called her "Shine" because of her happy, bright personality which complemented her golden blonde hair. Grandma Dora Redman raised 18 children and outlived two husbands. Dora birthed 11 children and raised another seven from her husband, William Preston's, previous marriage. Mother was a middle child. She was one-eighth Cherokee Indian. The Redman offspring spelled their last name differently. Some kept the *Redman* spelling while others adopted variations such as *Redmon* and *Redmond*.

At a family reunion years after my mom had passed, I heard a story that shed light on how the "Redman" name came to be spelled differently. Mom's highly educated brother, Foster, was engaged to be married, but his wife would not take his "Redman" name. She didn't want others to see her or her offspring as descendants of Cherokee Indians. Therefore, Foster changed the spelling of his name to "Redmond" to appease his fiancée and entice her to marry him. I find this odd as I've always been proud of my Cherokee heritage; however, it was not uncommon for children to be bullied or excluded due to their Native American affiliation. Perhaps Foster's fiancée only wanted to protect her children from ridicule. It's just sad that such a need existed.

Mother's parents thought it was important to educate the 10 boys. In order to accomplish that goal, my grandfather, Preston, came up with a plan. He financed the college education of his oldest son, and then passed down that mantle of responsibility to each graduate to fund the education of a younger brother.

Preston believed that sending seven girls to college was a waste of money. Girls were expected to get married and raise children. Men were the breadwinners. So while Mother's brothers went off to college, she and her sisters stayed home to work the cotton fields.

As expected by her family, Mother married Dad in 1930 during the Great Depression (1929-1940) when she was only 16. Her sister, Fann, was dating a young military man, Atlee. Private Atlee brought one of his friends, Private Smith, to the farm to meet Mom. Dreaming of a better life, Mom married Dad after knowing him for only eight weeks. Mom and her sister, Fann, had a double wedding in the cotton fields of North Carolina.

The way Mother tells it, she and Dad had a happy marriage before the war. Even though the world was suffering through the Great Depression, Dad's military position offered them security, food, and travel; their marriage offered love, companionship, and happiness. Mom and Dad tried unsuccessfully to have children, but after seven years and several operations, Mom gave birth to Betty Alice. The blond-haired, blue-eyed little squirt with an infectious laugh was the love of their lives until Bobby came along two years later. Mom and Dad lived in the Panama Canal Zone when Bobby was born. Their family was perfect, a girl and a boy.

During the first decade of their marriage, Dad was a gentleman as well as a good father and husband, according to Mother. He played golf on the military base where he and Mother socialized with other families. Dad was a 32nd degree Mason; Mom was an Eastern Star. They enjoyed a social lifestyle, and the two children completed their blissful marriage. From Mother's accounts, these were the happiest days of their marriage. They were intoxicated with love.

My Mother,
Eunice Viola Redman Smith

Mom and Dad were living in the Panama Canal Zone when Japan launched a surprise military attack on Pearl Harbor's naval base on December 7th, 1941. They thought it best for Mom and their two children to leave Panama to seek refuge back on the farm in North Carolina. They would be safe at Grandma's farm, as they expected Dad to be deployed to Europe.

Grandma Redman was a stern, round, heavy woman who didn't have much patience for young children. Eventually, Mom sent six-year-old Betty to a boarding school so it wouldn't be too hard on Grandma. Betty loved St. Genevieve of the Pines School. Now there was only one "young 'un" running around under grandma's feet.

Betty was excited to go to first grade. She would be away for months, only coming home on holidays and summer vacation. In preparation, Mother bought her new uniforms, all new clothes, a new book sachet, crayons, erasers, pencils, and a compass. Mother sewed Betty's name in all her clothes. Four-year-old Bobby felt left out and jealous. He wanted all these things, but mostly he was impressed by Betty's name tag stitched into each piece of her clothing. Mother transformed

Bobby's sadness into joy when she fastened Betty's name tag into his shirts.

I have vivid memories of the farm when we visited on family vacations. As I listened to stories from Mother and my older siblings, I imagined the farm as a magical place.

The old white clapboard farmhouse set 50 feet off the gravel road. The small front porch overlooked a horseshoe gravel driveway lined with purple irises. Two persimmon trees, an apple tree, and a grape arbor decorated the small front yard. The large original porch had been enclosed to accommodate relatives when they visited because it was close to the only heat source in the house, the wood-burning stove in the parlor. Beadboard ceilings six feet in height and maple wood floors helped to retain the heat. Two bedrooms were upstairs with several single and double iron beds in each room. Betty remembers rolling out from the warm feather mattresses under a thick shelter of homemade blankets to run outside to the outhouse before coming in for breakfast that had been prepared on a wood-burning stove. Fresh milk with rising cream complemented eggs from the hen house. Baths were administered in a tin tub on the large linoleum kitchen floor.

Summers were especially fun as aunts and uncles came by to visit Grandma and Shine. Four to six cousins went to the back fields to play in the vast space of the barn, down by the creek, gulley, and swimming hole. Betty was known to climb high in trees

Jill, Bobby, and Phyllis at Grandma Redman's farm: North Carolina

and sometimes fell out of a tree to land on a soft bed of leaves. Laughter, play, and freedom ruled the day. All of this happened before I was born, but I loved hearing the stories about Betty and Bobby's life before Dad returned from the war. The imagery of such happy times made me yearn to be alive during those years.

Listening to Betty and Bobby recount memories of their experiences living on the farm transformed my imagery into fascination. Although Betty had told me she loved St. Genevieve of the Pines elementary boarding school, Bobby told me she missed being away from the farm and looked forward to getting back every chance she got. That sentiment is expressed through the poem she wrote 40 years later. At a family reunion of the Redmons/Redmans/Redmonds, Betty delivered this rendition of her life on the farm when she came home from school:

Glorious Mornings

Eating breakfast in the big kitchen, heated by the old wood stove.
Baths in a tin tub on that warm linoleum floor,
Walking barefoot to catch the school bus.
Then, putting my shoes on without any fuss.

Waiting for summer was always the same:
Hearing that creek calling my name.
That gully was at least 12 feet deep;
Jumping and playing there made my life complete.

My cousins came often and we had a ball.
We dammed that creek with all we could haul.
Bobby, Kenneth, Joyce Ann, and I
Made a life of happiness without ever a cry.

The adventures were exciting as only we knew,
And we enjoyed each moment until we could feel the dew.
The next morning a small tap on the door.
Well, there's Ivy, Sam, Dick, little George, and more.
That gully's calling us, "Come out and play."
I bet that swimming hole's really deep today.

We got dressed as fast as we could.
Opened the door and there the Lineberger boys stood.
Jim, Bud, and Richard were there;
Ready for fun, to the barn we all fled.

Faster and faster and faster we ran,
And I was the first one to jump in the sand.
The creek was our next stop. There was room for us all.
We laughed, played - without ever a brawl.

When Michael came home from far away lands,
Spirits ran high cause we knew his plans.
To hang on grapevines, swing from tree to tree.
Then the final spot--the salvation tree.

Mom says, with a smile on her face,
Your Uncle Pete's coming home today, so I wait on the staircase.
Excitement runs wild. There's a lot of work to be done.
The hours pass slowly, but finally they come.

It's Fran, Linda, and Gary.
We knew where they'd wanna go,
So off we all went to the old swimming hole.

I know it's hard to believe how big that hole was,
But we thought sailing the world was a sight we could behold.
That gulley knew a lot of tales.
But it stayed quiet through the years without fail.

The creek knew and loved each one,
Protected us all, even the little ones.
Now forty years later, it looks a lot different.
The gully's not so deep and the creek - not a trickle.

Here we all are in 1994, and you could hear it saying,
We could do it once more.
Just shut your eyes; let your mind run wild . . .
All of a sudden, with youth in my eyes,
I pick up a dirtball and throw it at my brother.

Bobby looks at me and tries to duck,
And I see the grin on the face
Of my six-year-old friend.

~ Betty

During his military venture, every time Dad came to the States for a training event, he and Mom arranged a rendezvous to bring the family of four together for a long weekend or a week's vacation. One trip yielded a third pregnancy. During a 13-year span, Mom gave birth to five children. My younger sister, Phyllis, and I were post-war products.

Not only did the world turn on its head during World War II (1939-1945), but Mom's marriage took an atrocious turn as well. From the war letters Mom saved all those years ago, there was clear evidence of Daddy's love and caring for his wife and children before World War II. But as Mom put it, "The war changed him."

The whole world can become the enemy when you lose what you love.[7]
~ Kristina McMorris

Chapter 3:

The War Changed Him

As OFTEN HAPPENS WITH LONELY SOLDIERS during a war, Dad fell in love with another woman while stationed in American-occupied France. Months went by with no word from Dad. Worried, Mom wrote Dad's commanding officer inquiring about him, as she feared his death. In the next letter Mom received from Dad, he revealed his love for Odette and demanded a divorce. Mom begged him not to leave her alone with three children with no substantial way to make a living for her family. For reasons unclear to me, Dad eventually came home to his family, but he was not the man Mom had married. I wondered what had happened to change a loving father into a brutal beast.

Dad made his agonizing re-entrance into the family when Betty was 10, Bobby was eight, and Jesse Neal was 18 months. It only took a few days before both Betty and Bobby begged Mother to leave Dad. Unfortunately, she didn't have the education, confidence, or means to do it. I was born a year *after* my father retired from the Army.

I think Dad did love his kids, as best he could. I think he wanted us to be safe. But he was wounded and self-absorbed. Although I didn't often see it, my father had a soft spot. I remember seeing tears fall from his eyes when he watched a sentimental television program, but he never talked about his feelings. I think he longed for a different life, although he never said those words to any of my siblings. I recognize now that I didn't listen to my dad when he talked. I didn't like him. I didn't want to hear anything he had to say. My father rarely showed tenderness except to my sister, Phyllis, and sometimes Betty. He was judgemental, boisterous, and sometimes strutted like a peacock with his hands in his back pockets mimicking U.S. General Douglas McArthur, Chief of Staff of the Army during the 1930s. When introducing himself or bragging about his military rank of major, I'd notice him rocking back and forth from his heels to his toes, seemingly to gain height to his short stature of 5' 7".

Betty and Bobby grew up in a different decade from Phyllis and I. My older siblings were too young to remember Dad before the war. It didn't take my siblings long to figure out they didn't like this man dubbed "Daddy," who invaded their happy home living on Grandma's farm. When Bobby was 10, he spent hours perusing posters of "Most Wanted" criminals at the local US Post Office. As he studied criminals' faces, he thought, *Surely Daddy's picture is up there someplace. Anyone that mean has to be ***WANTED*** for something.*

After Mother completed her household chores each night, she took time to tuck me in bed and say my prayers. Again I would beg, "Mama, please get us out of here. I hate him!" But she softly explained that we had no place to go; she had no skills to make a living for us, because she hadn't graduated from high school. "We just have to buckle down and make this work," she said.

Looking back, I realize it wasn't that Mother didn't have talent and skills; her void was a lack of faith in herself. Though highly intelligent, she didn't have the confidence to go out into the world to make a living for herself and her children. Little did I understand the love she felt for Dad when they were younger, a committment that lasted through her last breath.

I suspect Mom felt stuck in her marriage. Although she was dependent on Dad for the family's financial security, Mother lived for us kids. Dad didn't like for us to be away, but when Dad took naps, Mother took us places. She taught me how to roller skate at the school down the street. She drove Phyllis and me to the State Capital and took us on a tour of the Legislative Plaza. This trip became a powerful memory for my future life as an advocate for education.

We even rode the city bus downtown once to Harvey's Department Store to shop. Before entering the towering stately building with ornate features, we walked past the large display windows artfully crafted to reveal the most current fashions for the coming season. As we carefully navigated the revolving door, we were met with the aroma of fresh roasting cashews which enveloped the entire area. Mother immediately guided us in the direction of the counter to purchase the nuts, a lifetime favorite for me. It was the first time Phyllis and I ever rode an escalator.

Mom gave diligently. She gave her all and never asked for anything. Growing up on the farm, she learned to work for the good of "the family." She toiled in the cotton fields to help put her brothers through college. She labored to put food on the table for the family. "Family" was the most important thing to her; it was sacred. She grew up with a mother who expected the children to sacrifice for the family. Everyone worked together for the good of the whole.

Living through the Great Depression and two world wars, Mother lived a meager life. She only had a few clothes and a couple pairs of shoes. She would rather have a hand-me-down or used dress that someone had given her than one brand new. I never heard her complain. She continually reminded me that Dad was different before the war. I was always assured of her love. Her tender kisses and warm embraces helped soothe me after yet another nightly battle with Dad. Although I could feel Mother's love, I also sensed her entrapment in this marriage, with no way out. Looking back, it must have been excruciating for her to be trapped in a marriage, knowing her kids were suffering. During these early days, my mother planted a seed that led to my craving for a better life.

Living in this abusive home and hearing my mother's rationale of lack of education as a justification to save us from this tyrant made me determined to do something different with my life. But there was a dark cloud hanging over me. Although I had determination, like my mother I lacked self-respect and confidence. I felt flawed from the core. As my life unfolded, I found inner guidance that led me to new opportunities and highlighted a path to make sense of my traumatic childhood. Mother often talked about how the man I called "Daddy" was different before the war. I longed to know more about this man. I wanted to know when and how her loving husband became my abusive father. My search for the "why" has never left me.

Chapter 4:

Death of a Soldier

THE PHONE RANG in the early spring of 1987. It was my sister, Phyllis. "Come to the hospital. Daddy's dying."

The bitter smell of antiseptic, covered by artificial fragrance contained in soaps and cleaners became more intense and diverse as I exited the elevator on the fifth floor. Across the hall, I saw Phyllis sitting alone. She had already visited Dad in the ICU.

"He's unconscious," she reported. "Do you want to go in?"

"No," I said. "I don't want to see him."

As Dad lay dying in the hospital at the age of 81, my thoughts raced. Dad had shown little love or support for me during my entire life. Mother's parting request on her deathbed at age 64 had been an appeal for me to take care of him. Given their tumultuous marriage, it was difficult for me to understand how she could honor him this way. She must have known how much she was asking of me because she knew how much I hated him, but she also knew how much I loved her, and that I'd do any-thing I could to grant her dying wish. I was true to my promise but also thankful I had two sisters and a brother to help carry the burden. Even though I couldn't stand to look at him, for nine years I'd cooked breakfast for Daddy every Sunday after my two daughters and I took him to Mass. His Chrysler Imperial was only driven one day a week when I took him to church.

Standing up to Dad had been a part of my DNA since I was knee-high to a grasshopper, but one experience stands clearly in my memory. I was in the process of enrolling at Vanderbilt University to begin working toward a Doctorate Degree in reading education. Reluctantly, I asked Dad for some information that I thought would be required to complete the application. On the way to church, he informed me that he would not divulge any of his personal information. Within seconds, I checked my rearview mirror as well as my side mirrors and whipped that huge, heavy Chrysler into a u-turn in the middle of a 4-lane highway on Gallatin Road. Luckily on Sunday morning, there wasn't much traffic.

I said, "Ok! I'll just take you home!"

It scared the bejeebers out of Dad.

"Ok! Ok! Ok!" he shouted. " I'll help you!"

It felt good to be the one in control of this run-in.

My thoughts continued to vacillate. A very different memory began to take shape - a time when my father was there for me. When I was going through my divorce, my weight fell from 110 to 87. I eventually took my daughters to Betty's house and put myself in the hospital when Dad visited me. I recalled Dad sitting in a chair leaning forward, listening to me sob about my divorce. He was thoughtful, perhaps remembering his own near divorce, although he didn't speak of it. His eyes were soft, kind, loving, understanding. As my eyes met his - a rare moment - I saw tenderness. Mom had passed away by then, but Dad and I shared an affectionate moment that I will carry with me forever. Perhaps he saw the pain I was enduring from my divorce. Perhaps he thought about the pain he had caused Mother as he saw me lying in the hospital bed, just skin and bones.

And now my dad was dying. We'd had a tumultuous relationship. He had not been the loving father I yearned for, and I suspect I was not the daughter of his dreams.

The nurse accompanied Phyllis and me to a private conference room. I knew what that meant. The doctor came in to confirm Dad had passed. At long last, this 39-year chapter of my life was over. Breathing into that awareness brought me a sense of relief. My father could no longer rob me of my sense of self or haunt me with his demeaning words about my imperfections. It was up to me to change my internal dialogue from his voice to my voice. I thought of my mother and felt her appreciation that I'd fulfilled my commitment to her last request. My youngest daughter, Phaedra, loved her "Pop" and needed to grieve his loss. My children had lost both grandparents. Our family needed time to mourn.

After Dad died, my siblings and I found a box of letters including Dad's military records. In this box lay the secrets I'd been seeking – a glimpse into my dad's life before the war. The letters revealed a part of my parents' lives I'd never known, and I began to discover the man Mother had referred to through the years. The puzzle pieces to Dad's anger began to take shape, although new questions emerged.

From the letters Dad wrote to Mom and from his compilation of military records, I learned that Dad's military birth date was March 8, 1905; however, his accurate birthday was Feb. 26, 1906. Dad enlisted in the Army in 1926 at his birth age of 20 - military age of 21. Diminutive at only 5'7" and 129 lbs., Dad was several pounds under the minimum requirement for military service. He consistently struggled to gain weight. According to his military records, Dad was assiduously diligent,

Private Smith in 1926

Notebooks containing Dad's love letters and military records

industrial, and worked at peak efficiency. Perhaps he found it difficult to gain weight because it was difficult for him to calm down enough to eat. I remember that Dad used to eat raw eggs and take Vitamin B12 shots to help him maintain and gain weight.

My siblings and I took turns with the compilation of records and letters. Phyllis chronicled each document and letter spanning from 1926 - 1987, and my sister-in-law, Anne, inserted them into sheet protectors and five 3" binders to house all the materials.

When I read the evaluation reports from Dad's supervisors, I was shocked at the young man my dad had been. I knew he had a sharp, inquisitive mind, but I was impressed with the description of his "convivial spirit." *Friendly and agreeable? I wish I had known him then!* Dad had only completed the 9th grade, but Mom said Dad could do anything he put his mind to. He taught himself to play the piano and guitar. He taught himself geometry and algebra, as well as how to fix televisions and radios. He'd even built a television and a Ham Radio.

During his first nine years in the Quartermaster Corps, Dad worked as a principal clerk in charge of records, reports, and fiscal matters in the commissary. He later worked in the supply division as the Chief Clerk of the Quartermaster's Office and was Acting 1st Sergeant, Supply Sergeant, and Company Clerk in charge of procurement issues. Dad loved the military and became an excellent instructor of military and civilian personnel. He was highly recommended by the officers for whom he directly worked. Due to the war, Dad climbed the ranks from an enlisted private to become a commissioned officer with the rank of major in 17 years.

Dad died alone at the age of 81 in 1987. I couldn't stand to look at him. I'd hated him for the biggest part of my life, but now this decision haunts me. Thirty years later, I wonder if he might have had something important to say to me. Perhaps he would have apologized for his behavior. Perhaps he would have said he loved me in a way I could have heard and understood. Although I don't know what he was thinking as he was passing from this earth, I do know that I regret not being there for him. To just sit - to listen - to watch - to see.

But after years of entertaining my regret, I decided to change directions. Rather than lamenting my lack of willingness to be with my Dad during his last hours, I made a decision not to deny my past but to seek the strengths my dad had instilled in me. *Were there any? Were there any rubies in the rubble?*

Chapter 5:

A Glimpse

FINDING THE LETTERS AND MILITARY RECORDS were a treasure. When I was a child lying next to my mother after a hellacious fight with Dad, she often reminisced how Dad was different before the war. Now, in front of me lay solid evidence of the man Mom referenced, but I couldn't fathom. Compassion and curiosity began to creep into my consciousness. Through Dad's letters and military records that date back almost a hundred years, I not only got to meet the father I never knew, but I began to consider similarities in this man and myself - some positive, some negative. Dad's life, uncovered through letters in his own beautiful handwriting, excavated evidence of just how different he was before the war. His love letters were indicative of his devotion to his family - something with which I had no direct experience during my lifetime. My siblings and I are still putting the pieces together to help us understand our parents and how living with them affected our lives as children and as adults.

Mother and Dad met on July 4th, 1930. They married after only two months. Betty was born seven years later in 1937 in Norfolk, Virginia while Dad was stationed at Fort Myer. Betty was the apple of Daddy's eye. Two years and three months later, Mom gave birth to Bobby in the Panama Canal Zone before the U.S. entered WWII. Bobby was Daddy's little soldier.

With the war raging in Europe, Dad didn't know when he would receive orders to ship out; therefore, Mom and Dad decided it best for Mother to flee Panama in 1942 to secure a safe harbor for the children. Mother took Betty and Bobby to her family's farm in North Carolina. Dad writes:

It's awfully lonesome here without you and the babies. Everywhere I go I see places we were together when you were here and naturally I feel blue and wish either you

Mom (Eunice), Betty & Bobby

were back down here or I was in NC with you. I also miss Betty and Bobby more than you can ever imagine. I have your pictures on the table in my room. I believe seven years is enough to spend down here in Panama anyway. I don't feel as good as I did at one time. I don't have the pep I had when you were here, and believe a change of scenery would help me a great deal. Sensing Dad's depression helped me to see my father differently.

Dad served 11 years as an enlisted man and went up in rank from a private after six years, then staff sergeant after only two. He was promoted to tech sergeant after another two years, then quickly on to master sergeant after only one year. He then became a warrant officer. In 1942, Dad was recommended for admission to the officer candidate school by Lieutenant Colonel Hollis, who wrote, "With your fine record, you have an excellent chance for a promotion." This was a rare opportunity for Dad to become a commissioned officer without meeting the requirements for Officer Candidate School.

Due partially to the U.S. entry into WWII, Dad was temporarily promoted to captain in 1942 while serving in the Panama Canal Zone because of the "present emergency." Additionally, Dad had received high scores on his test for captain.

"By direction of the President you are temporarily appointed and commissioned," read the notice from Washington, D.C. Dad was sworn in on April 12, 1942. He wrote to Mom:

If the letter announcing my promotion doesn't assign me to a station in the states, I intend to apply at once for a transfer. Although I'm proud of my promotion, I feel lost without you and the babies. I sure hope that I get to go to the states and get a station in some depot or Washington so I can be with my family again.

In the next letter, Dad stated:

You should see my bars and the gold braid! I don't know where I will be assigned yet. I've been busy buying uniforms today. Coats cost $40 each. Shirts cost $15 each and trousers, $16.50. (Those prices seemed extravagent for 1942.) *Sure hope I get to see you and the babies soon but don't know when that will be. I always write every day. Glad you received my six letters. Write to me every day, dear! Love and millions of kisses, Daddy*

P.S. I went over and had my picture taken in my captain's uniform today. With this cold and the way I felt, I guess they will look like the devil. I haven't heard if I will be assigned back to the states but am hoping to receive that appointment one of these days. You better write every day for I do love you so much!

On temporary assignment to New Orleans in July 1942, Mom and the children traveled to New Orleans to meet Dad for a rendezvous.

From Dad's commanding officer in 1943:

"Captain Smith has unequivocally exhibited exemplary characteristics of aptitude and application in the manner of performance of duties and has established by diligent and earnest effort, consideration for promotion to the higher grade. His promotion is definitely in the best interest of the service for the reason that he is considered to be the best-qualified officer in the command available for the position and grade to which promotion is recommended."

Dad wrote letters home almost daily. In April 1942, he wrote 18 letters to Mom. Each time *sending millions of kisses and lots of love.* Each time requesting Mom to write each and every day. *You just can't imagine how much I miss you! I would just give anything in the world to see you - for just one minute.*

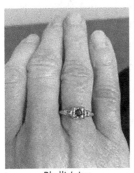

Phyllis' ring

During my entire life, I'd never experienced Dad as a romantic until I read and was consumed by his letters. On their 12th wedding anniversary, Dad recalled the events of their marriage. All correspondence was censored by the military, so he had to be careful just how much he described in writing. I don't recall Mother ever wearing rings on her callused hands. Before her death, Mom gave her rings to my younger sister, Phyllis. Since the original diamond had been lost, Phyllis' husband, Emmet, replaced it with her birthstone and gave the sapphire ring to her on Christmas of 2020. Both the engagement and wedding rings were engraved with "RLS to EVR" (Robert L. Smith to Eunice Viola Redmon), and the date of their wedding. Phyllis carries on her hand a symbol of the love our parents had for each other before we were born. A love none of the siblings experienced living together as a family, yet rekindled in our hearts after the letters were discovered.

Sept 8, 1942

My dearest wife of a dozen years: How I wish I could be with you on this memorable date. You've grown more sweet and lovely as the years go by. I love you more and more with the passing of each year. You are the jewel that keeps me going. You will always be my only love. How this date brings back memories of a dozen years. Getting up early, going to New York, having the flat tire, getting the license, and being married at 12:20 p. m., having dinner with Bill, going back to Cleveland, stopping and having a cherry wine on the way back home. The serenade, the company that night, Betsy Ross, etc. This date brings back to me all those things plus many more I can't mention here. All are pleasant memories for me. Honey, I'd give anything to be with you for just one moment today. When this war is over, I will never let you and the kids leave me again.

As I read these letters after my dad's death, I can feel my hatred dissipating; I'm falling in love with this man! I only wish I'd know this version of my father during my lifetime.

On April 23, 1944: *My dearest little dream girl,*

You said the postmaster said you weren't putting enough postage on the letters. Tell him if he will read his postal regulations and learn what the government is paying him to know, he will see that six cents per one-half ounce are all that is required to write to anyone in the military service. Tell him to wake up. Honey, this was the sweetest letter I have received from you since you left here. How I would love to hold you in my arms tonight, you know? I would just love you to death.

As I read more of these letters, I came to understand that Mother and Dad were both concerned about marriage fidelity. In each letter, Dad reminded mother, *Be a good girl.* Although I didn't have letters Mother wrote to Dad, his response to her indicated she also had similar concerns. *We have five girls in the office, dear, but don't you worry. None of them could ever take even one little corner of your place. No one even appeals to me but you. I never ever think of anyone else.*

When Dad returned to the states for additional training, his enthusiasm with mother was evident in this letter:

You'd better get some weight on before I get there, for you will lose weight when I come to see you. You know? No sleep, sit up and talk all night. The last three of your letters were not censored. Are mine? Keep the letters coming. Your loving husband with loads of kisses.

July 4, 1944, on the 14th anniversary of when Mom and Dad met:

Today brings back pleasant memories to me as of July 4, 1930, when I first met you and we were over to Mrs. Beams. You wore a white dress that night. I can see it just as plain, and you too. You have grown more dear to me ever since this day. I may not have shown it at all times, but really, I have always known what a nice life and happy marriage we would have. No, you didn't ask for the $20, but you needed it worse than I. You can always have anything I've got. Mother couldn't make her car payment in May of 1942. It was 2 months overdue.

Dad's military records were stellar; he was described by his commanding officers as: "reliable, industrious, trustworthy; and, in the performance of duties was excellent, loyal, and willing; he was a man with a very high sense of honor, integrity, and moral character, a gentleman in the very real sense." His commanding officers went on to write that Dad had "an extremely high sense of responsibility, superior in intelligence, initiative, and leadership as he handled men cooperatively; his loyalty, attention to duty, general bearing, and neatness were exceptional!"

Major Robert L. Smith

After Dad received his commission as captain, he occupied the position of Assistant to the Quartermaster Supply Officer as Property Officer. Ten months later, he was promoted to major in 1943. In 1944, Dad's commanding officer stated:

"In comparing this officer with all officers of his grade known to me, I would place him among the upper third. He is an officer with several years of experience in supply work, possessing excellent general knowledge of the handling of supplies and supply procedures. He is an excellent officer. I have found him to be extremely thorough, dependable, responsible, and loyal. He is quiet but follows through. When he brings up points, they are always well worth consideration. He is very much a gentleman."

On October 22, 1944, Dad wrote to Mom from Southern France that he handled all reports and the vast equipment pool. *The 63rd is the depot here. We are known all over Europe. Equipment includes forklifts, trucks, tractors, pallets, floats, etc. We are open 24 hours a day. The depot never closes.*

Dad at Christmas

Another colonel wanted to transfer Dad to work with him, but Colonel Moore raised the ante and got to keep Dad at the 63rd Depot.

Although I never knew Dad to have friends, Dad wrote:

I sure miss Mr. Jackson. He and I got along grand. We had our walks in the evening, and then we would sit and talk for hours. I don't know anyone here. I am writing to you, which is the only good time I have now. Do Betty and Bobby still remember their Daddy?

Oh yes, do you remember one month ago tonight? I got to see you on leave and what a night that was! I will never forget it. Hope we can be together again soon. I wrote to Colonel Wilson again today. I asked him for any assignment in the United States. I guess he will grow tired of being bothered with me, but you never get anything until you ask for it. Maybe I'll get lucky. Let's hope so anyway. If and when I get to come back, I'm intending to ask for 15 days' leave. I don't think I ever want to be away from you for even one night. In fact, I never did. I haven't heard from you in three days. I hope nothing's wrong. Your letters may be held up due to censorship.

Over thirty years later, I sit with the revelation of this new glimpse of my Dad and the moment in time that changed my life even before I was born. I understand I'd measured Dad as harshly as he'd measured me. As a result of these letters discovered after his death, I began to notice a spark of understanding and compassion. I wanted to know more.

I hate war as only a soldier who has lived it can,
only as one who has seen its brutality, its futility, its stupidity.[10]
~ General Dwight D. Eisenhower

Chapter 6:

Reminiscing Time

MEN ON THE FRONT LINES were given mail priority. Sometimes Dad received over 10 letters at a time, but it also meant that sometimes, with his travels, he did not receive a letter for a month. That was hard on him. Dad played the banjo to entertain himself. Some days he wrote Mom two letters in one day; *The sooner we kick the hell out of these Germans and Japs, the better it will suit me.*

Chaplain McGohan is our Catholic chaplain here, and I think he is one of the finest men down here. He seems to think lots of me, too. He is the one I told you that used to come over to my room and listen to the news on my radio. We have been getting good news lately. Hope it continues that way. The better the news, the sooner we get together again. I'm sure lucky to have such a sweet family. Most men are not as fortunate as I am.

May 1944: *I love you all beyond your imagination . . . . There is a ration on liquor. We can only get one quart per month.*

After one of Mom and Dad's rendezvous in March of 1944, she found herself pregnant with her third child. Dad was someplace in Europe but his mailing address was NY, NY. In combat, all mail goes to the APO, which means Army Post Exchange. Since the men were on the move and operations were undercover, the mail went to the central post office, and then the Army knew how to locate the servicemen. This also contributed to mail arriving late.

June 16, 1944: Preparing for sea: *I want you all to be happy while I'm away and you just must be for the sake of the baby and yourself. I'm hoping we may soon be together again. The news seems good on the war front.*

Airmail postage was free when writing to military personnel, which encouraged increased correspondence between civilians and soldiers.

On July 4, 1944: Dad wrote: *I hope I'm home by the time the baby is born.*

On July 6, 1944: *I never knew how to appreciate home until I left.* He says he's living in the city but can't tell her what city.

July 7, 1944: Dad visited Liverpool, Hereford, Cheltenham, and Birmingham. He reports lots of grassland, cattle, and sheep.

I guess you are reading in the papers about these robot planes or "Flying Bombs" as they call them here. I haven't seen any of them yet and wouldn't like to meet one of them. Did you hear or read about Churchill's speech on them yesterday? I don't think they will last very long. What are Miss "Priss" Betty and "Pickled Pear" Bobby doing? It doesn't get dark here until 11:30 at night. Day breaks about 5:00 a.m.

July 9, 1944: *Just think, four weeks ago we were together and I took Bobby out to camp to look at our equipment, and he wanted to go looking for the Japs. I sure would like to take that trip today - nothing would suit me better. Also, you and the children and I were looking for a place to stay and I was so nasty, for which I am very sorry, and we finally got that room in the Chesterfield Hotel. I'll never forget those days and especially the last two mornings. I'll also never forget the last time I saw you and the children. You were looking at the staircase when you said "bye" and Bobby and Betty were running upstairs with my soiled clothing, which I brought down. Bobby gave me a dirty look when Betty grabbed it and started away with it. I'll never forget seeing their little legs as they ran upstairs.*

You can hardly buy anything here. I have a ration card for purchases at the PX. We get one pack of cigarettes per day, 20 bars of candy, three little packages of cookies, and two small packs of chewing gum per week. So far this is enough. You can't buy anything in any of the British stores I've been in, so it looks as though it will be hard to send any souvenirs at present. However, I'm enclosing three English coins for you all: the threepence piece is worth a nickel, the sixpence - a dime, and the one-shilling piece is worth twenty cents in American money. I hope I will always remember how much I miss you now when I get back to you and feel like being grouchy.

I'm not allowed to tell you the date I left the states, the date of my arrival nor how I came, and where I left the land. So that will have to be a secret until the war is over and I can see you and tell you personally. I'll have plenty to tell you then, I hope.

July 10, 1944: For five weeks, neither Mom or Dad are receiving the other's letters. Finally, mail comes and Dad writes: *Finally, I recieved 16 letters today. I can rest knowing you and the babies are well. If you want to stay with your mother until I get back, it's ok with me. I want you to have the very best of care when the baby arrives.*

July 12, 1944: Mother traveled by train from Concord, North Carolina to Gallatin, Tennessee where Dad's family lived and where she recieved this letter. *Tell Bobby I'm wearing the sheepskin he slept with the last night we stayed in Hotel Chesterfield. Tell Betty I am wearing her good luck piece on my dog chain.*

July 14, 1944: *Today reminds me of different dates. Two years ago, I called you from New Orleans, Louisiana, and spent a couple of weeks there before I left for Panama. I hope I get back home as quickly as I did then. One month ago today I had my last big kiss before leaving you and my precious babies.*

July 16, 1944: *Honey, you said you hope I don't drink at all while I'm over here. Well, just for that, I am up the pole. I will not drink another drop of even beer until I see you again. Please believe me. I mean it.*

In some of his correspondence with Mom, Dad talked about how Mother would serve him breakfast in bed. I rarely saw them treat each other with any tenderness. Oh, I wish I'd known them then!

July 19, 1944: *I'm thinking of increasing my bond allotment to $200/month instead of what I am taking, or sending you the money and letting you buy the bonds.*

July 20, 1944: *I just heard over the radio they have attempted to kill Hitler. I sure wish they had succeeded. Honey, I don't want you to worry, especially in your condition.*

July 21, 1944: *All indications point to a nuclear collapse in Germany from radio reports heard here. The Japs are having their troubles too. Are you getting to be my big fat mama now? How are my "snaggle-toothed Janie" and "Soldier Boy June Bug" getting along? In addition to my other duties, I am a censorship officer for 42 enlisted men here with me. Altogether we write 100 letters a day, I have to read and sign everyone's before they're mailed. Some job! I love you so much and I'm not even drunk.*

July 31, 1944: *I would've liked to have seen Bobby playing soldier. Tell Betty her daddy sure does love her, and he'll be back just as soon as he can. I'm still in England and now occupying a room in a farmhouse until I can get a room on the post. I have to pay a shilling or 20 cents a day for the room, but I haven't met the family yet. I've seen them but haven't met them.*

Although I rarely recall Mom and Dad ever celebrating anniversaries or each other's birthdays, Dad remembered their anniversary and Mom's birthdays in his letters to her. On August 1, 1944, Dad sent Mom a Western Union birthday wish.

August 6, 1944: *You get the best care you can when the baby arrives. Don't let the money worry you. I want you when I get back and I want you healthy. So go to the hospital and stay until you can come out.*

My mom was always a penny pincher. Living during the Great Depression most likely influenced her relationship with money. I'd also seen Mom and Dad fight over Mom wanting to send $20 to her mother in North Carolina, so it seemed out of character for Dad to tell Mother not to worry about money.

Dad's description of the war made me feel like I was there.

August 19, 1944: *I'm using my footlocker as a writing desk. Swarms of planes are overhead now. They are on their way to bomb . . . . I can hear guns in the distance but it's a good distance.*

August 21, 1944: *It's been raining here for two days and the mud is half knee-deep. If you ever saw a muddy hog pen, you can imagine what it's like here. The mud is thin, sloppy, and cold as the devil. No lights, no running water, no conveniences, We use our helmets to wash our face and hands, to take a bath, to dig fox holes if necessary, and of course to wear on our heads. We're having a good time compared to the old Doughboys (Infantrymen) on the front lines. Understand, I'm not kidding. We work! We are working with German prisoners here in France. I don't know any German language and don't want to know any. They can all go to hell as far as I'm concerned. They started this war and I hope they pay for it.*

August 22, 1944: *I'm not interested in any women except you and Betty Boop. Don't drive the car. It's not safe. I'm sending an extra hundred dollars to the bank for you this month.*

I love hearing Dad reassure Mother. His desire to ensure her safety made me think of him differently. There was indeed a time he cared for my mother. I was beginning to see that my dad wasn't all bad!

August 23, 1944: *It's only been two months since I saw you last and it feels like 10 years. I try to work and sleep as much as possible so I don't get so homesick. I sure would love to be where I could hear our radio again. I don't get much news here. What do people think of the progress we're making? There are plenty of foxholes where I am but haven't had to hunt one and hope I don't have to. I signed the pay voucher today and an extra $100 is going to the bank. You can consider that an anniversary present as I can't send anything from here.*

August 24, 1944: *I have a nice bed in a small wall tent. There are two of us in the tent and we have enough room for our footlockers, barrack bags, equipment, and suitcases. It isn't so bad now. There aren't any towns around here. I have seen all of England and France that I want to see.*

After the Great Depression, money was tight for Dad's family. One of his brothers, Austin, asked to borrow money. Mother was soft-hearted. Dad warned Mom not to get involved in Austin's finances.

August 26, 1944: *You spoke of Austin getting in debt. Don't start lending them money cause when we start housekeeping we will need all we have as my pay will be cut to less than $300 a month. I am sending an extra $100 per month home now so you should have plenty and save a little. You be sure and use all you need for anything you need but don't lend it out. I sure would love to see Bobby in my uniform. I bet he is some cute boy in it. Also, I bet Betty is some cute girl now that she is in a big school.*

Why don't you just put that old car in the garage and forget about it until after the baby comes? Then you can start driving again. I want you to have the best of care and if you don't think there is a good hospital, I want you to find a good one.

September 6, 1944: *We went to the USO show last night. We got to see Judy Garland, Humphrey Bogart, and Lauren Bacall. Bing Crosby sang God Bless America. Big tears rolled down my face. I thought of you and Betty and Bobby singing it when we were in Savannah. I sure would love to hear your voices singing those beautiful songs again.* I loved hearing about my dad's tender streak.

September 7, 1944 [Wedding anniversary]: *I remember 14 years ago tonight. I'll never regret it as long as we live.*

September 8, 1944: *Do you remember what happened 14 years ago today? I sure do. That will be a day I'll never forget or regret. I'm really proud of the girl I married that day. I could have looked a thousand years and not done as well. I love you with all my heart and never doubt this for one moment.*

This war is an awful thing. I'm not kidding myself or anyone else that there isn't anything funny about it, but I'd go through anything for you and to keep my kids from going through another one in 25 years. I'm hoping that it will be over soon.

The first time I read this letter, my heart swelled and emptied through my teary eyes. Retaliation against the Japanese government was an important reason to fight in this war, but Dad also hoped his kids would be spared future worldwide conflicts due to the progress made during WWII. My hatred for my father began to dissipate.

September 10, 1944: *Received your three letters now and at the same time, orders to move quickly. If you don't hear from me for a few days don't worry. I'll be ok.*

September 14, 1944: *We are pretty nicely located in France. At last, I can tell you where I am. I'm in Paris. I believe it's the 4th largest city in the world. I'm going to try to get some perfume here for you.*

September 24, 1944: *I haven't heard from you for almost 2 weeks. We have been moving so fast our mail has not yet caught up.*

September 28, 1944: *Give me some more time to think about the baby's name.*

October 1, 1944: *These languages are getting confusing in my head. First of all English, then Italian, then German, then French, then Polish. What a mess!*

I'm intrigued that even though my father only had a 9th-grade education, he was able to speak so many languages.

October 6, 1944: *Oh about the name, Viola Elizabeth if it's a girl. How about Jesse Neal if it's a boy? These are only suggestions.*

Oct 11, 1944: Dad talked about different French words/phrases he's learned.

As I read these letters, my mother's voice resonated in my head: *the war changed him*. What had happened to change my dad from this loving father before the war to the man I despised?

When Dad received orders to Germany, a woman named Odette followed Dad to Germany as his secretary and was assigned sleeping quarters with other females by Colonel Thornton. Odette was estranged from her husband. Dad stopped writing to Mom by the end of 1944. Jesse Neal was born on December 21, 1944. From Dad's own account to the military, he had an affair with a French woman, Odette, while he was stationed in Paris. Looking back at Dad's military records, he admitted the affair, which he stated lasted from September 1944 to September 1945. Dad continued to write to Mom almost daily during September - November 1944. It appears Dad and Odette, as well as Mom and Dad, had an on-again-off-again relationship for the next two years. It is unclear when Odette left her husband or if she and her husband were already separated when she began to work as Dad's secretary in September of 1944.

Chapter 7:

Changing Tides

WORLD WAR II ENDED on September 2, 1945. There were no letters or information about Dad for an entire year. What was going on with my father? My mother didn't know if he was alive or dead. In September 1945, Mother wrote the chaplain:

It's with a very heavy heart and a great big prayer that I again write to you. Some time ago I wrote about my husband, and I received your letter of June 4, 1945, and also several from him saying the affair with the very pretty young lady was finished. I was a very happy woman. In a letter I received on the 23rd of July he wrote again wanting a divorce. I don't know what to do. He wrote to his sister to say he was going to Reno to get a divorce. Please chaplain, can't you get him transferred back to the states? I don't want this to go on his record or I could get it done myself. If I thought he didn't love our three children and me I wouldn't bother with this embarrassment. Please try to understand. I don't want him without his love. But I don't believe this affair is love. Enclosed are a few little notes he wrote after seven years of married life. Please send him back to me.

It must have been agonizing for my mother to have no information concerning my father. With another nine months of time passing - still nothing. She never gave up trying to locate him.

On June 1, 1946, Mom wrote the Secretary of War saying:

Dear Sir: I am distressed about my husband. The last I heard from him was February 14, 1946. At that time he was in Darmstadt, Germany and so far as I know, he is still there unless he has been killed or something happened to him. I'm afraid he has become infatuated with another woman. If he is still alive, I want to know the facts, and why he doesn't write to the children or me. I have three children by him, one born after he entered the service for overseas duty. At one time he wrote that he wanted to be divorced, which I refused. Is it possible he has been returned to the United States? If so, he has not let me know of it. Please conduct an investigation. Find out all you can: where he is, whether dead or alive, if he is still in Germany or back in the United States. If he is still in Germany, can't he be transferred to our country? Please let him come home. Your full answers to all questions will be greatly appreciated.

From what I can tell, Dad hadn't met his new son, Jesse Neal, who was now 20 months old. Mother sought a lawyer and was told she could not get alimony. She refused to grant the divorce, and to my knowledge, the divorce never occurred. However, Dad's sporadic relationship with Odette seemed to continue.

At long last, on September 27, 1946, a letter came. Mom and Dad's relationship was on again; however, his tone was different. It must have been difficult for Mom to receive warm letters followed by Dad's coolness. His letter stated he was applying for the kids and her to come to Europe.

Darling family, This is the third letter I have mailed you and, still, I receive no answer. What is wrong? How are you and the children? I made an application for you to come over here, and they said it would be December before transportation would be available. It has been about three weeks since I've heard from you. Please write and give me the low down. Please receive all my best and write soon. Your husband, Robert. I noticed there was no "a million kisses, all my love, write to me every day," only "give me the low down," signed "your husband."

Bobby remembers Mom preparing the children for the European trip. Betty was almost nine; Bobby was six and a half, and Jesse was three months shy of his second birthday. Dad had still not met his new baby boy. They took the necessary inoculations. Mom bought new winter clothes, including a wool suit for Bobby, to prepare for the cold climate in Europe. The trip was planned but never materialized.

December 29, 1946: *Darling family, I will write you a few lines to let you know that I am thinking of you all today and certainly wish I were with you. I love you and am sorry to have caused you all the trouble. I will be leaving here on the 6th of January for home. I hope you have all had a nice Xmas. I didn't. Don't write anymore after you get this. Excuse the short letter, darling. Will see you soon. Happy New Year to all. Please receive all my love. Love and a million kisses, Daddy.*

In December of 1946, Dad was stationed in Mannheim, Germany. Odette and Dad worked together until December 1946, when Dad requested and received orders to go stateside.

Was Odette angry that Dad was planning to leave her? Mom lived through two topsy-turvy years of Dad wanting a divorce, Dad wanting Mom to join him in France, and Dad apologizing for the affair, and then wanting a divorce again. However, bouncing between extremes would only continue. *What was going on?*

Chapter 8:

A Moment in Time

HOW WOULD MY FAMILY'S LIVES HAVE BEEN DIFFERENT if not for Dad's affair with Odette and the heartache that ensued, affecting two families 4,352 miles apart, spanning the width of the Atlantic Ocean? We will never know the exact moment in time that caused a chain of events that could never be reversed. The infamous years of 1945-1947 not only affected my mother and her three children but also would create a thunderstorm of problems for two children yet to be born: my sister, Phyllis, and me.

In March of 1947, Dad returned to the states. Rather than joining his wife and children in North Carolina, he moved to Gallatin, Tennessee to be with his parents and siblings. Mother was unaware Dad had returned to the states. One year before I was born, Dad wrote to Mom while she was living with Grandma Redmon. On October 2, 1947 Dad wrote:

Dear Eunice,   *10 /2/47*

I will write you a few lines after our conversation over the telephone one week ago tonight when you so graciously hung up on me. Thank you so much for doing so. I have terminated the allotment to the bank, which you didn't think of when you changed the account. Today I understand that you had the Red Cross looking for me. Well, that will not do you any good. You have caused me enough trouble with your writing to chaplains, Red Cross, etc. Please consider this final for you and me. In fact, it was finished two years ago except for the bank account which you so neatly tied up, but this is all the same with me. If you remember I asked you for a divorce in March of '46 and you ignored my request for a couple of months. I understand you saw a lawyer in Gallatin and asked if you divorced me if you could get any alimony, and they told you "no" so you refused me then.

I am in the states now, and I will not see you again. So I hope that you have made good with the money that I previously sent. I shall continue to send money to the kids. But the bank account is finished. I told you that I love someone else and that still goes. Just forget me and consider it a bad deal. Good-bye. Good luck; and, may you have everything that you want except me, if you still want me. I am going to Reno when I leave so don't look for me to come there. If I don't return to Europe, Odette will come here.

    -Smith   ~~

I spent hours combing through military records to try to understand what happened to rekindle my parent's relationship after that stinging letter.

From March 28 – August 16th, 1947, Dad lived in Gallatin with his parents. He took Aviation Flight lessons from his brother, Cordell, at Cornelia Fort Airport in Nashville for five months. Dad flew almost every day and earned a Visual Flight Rules (VFR) pilot's license. Dad said for all the money he'd spent on flight lessons, he could have gained a terminal degree in college.

In April 1947, Dad drew up a divorce agreement providing $100 a month for child support for three children. His sister, Jessie Valencourt, was his witness. Mother never signed the document. I'm not sure Mother ever felt comfortable around Jessie after seeing that document.

That same month, Dad submitted a request to return to active duty. Thirty day later, he learned that Odette and her husband had filed formal allegations against him. *Was Odette torn between her husband's demands and Dad's hesitation?* In May of 1947, the Army started an investigation of allegations made by Odette and Justin Iehl. The investigating officer concluded that Major Smith:

> "-Induced Odette Iehl to leave her husband in December '45 to enter the American Occupied zone in Germany to be employed as his secretary.
>
> -Had a liaison with Odette while she was estranged from her husband during the period of December '45 through '46.
>
> -Attempted a further estrangement between Odette and her husband on the 24th and 26th Dec. of '46 at Niederbuhl, Germany.
>
> -Appeared drunk and disorderly at Niederbuhl, Germany on the 24th of December, 1946 in front of the residence of Justin and Odette.
>
> -Carried a pistol into the French Occupied Zone on the 21st of December '46 and pointed his weapon at Justin.
>
> -Ordered military personnel to use a government vehicle to transport Odette from Karlsruhe, Germany to Mannheim, Germany on or about the 10th or 15th of January 1946."

My dad's testimony relating to charges made by Odette and her husband was taken by an assistant inspector general of the Third Army on the 2nd of May 1947, while Dad was on terminal leave in Nashville, Tennessee. According to Dad's testimony, the assistant inspector general recommended that Dad take the Fifth Amendment and told my father this would not hurt him. Their conversation took place in the hallway; they did not even go into an office for the affidavit. Dad didn't think it was a big deal so, as advised, he declined to answer many of the allegations on the grounds that his answers might tend to incriminate him. However, Dad would not take the Fifth Amendment on two of the allegations. He denied pointing a pistol at Justin Iehl, and he denied being drunk at the time and place alleged. Dad also stated that Odette's mother "threatened to make trouble for him because he was seeing Odette." This moment in time was devastating to Dad's career, and it followed him for the rest of his life as he tried to correct the record.

During the period of 12th - 14th of March 1947, the investigating officer recommended that necessary steps be taken to revoke Dad's commission in the Officer's Reserve Corps. He further recommended that "a copy of the case be filed in Major Smith's file for future reference in any evaluation of his service." The Pentagon recommended that Dad not be reappointed as warrant officer in the Regular Army, but such a drastic move needed to be reviewed with other legal opinions sought. Three additional adjutant generals and one judge advocate general reviewed the records but drew different opinions and concluded that Dad was entitled, as a matter of legal right, to be reappointed to the Regular Army.

On June 24, 1957, the judge advocate general found a caveat: "Under the provisions of paragraph 11, AR 610-5, the Secretary of War may revoke the authorization of a warrant officer who has less than three years of continuous service as a warrant officer of the Army." Dad had served in the European Theatre as a Quartermaster Officer from the 21st of June, 1944 until the 1st of February, 1947. His time was four months shy of three years.

The Army concluded that Dad should be offered the opportunity to re-enter the military as a warrant officer, as he was entitled, and at the same time be advised that, if he accepted the offer, action would be taken to terminate his commission under the previously mentioned regulation. "If Major Smith, nevertheless, accepts the proposal, it is recommended that action be taken by the War Department to terminate the appointment without delay, under the provision of paragraph 11a." Due to the allegations filed by his previous lover and her husband, misconduct had been reported by Second Legion French Gendarmerie and sustained by the Inspector General, Headquarters Continental Base Section, European Command, and the Inspector General, Third Army. Dad lacked 10 days serving 21 years in the United States Army. He was not one to let the dust settle under his feet. He had already written to Senator Al Gore, Sr. about his concerns. *I wonder if Dad was worried since he did not have legal representation at this point.* On June 26, 1947, just two days after the Judge Advocate General found the caveat, the Army received a letter from Senator Gore recommending a favorable outcome for Dad as he had never been tried by either a Special or General Court-Martial.

Dad knew the military. He was bold - unwilling to settle if he thought he was right. On July 9, 1947, Dad received the invitation he'd fought for. "You are reappointed warrant officer. You have an opportunity to accept or decline." Dad accepted the appointment with the intention to retire. In order to make an application for retirement, one has to be on active duty. Dad had found the best way out of this present mess he'd created. Statement from an adjutant general:

"Had Major Smith been brought to trial before separation as an officer, it is doubtful he would have been dishonorably discharged. His prior service of 21 years appears to have been honorable and efficient. Revocation of his reappointment will probably only change his status from warrant officer to master sergeant. The service has little to gain by this rather dubious action. I recommend reappointment and retirement as a warrant officer. It is pertinent to note that one Congressional inquiry was received, and answered several weeks ago."

On May 10th of 1947, a report noting Dad's service decorations and citations was documented. He received: American Campaign Medal, European African Middle Eastern Campaign Medal, WWII Victory Medal, Army WWII: Occupation Medal.

After returning to Gallatin, Dad kept in touch with Odette. I can only imagine how much it must have hurt him for her to join her husband in bringing these charges against Dad. *I wonder why the relationship was so topsy-turvy. Was Dad torn between his love for Odette and Mom, or was Odette torn between her love for Dad and Justin? Or both? I wonder if Dad hurt Odette by returning to the States and not staying in Europe. I have no doubt about the hurt my mother felt due to the betrayal by the man who wrote that he would never leave her, the man who professed "love and a million kisses" in daily letters but who had now defiled her marriage.*

During the war when Dad was promoted to captain and major, those positions were temporary, given the needs of the war; however, after the war, Dad returned to his permanent rank of warrant officer.

Although Dad received his reappointment in the Regular Army on May 29, 1947, taking his oath of office had to be postponed. While on leave in Gallatin, Tennessee, he began to bale hay for local farmers, when he developed health complications that resulted in pneumonia. Dad grew worse before he sought medical attention. His situation grew dismal, and his family feared that death was imminent; therefore, Pa Neal called Mother in North Carolina to ask her to come to Gallatin to be with Dad in his final hours. Mother made arrangements with her sisters to care for her children while she traveled to Gallatin.

Mother was a healing presence for my father. Through her constant care and attention, Dad gained strength with her by his side. As a result of his healing transformation, my parents reunited. They began to plan a new future together and wanted to purchase a gas station or small grocery store where they could start over and make a living for their family. Mother returned to North Carolina to collect her children.

You have to understand that PTSD has to be an event that you experience, a very traumatic event. And actually, there is evidence that brain chemistry changes in certain individuals where it's imprinted indelibly forever, and there's an emotion associated with this which triggers the condition.[13]
~ Dale Archer, Doctor and Psychologist

Chapter 9:

Post War Era: Living with Dad

As I WAS TRYING TO MAKE SENSE OF THE EVENTS OF Dad's post-war era in my mind, I wondered what had happened to my older siblings while Mother was in Gallatin caring for Dad during the time he had pneumonia. Because this happened before I was born, I called Bobby and asked him to reach into the recesses of his memory and dig up the details of that time over 70 years ago. With pen in hand, I scratched down his narrative in cursive as fast as my fingers permitted.

When Pa Neal asked my mom to come to Dad's bedside, she made arrangements for Bobby to stay with her sister, Eva, who had three boys of her own. Betty and Jesse Neal stayed with Aunt Fann who had a daughter about Betty's age.

Aunt Eva lived at Horseshoe River Bend on the Pee Dee River in Charlotte, North Carolina. Each day she took the boys out on the boat to cool down during the dog days of summer. Eva's boys were accustomed to jumping off the boat while it was moving. One hot, humid day toward the end of August, they called for Bobby to join the adventure. She knew Bobby couldn't swim so she handed him a lifejacket and instructed him to put it on and jump off when he was ready. She forgot one important detail; she neglected to inform seven-year-old Bobby how to secure the lifejacket. Bobby got up his nerve. He jumped in. The lifejacket damn near drowned him! Bobby was upside down in the water, and the jacket was on top of him, holding him underwater. Eva's boat returned to the place where Bobby had jumped in. She and the boys dragged him out of the water. Bobby never forgot this lesson. As a Fire Science Engineer later in life, he remembered how important detailed safety instructions are, and he never skipped any steps.

After Dad regained his health, Mom returned to Concord to gather her three children. She announced plans to take them on a train trip to Nashville to bring their daddy home. Although the children didn't remember their father, they were excited to meet the man Mom had talked about - the one who loved them, the one who'd sent them "millions of kisses" in so many letters.

On October 14th, 1947, Dad received his reappointment as warrant officer, Regular Army. It was a big pay cut to go from major to warrant officer. Dad signed his oath of office and was assigned to Ft. Bragg, North Carolina pending retirement. Excitedly, Mother and the children boarded the train to Tennessee to reconnect with a dad they didn't remember - a dad they hadn't seen in over three years. After all this time, Dad would finally meet his youngest son, who was now almost three years old. Seven-year-old Bobby fell in love with trains. The sound of the train rolling over the tracks as well as the back and forth motion rocked him to sleep - a memory he never forgot.

Bobby doesn't remember his initial encounter with Dad because it was over-shadowed by what was to come. Once in Gallatin, they all loaded up in Dad's 1938 Ford rattletrap for the trip back across the mountains on a two-lane highway to Con-cord, North Carolina. Jesse Neal was in the front seat with Mom. Betty and Bobby were having a high time in the back seat, roughhousing and playing when Dad began to show his true colors. With wide eyes, Dad barked in his sharp, thunderous voice, "Put your face up here! I'm going to slap the shit out of you!"

Both Betty and Bobby shrieked, hoping to palliate his anger. Mother fell into silence. This was their first introduction to the father who had been more legend than flesh. This was their debut to a new life carved out for them - an age where time feels infinite - a life that would affect them through at least the next 40 years, if not an entire lifetime. *Mother, what have you done to us?*

Soon after arriving in Concord, Dad purchased the Allen Service Station and grocery store with his life's savings. The property came with family living quarters behind and above the gas station/convenience grocery store where they sold milk, eggs, butter, bread, soft drinks, and other staples. The apartment was clean but lacked amenities. The back door to the store opened into a living room void of furniture, a space once used to store animal feed. The downstairs kitchen had no hot water. Mother had to heat water on a wood-burning stove for baths and cooking. This was not uncommon, given the time and location. One large bedroom upstairs spanned the entire square footage of the store below. Two double beds were utilized to sleep five people. Mom and Dad slept in one bed; Betty and Bobby slept in the other bed. No one remembers where Jesse slept.

A single, 200-watt light bulb glared as it hung in the large upstairs bedroom. Each night, Dad drank beer and listened to his loud Ham Radio into the wee hours of the morning while his wife and three children tried to sleep. Looking back, I wonder if he was keeping up with friends from Europe or if he was trying to make contact with Odette. He was not willing to turn down the volume, or turn off the bright light. I suspect Mother would not have dared to confront Dad about this, since she would no doubt have been physically punished. Sleeping with the lights on could have been a factor of post-war PTSD. It was not uncommon for WWII vets to sleep with the lights on in order to feel safe. However, the chaos made sleeping difficult for Mother and her children. I'm sure this was a contributing factor in their educational decline during this time.

While my parents were busy selling food in the store and pumping gas, Dad tried to keep two-year-old Jesse Neal in the living room and kitchen. He was not permitted in the store. Mother checked on Jesse often, but her time with him was controlled by the demands of the business. It was difficult to keep a toddler from his mother since he could turn the doorknob and enter the store. In order to confine Jesse, my father hung a mousetrap on the doorknob from the living room to the store. When little Jesse reached up to turn the knob, the mousetrap went off with Jesse's fingers caught inside. He let out a blood-curdling scream! Dad's attempt to control a two-year-old had failed. Perhaps he was able to prevent Jesse from entering the store, but his screams caught everyone's attention.

On November 30, 1947, my father, Major Robert Lewis Smith, retired from the Army under Commander-in-Chief, President Harry Truman. Dad served for 21 years, six months, and 12 days. Upon retirement, Dad weighed 130 pounds, and was 41 years old. He'd gained one pound in 21 years. Pa Neal wrote to various dignitaries trying to get Dad's name changed back to his birthname, Thomas Martin Neal, but Dad was unwilling to cooperate, as his new identity had been solidified.

No preparations were made for Christmas in 1947. Two of Dad's socks were hung on the clothesline in the bedroom. In the socks, Betty, Bobby, and Jesse found their Christmas presents: oranges, apples, and a bit of candy taken from the store inventory.

My older siblings discovered a father who was angry, boisterous, and a child-abuser. Hearing that Dad had been a loving husband and father before the war - before they even had memories of him - provided little comfort. "Daddy" was different from the way Mother had described him. As I now hear events shared through my older siblings' voices, I can't help but wonder what haunted Dad. *What had changed him from the loving husband and parent demonstrated in his letters to the nasty loudmouth he had become?* What's clear is that home life for Mother, Betty, Bobby, and Jesse Neal was now a deluge of loud noise: yelling, screaming, and fighting. Betty was in fifth grade; Bobby was in third. They both failed their respective grades that year.

Being retained in the same grade affected both my siblings. They began to think something was wrong with them. They both began to hate school and tried to spend as little time as possible with books and learning. It wasn't until Bobby was in his mid 30's before he had enough faith in himself to seek a college education. It was traumatizing to be raised by a demeaning, autocratic father. That, coupled with the instability of the family, had long-lasting effects.

I WAS BORN IN OCTOBER OF 1948. Mother went by ambulance to the hospital to give birth to me. Dad didn't come. At age 11, Betty took care of four-year-old Jesse Neal. My birth was uneventful. There were no complications, no visitors, no flowers. Mother and I returned from the hospital by ambulance. Bobby remembers how distraught she was to find the house a total wreck. No care had been taken while she was away. Not one dish had been washed. There she was with a brand new baby and no preparations for where I would sleep. Mother placed me in a chest of drawers - a common practice at the time.

Mother couldn't think of a name for me. At the hospital, a cleaning lady suggested the name "Jill Anita." That's how my name was chosen - at the last minute, a desperate afterthought - but I love my name.

The winter of 1948 was long and dark. No plans were made for Christmas. Betty and Bobby went out to the woods behind the store to cut a Christmas tree; they decorated it with a garland made of paper chains they'd colored and glued together. Betty wrapped fruit and any junk she could find, sometimes just empty boxes, and put her presents under the tree.

When school resumed after the holidays, the students were excited to share stories about their Christmas presents. The teacher decided to seize the moment and began to call on the students in alphabetical order. Bobby grew weak in his knees. There was no way he was going to share his disappointing experience. For once, he was thankful his last name began with the 19th letter of the alphabet. He grappled with how to save face in this perilous moment. As he listened to his peers recount their magical experiences, Bobby fabricated the story he would tell. By the time he was called on, he spoke convincingly about his best Christmas ever - even while his knees were hanging out through the holes in his britches. Bobby spoke about his new Shetland pony with saddle and bridle, new boots, a toy gun, a bicycle, and an electric train. He was so convincing, he almost believed it himself.

Bobby carried this dormant memory into the future. Years later when his own children were grown and gone, an experience occurred that brought back the memory of that painful Christmas. Bobby's wife, Anne Gayle, had purchased an expensive gift for him that was too large to fit under the tree. She hid the main present in the garage. In order to prolong the fun and excitement, Anne wrapped several presents to put under the tree. Each present was numbered and contained clues about where to go next to find the real present. After Bobby opened three "empty" boxes containing only a clue written on a single sheet of paper, she noticed tears in his eyes. The experience of opening those empty boxes had taken him back to that agonizing Christmas when he and Betty unwrapped only empty boxes on Christmas morning. This was one of the few times Anne ever saw Bobby tearful.

In 1949, Bobby dreamed of receiving an electric train set for Christmas. Mother had insisted they spend part of the holidays with Grandma Redman 15 miles from the service station. Betty was fast to inform Bobby that there was no Santa Claus. He didn't believe one word of it until, while packing to go to Grandma's house, he saw Dad loading an electric train set into the car. Christmas magic began to fade. On Christmas morning, Bobby hurled himself out from under the warm blankets, sprinted to the parlor where the Christmas tree stood, and found Dad putting the train set together. Excited, Bobby pitched in to help and started assembling the train track. Without warning, Dad beat the holy crap out of his eight-year-old son. As my brother portrayed this story to me many years later, I could barely unscramble the words as they touched my ears and bruised my heart. *What could have triggered such a response?* Most parents would have assembled the train set before going to bed on Christmas Eve, so their young child would wake up to find that Santa had come. *Was Dad just a dang bully?* Although he was small in stature, he seemed to take pleasure in towering over someone so much smaller. Any enjoyment of that electric train dissipated for Bobby. Not only did he lose his belief in Santa Claus, but he also lost any hope of his father's humanity. This crisis served as a relic of a lost childhood. Bobby never wanted to play with trains again.

From my perspective, Mom's life had been a living hell, but perhaps she was glad to have Dad back. I certainly don't understand why - except that she loved him, and he brought money into the home, which was important for her feelings of security. Her life had been difficult with three children and an often-drunk, often-abusive husband. At age 11, Betty was expected and willing to cover the babysitting responsibilities for Jesse Neal and me.

Life sped on. Dad never discussed his wartime experiences with me. If he did, I didn't hear a word he said. My hatred was so strong that I tuned him out when he spoke. Phyllis remembers hearing him talking about his travels to Europe, Switzerland, France, and even some of the events of the war. My other siblings have no memory of hearing his recollections about his wartime travels or experiences.

In October 1949, Congress enacted legislation promoting all WWII retirees to their highest rank during the war. Rather than being reinstated to the rank of major, Dad was restored to the lower rank of captain because that was the "highest rank he'd performed satisfactorily" before the affair. Since Odette's accusations were now part of Dad's military record, he began to pay the financial price for his indiscretions. The official paperwork from Washington, D.C. read, "It is not in the best interests of the service to reappoint Warrant Officer Smith to Major."

The accusations made by Odette and her husband had blemished Dad's record. He not only betrayed Mother; Odette betrayed him. His postwar rank of captain accompanied a nice pay raise, but he was disappointed that he did not receive his full reinstatement as major. Although he was awarded three years of back pay to adjust his postwar rank, not recouping the financial benefits of the rank of major was a blow to his ego and pocketbook.

Bobby remembers that one brisk fall morning in November of 1949, Dad drove the old 1938 Ford tin lizzie to Fort Bragg to complete the final paperwork for his retirement from the Army. Oddly, he didn't come home that night. When he did return the next day, his head was bandaged. Dad claimed the brakes had failed, and he'd totaled the car. In all likelihood, drinking had something to do with the accident, but no such details were revealed. Dad used the money accrued from his promotion to captain to purchase a 1950 Nash for $2,025.00. He financed the unpaid portion for $180.00 a month. The four-door, gray Nash looked like an upside-down bathtub. It was futuristic and could cut through the wind effortlessly. Jesse Neal loved the car so much that my parents referred to it as "Jesse's car."

Chapter 10:

Jesse Neal

MOTHER TOLD ME THAT JESSE NEAL WAS EPILEPTIC. "He would be sitting in a chair and just fall to the floor for no apparent reason." Epilepsy is a result of a change in the normal electrical activity in the brain. Seizures can last for a few seconds or even minutes. They manifest in a variety of ways such as rapid blinking, staring into space, falling, or loss of consciousness. Betty and Bobby don't remember seeing Jesse experience a complex seizure, but according to Bobby, Jesse was prone to accidents.

Bobby recalls that when he was seven years old, he was riding in the front seat with Dad traveling on Highway 29 to Concord, North Carolina. Four-year-old Jesse was in the back seat standing on the floorboard. Dad and Bobby heard the back door slam shut. Startled, they looked in the back seat to discover Jesse's absence. Jesse had fallen out! At 20 mph, Dad slammed on his brakes. They found Jesse on the side of the road. He'd landed in a grassy area. Although he was scratched up a bit, he was not hurt. Dad never bought another four-door sedan again until all the children were grown and gone.

That same year, Mother and Jesse were walking on a sidewalk in a residential area on the outskirts of Concord, North Carolina. Even though she was holding his hand, Jesse darted out between two parked cars and was hit by an oncoming car. Mother raced after him and pulled him back before he was badly hurt. The bumper of the slow-moving vehicle hit Jesse's knee, which caused significant swelling. His knee turned black, followed by purple, and then finally amber. Mother took him to the doctor several times to drain the fluid from his knee. It took several months to heal completely.

Jesse loved to ride on the fender of Bobby's bicycle. When Bobby hit a bump, Jesse's little body bounced around a bit. On one occasion when they hit a small obstruction, Jesse nearly bounced off the fender. He caught himself by gripping his legs and feet together while squeezing his thighs. Jesse's bare heels were scratched by the spokes; he began to cry. Bobby pulled the bike over and tended to Jesse's heels, which were red and scraped. With Bobby's soft reassuring voice, Jesse's tears dried up quickly, and they were on their way again.

Things were looking up for my parents. With money in their pockets, Mom and Dad were ready for a move. They wanted to purchase a home in a neighborhood with a yard for their children to play. After WWII ended, Congress realized that nearly 16 million men and women would return to American soil. Veterans flooding the job market all at one time could cause another depression and widespread economic instability similar to the aftereffects of the 1929 stock market crash. Therefore, President Franklin Delano Roosevelt signed into law the Servicemen's

Home in Kannapolis,
North Carolina

Readjustment Act of 1944. It was dubbed the GI Bill of Rights because it offered federal aid to help veterans buy homes, get jobs and pursue educational opportunities. It was intended to help servicemen adjust to civilian life again. With the help of the GI Bill, our family moved to Kannapolis, North Carolina in 1949. Dad and his brother-in-law, Atlee, helped build the "City Service" gas station and grocery store on Highway 29. Dad bought a home on Pennsylvania Avenue. This was just a quarter-mile from his new service station. The house had white asbestos shingles and a covered front porch. Although there were no trees in the yard at the time, Mom planted a small twig in the front yard that later grew into a big oak tree. Inside the house, a large kerosene heater in the hallway opened to three bedrooms and kept the entire house warm. Mother's sister, Fann, and her family bought a similar house in the same Royal Oaks subdivision. Government legislation, such as the Federal Housing Administration and Servicemen's Readjustment Act, helped to fuel the housing industry. Millions of Americans across the country were buying single-family homes. Builders could hardly keep up with the need for housing. With small yards and similar house plans, the Royal Oaks subdivision had a cookie-cutter appearance exhibiting the lack of artistry in post-war homes. All the streets of the neighborhood stretched out in rows named after states. A small airport remained in the vicinity behind the subdivision with old broken-down airplanes from the war. Bobby and his cousins played at the airport graveyard, the backdrop for a thousand imagined battles.

In Kannapolis, Dad worked at a business called The Question Shop where he repaired televisions and radios. I later learned the name was built around the premise that there was no doubt the owner could fix the television. The real question was if customers could afford the service.

After working at The Question Shop during the day, Dad taught at a radio electronics school at night. He instructed civilian men how to repair televisions and radios. Mom ran the grocery store/gas station. With Dad's pension, new business, and moonlighting an additional job, the family had four incomes. This enabled them to purchase everything they needed to set up housekeeping. Mom even got a new washing machine with the extra resources.

Dad was gone from home most of the time, except for weekends. Bobby and Betty remember this time fondly. Dad's busy work schedule offered the family a reprieve from listening to him blow off steam. At age 12, Betty continued taking care of Jesse Neal and me. I was 18 months old. Jesse was five.

10-year-old Bobby

IN JUNE OF 1950, ten-year-old Bobby and a couple of his new friends were looking for something to do. They walked down to the City Service gas station, located a block from the end of the subdivision where we lived. Mom was minding the gas station, as well as taking care of Jesse while expecting her fifth child. When Bobby and his friends arrived, Mom suggested they take Jesse with them, go down to the nearby vacated swimming pool to catch tadpoles, and put them in a jar to watch them turn into frogs. The shallow end of the pool was completely dry, and it appeared to only have a little bit of rainwater in the deep end. With jars in tow, my two brothers, along with friends, set out for the pool located 100 yards from the new gas station. They found lots of tadpoles. Neither of my brothers knew how to swim, but the water only came up to their ankles. Jesse Neal continued to walk out into the pool when suddenly he was in water over his head. The bottom of the cement pool was layered with moss in cloudy water. Bobby continues the story:

"The bottom of the pool at the deep end was slippery. I watched in terror as Jesse disappeared into the brackish water. I immediately went in after him and instantly caught him, but the water was deep; it was over my head.

I couldn't swim; Jesse was flailing about trying to stand on me so that he could get some air. I was drowning, and Jesse was holding onto me, pulling me down. I couldn't get my head above water. I tore loose from him and grabbed hold of the ladder. I tried to reach him, but he was too far away. If only he'd been two feet closer, I could have reached him. I looked under the water and could see him moving his arms, his head just under the water, and his blond hair on the surface. I can never unsee that picture in my mind. It's tormented me for years. My friends ran to the gas station to get Mother. She called for help from the man who owned the store next door. He quickly came with her to help us. The neighbor couldn't see beneath the water so he walked around inside the pool. I remember the water was only up to his armpits, informing us the pool was not very deep, but we were little guys and

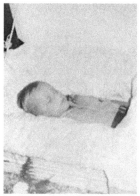

Five-year-old Jesse Neal

none of us could swim. The neighbor found Jesse and pulled him out of the water. He stopped a car on Hwy 29; the driver administered CPR but to no avail. Jesse was taken to the hospital, where he was pronounced dead.

Jesse lay in the living room while Dad shouted to Mom, 'This is your fault!' Mom sat up with the body all night. Our cousin, Kenneth Beam, and his father, Atlee, dug the grave in Cleveland where Jesse is buried. How I wish this had never happened." I was only 20 months old and don't remember my sweet brother.

Bobby had done all he could but was unable to save Jesse Neal. When Mother was informed about the accident by Bobby's friends, she ran 100 yards as fast as she could, even though she was six months pregnant. Our family and community grieved the loss of our five-year-old brother. My sister, Phyllis, was born three months later in 1950. It was a traumatic experience for the family, but especially for Mother and Bobby. They were already in enough pain losing a son and brother. The trauma Bobby felt while trying in vain to save his younger brother's life must have been excruciating, yet my father blamed him and Mother for Jesse's death. I don't like to question my brother about this experience, because I can still see the grief in his eyes, even though he knows there was absolutely nothing he could have done differently to have saved his brother.

Within months, Bobby joined the Boy Scouts of America and became an excellent swimmer. Over time, Bobby made it his personal responsibility that no other sibling would drown like his brother. He taught me how to swim, how to save another if drowning, how to administer artificial respiration, and how to navigate water safely - all the things he had not been able to accomplish for his brother. Bobby continued to think, *If only I'd had this training earlier, I could've saved Jesse.*

During the days of my youth, a picture of Jesse Neal riding a horse sat on our piano. As a child, I admired the picture and dreamed of a horse ride. When I was very young, I remember asking Mother, "Who is the little boy on the horse?" She told me it was my brother who had drowned when he was five years old. The picture had been taken just two weeks before the accident. Seeing the pain in her eyes, I asked no additional questions. Growing up, we never talked about Jesse's death. It seemed too painful to ask Mother for details. It wasn't until 1978 (28 years later), after Mom died of breast cancer at age 64, that I called Bobby to ask if Phyllis and I could visit him at his home in Georgia to hear about the events of Jesse's death. As a grown woman with children of my own, I finally learned about Jesse Neal's mysterious death, thanks to my brother's willingness to share his horrific and devastating experience with me.

Picture of my brother, Jesse, that stood on the piano

I learned that my parents sued the owner of the pool, which had no fence to keep young children or animals away. They won the lawsuit and were awarded a settlement due to the owner's negligence. The owner of the pool never paid.

Meanwhile, Dad tried to get his military records corrected. If successful, it would have boosted Dad's broken ego. He wholeheartedly believed he deserved to be reinstated to the rank, grade, and pay of major.

TIME MOVED THE CALENDAR FORWARD TO A NEW SCHOOL YEAR. It was still hot outside as the morning sun chased the dew away. If only the sunlight could chase away Bobby's feelings of isolation and loss! Witnessing Jesse's death was a life-changing event for Bobby, but Mom and Dad's pain was too intense for them to face or even discuss their agony; therefore, not another word was spoken about Jesse. At only 10 years of age, Bobby was completely isolated with no one to talk with about his anxiety, which manifested in nightmares. Coping with such emotional upheaval negatively affected Bobby's ability to focus on school. In October, Bobby brought home a report card revealing poor grades. He remembers, "Dad beat the holy crap out of me, and that was the last time he ever saw my real report card."

My traumatized brother, who later became an engineer, may not have been school smart in those days, but he was most definitely streetwise. Bobby was good at devising stories to get him out of tight spots. He convinced his teacher that he'd lost his report card; she issued him a second. Bobby had a plan to save himself from more beatings. Betty began to forge Dad's signature on all of Bobby's authentic report cards. With the extra card in hand, Bobby presented a falsified progress report to Dad with manufactured grades. Bobby didn't make himself out to be a straight-A student; he entered grades that were more believable: one A, two or more Bs, and the rest Cs. For the next nine years, Betty signed Dad's name to Bobby's accurate report cards, while Bobby offered Dad a modified replacement for his signature. This method ensured Bobby's escape from any more whippings for poor grades. Bobby didn't backtalk Daddy as I did; he just outsmarted him.

In 1951, with more money in his pocket, Dad bought a new, two-door, black Chevrolet with a red/grey interior. It had an automatic transmission called "power glide." That rainy Christmas Eve didn't dampen anyone's spirits. Betty and Bobby remember this as the best Christmas of their youth. On Pennsylvania Avenue, Dad came home with two new Hawthorn bicycles. Bobby's bike had a basket, luggage carrier, horn, and a light. At 11 years old, Bobby was so excited he could hardly sleep. Lying in bed, he woke up several times during the night to see that big wheel lit by the moonlight shining through the window of his room. This was his ticket to freedom. Bobby rode his bike a mile to school each day and kept it polished. The family was finally settled after the trauma of Jesse's death.

Maybe it's not always about trying to fix something broken.
Maybe it's about starting over and creating something better.[15]
~ www.idlehearts.com

Chapter 11:

Starting Over in Tennessee

I HAVE FEW MEMORIES OF WHEN OUR FAMILY MOVED to Tennessee in 1952. I was only four. It was a mysterious time. Seeking answers about my childhood, I called Bobby to vicariously re-experience the days of my early youth. Bobby remembers that one morning at the crack of dawn - all out of the clear blue sky - Dad instructed, "*Get in the car! We're loading up to move to Tennessee.*" There were no explanations, no time for Betty and Bobby to say "goodbye" to their many friends, no memories of any fights that night between our parents. No memories of a moving truck. No talk of selling the house. We just all piled into the car, drove away from our Pennsylvania Avenue home, and moved to Nashville, Tennessee.

This brings up more questions with no answers. *What did they do with their furniture? Was my Aunt Fann, who lived in the neighborhood, aware of the move? Were they running away from something? What was the immediacy of this move?*

Using the GI Bill, Mom and Dad bought a brand new home in the Marlin Meadows subdivision in the small town of Madison, nestled on the outskirts of Nashville. They bought new furniture, new window coverings, a washing machine, a dryer, and a new lawnmower. Our home was three miles down Neely's Bend Road, known to Madisonians as "The Bend." Dad rented a building in Gallatin and opened his television repair shop called The Question Shop, located over 20 miles from our home. In those days, it cost money to make a long-distance phone call. Dad thought it best to live far enough away so he wouldn't be disturbed in the middle of the night or on weekends when someone had television problems. I suspect that had happened frequently when our family lived adjacent to the store in Concord and even in Kannapolis.

I'm not sure if this is my true memory or a memory of what I've been told. In my mind, I clearly see grass, three feet high on the acre lot on Coggin Pass. *Was it grass, or were they tall weeds?* The grass was blooming and resembled wheat. Bobby

Lively lad
used to cut
tall grass.

used a sling blade, which was probably the most efficient way to level the grass. I clearly remember the swish, swish, swish on those hot summer days.

There were no trees or shrubs on the acre lot. I doubt Dad helped cut the grass as I never once saw him behind a lawnmower. I imagine Bobby had blisters on his hand, and it must have taken many days to cut the grass low enough to be able to mow it. Our gravel driveway came directly off the busy Neely's Bend Road. The house had three bedrooms with separate living and dining rooms. Oak floors were laid throughout the house. Wall heaters in each room allowed for individual room temperature control. Through the years, Mother planted trees and shrubs. She dug up baby pine trees in North Carolina and transplanted them along the side of the yard. Family and friends in N.C. said, "Oh, those pine trees won't live long in Tennessee, but they flourished and still stand tall today.

Home on Coggin Pass, Madison

IT WAS AN UNUSUALLY WARM OCTOBER for Halloween trick-or-treaters as the harvest moon pierced the starless, black sky. Historically, Mother would take us to various neighborhoods and wait in the car while Phyllis and I did our bidding for candy at the front doors of homes open for goblins. I'd been sick with the flu and home from school for two days. I must have been complaining about all I was missing. Bobby could tell how disappointed I was. I could see Mother and Bobby talking together in the other room, and then Bobby came in with a sheet. He invited me to climb on his shoulders. Mother threw the sheet over my head and measured where both my eyes and Bobby's eyes were located behind the sheet. I climbed down while Mother cut two circles out in the sheet for my eyes and a rectangle for Bobby's view. Bobby and I colored around the circles with black Magic Markers. I drew on some eyelashes. Once again I climbed on Bobby's shoulders. Mother draped us with the sheet and Bobby walked me around the yard several times. I followed his lead with ghost sounds - "Ooooo!" moving up a jagged scale of eight notes. I perceived myself as the biggest ghost in history. Because Bobby loved animals and they loved him, there was a parade of dogs and cats following us around the yard after just a few minutes. It was my best Halloween - ever!

Many memories of Bobby and Betty's last years at home flood through my mind, but Friday night football conjures sweet times when all of Madison filled the Madison High School (MHS) football bleachers to cheer for the Rams. Bobby played football; Betty played the clarinet and marched in the band as a student in the first graduating class at the brand new MHS. The Madison community proudly referred to ourselves as "Hillbillies" and came out in droves to support the kids. Traffic filled the roads. Cars parked in front of houses on side streets as the parking lots were bursting at the seams. My father didn't miss a football game; neither did I. Just walking through the gates, hearing the buzz of voices from smiling faces while the drums beat to a rhythmical cadence, sent a chill down my spine. Mother made me an orange dress to wear to the football games though she rarely attended. I suspect a few hours at home alone was a welcome reprieve. Dad even bought us cokes and popcorn. Tears flooded my eyes when the band played the Star-Spangled Banner and everyone stood at attention with respect. I didn't watch the football game unless Dad announced that Bobby was in. My eyes were on the cheerleaders. How cute they were! I was fascinated with their agility and skill. I was equally fascinated with the marching band, although I could never identify my sister as I watched the intricate moves forming patterns across the field. Friday night football seemed to have been a holy time because I felt free in the open air with Dad on his best behavior. This is one of the few places I felt at peace in his company.

I was surprised to later hear from Bobby that Dad never discussed football with him. No discussion of the plays. No "atta boys" or even "Why didn't you catch that ball?" He never asked Bobby how he felt or if he'd had a good day. But at the game, Dad seemed different to me. My brother was fast on his feet but had a smaller frame like my mom and dad. He spent a lot of time on the bench but when he played, my sister and I perked up and paid attention to the game, although we often didn't understand what was going on. We just heard, "Bobby's in!" and we started looking for our brother.

Years later when we were both adults, Bobby visited me at my home in close vicinity to the high school. After running a few miles together, we decided to run down the football field. Bobby said, "Man, this is eerie! I remember running through this field, seeing a big guy a hundred pounds bigger than me coming straight for me." His eyes grew big as his forehead lifted. "Scared the holy shit out of me!"

Betty and Bobby started school at the new state-of-the-art Madison High School. Betty was in 10th grade; Bobby was in 7th. The sophomore class would be the first to graduate using the phased-in approach. When MHS first opened, it originally included students in 7th through 10th grades, adding a new grade each year to complete grade 12. Betty claimed she was a senior for three years because she and her peers were in the highest grade for three consecutive years: sophomore, junior and senior. She graduated in 1956.

Madison was a hoppin' place in the 1950's, with a population of 11,200 and 175 businesses. It was home to an array of country music artists including Maybell Carter, Kitty Wells, Earl Scruggs, Everly Brothers, John Hartford, Hank Snow, Loretta Lynn, Patsy Cline, Lester Flatts, and many others.

Mrs. H. L. Bateman, 38-year principal at Stratton Elementary, started the celebration of Madison Hillbilly Day in 1953 to help benefit her school. It was such a hit that it became an annual event that continued through 1976. Attendance increased from a few thousand to 85,000 and finally to 150,000. Proceeds benefited schools across the area as well as the Madison Little League Baseball Park.

I remember in the early years of Hillbilly Days, men were required to wear a bandana around their necks or they would be thrown into "Hillbilly jail." When arrested, pictures were taken of the "convict" behind bars, and then the "convict" was released to enjoy the festivities. My father took it seriously and kept his neckerchief nearby when traveling to The Question Shop on those Saturday mornings in October. The attire for Hillbilly Day attendees included men in overalls with straw hats and long beards with corn cob pipes, women in long skirts with hats and bonnets, and children in pigtails with painted freckles donning sombreros.

Thousands of young and old lined both sides of Gallatin Road to watch the Hillbilly Day Parade that featured local marching bands, old automobiles, wagons pulled by mules, floats to advertise local businesses, and candidates for office. Dignitaries who participated in the parade included State Representative Richard Fulton, Mayor Beverly Briley, Mrs. Frank C. Clement, the governor's wife, and a variety of judges and court clerks.

Our family could be found weaving in and out of the crowd of hillbillies. Betty was in the MHS marching band wearing her orange and white uniform; Bobby could be found along the parade route socializing with his tribe of friends. After the parade, Mom would watch over Phyllis and me as we rode the Ferris wheel and then feasted on hamburgers, corn on the cob, and cotton candy.

I loved it when Bobby spent time with me. As early as I can remember, we played games like "Keep Jill Off My Bed." I would try to get on his bed, and he would joyfully push me away. Both of us laughing, I tried again from different paths; he used his long arms and legs to keep me off his bed. If I got on his nerves, I never knew it. Finally, he would say, "Go on now and don't get me in trouble." Somehow I understood and let him enjoy lying on his bed in peace.

Bobby was a Mama's boy, and he was proud of it; I was a Mama's girl. Mother was my lifeline. We were devoted to her! When Bobby was 15, he worked on a milk truck. He got up at 3:30 in the mornings to help deliver milk to residents down Neely's Bend Road. In return for his work, he received a small paycheck and the family received milk. Bobby learned the importance of family and how everyone was expected to work together for the good of the whole. After his milk route, Bobby headed off to MHS where he practiced football after school. Each week when Bobby got paid, he gave his small check to Mother to help buy groceries. Like Bobby, I wanted to take care of Mother. Through the years, all of us kids begged her to leave the devil we called "Daddy;" however, Mother stayed with him. In the 1940s and '50s, divorces were rare. Mom accepted her life and seemed to surrender to its circumstances.

Since Betty was two years older than Bobby, they had their own separate friends. As Betty and Bobby grew older, they spent more time away from the house. Betty worked at the Montague drive-in theatre, so we didn't see much of her. She was either at school, band practice, or working. When she had any free time, she hung out with her friends. My older siblings seemed to have had a lot more freedom and flexibility than Phyllis and I ever had when we were their ages. Bobby had friends who would drive by, call for him, and he'd jump in their car. As he was leaving, he'd yell to his younger sister, "Jill, tell Mother I went with PeeWee." Eight years later, when I was his age and asked Dad for permission to go anywhere, his answer was always a resounding, "No!"

Before the time of remote controls, Dad would call out to Phyllis or me to come to his bedroom and turn the TV channel or adjust the socks on his feet. Country living in the early 1900s didn't offer indoor plumbing, and Dad was not in the habit of bathing. I suspect his socks had stuck to his feet. Phyllis and I began to hate the sound of his voice calling our names. By the time I was 12, Dad stopped calling my name. He defaulted to Phyllis. Even though I was relieved he'd stopped bellowing to me, ignoring me felt even worse.

Coco, Flicka, Corkey, Jill, and Phyllis

Growing up on the bend, we had a dog named Coco. It was customary for Flicka, the cat, to snuggle

Easter Sunday 1953
Betty, Bobby, Phyllis, and Jill

on top of Coco's soft brown fur as they lay in the sun together. Even though there was turmoil inside the walls of our home, outside the animals seemed to know peace and love. Coco got into a fight with another dog. Because my parents didn't spend money on animals, Bobby took matters into his own hands and crazy-glued Coco's wound. The dog recovered! After that, Mother dreamed of Bobby becoming a veterinarian. She began to save as much money as she could to send him to college for that vocation.

Easter was a time for new clothes. This was also a time Betty and Bobby took us to church. I don't remember Mother or Dad joining us, but it was important to Mother that we attend.

In preparation for Easter, Phyllis and I received two ducks one year and two chickens the next. As the ducks grew older, we eventually took them to Old Hickory Lake to release them back to their natural habitat. The chickens were a different story. One chicken killed the other and then became the best watchdog we'd ever had. That rooster would not let anyone cross our yard. He would come after any invader, human or animal. We all began to fear that dang chicken. My sister-in-law, Anne Gayle, remembers that Mother would throw a pot of hot water from the back door before making a run for the car. She wasn't always successful in escaping the grasp of the chicken. Bobby had built Phyllis and me a little treehouse in the backyard with stairs up to the platform. Once we saw Mom run up the stairs to escape the pecking of that awful fowl. At last, Dad caught the chicken, wrung his neck, and we ate him for Sunday dinner.

Brothers are like streetlights along the road. They don't make the distance any shorter, but they light up the path, and make the walk worthwhile.[16]
~ Unknown

Chapter 12:

Bobby

Since dad bought a new car every few years, in 1954 he bought a Buick. The notes were $365.00/month; he paid it off in six months. As Bobby approached age 16, he dreamed of driving Dad's beautiful sky-blue, 1954 Buick Century. My brother thought the car was a jewel; he washed it every few days, waxed it once a week, and kept it clean from bumper to bumper. Dad allowed Bobby to start driving the sedan the day he turned 16 and got his driver's license. Bobby liked nothing more than cruising around Madison Square in Dad's hard-top convertible. Being seen by his friends in this cool car made him feel important. After enjoying a hot dog and a root beer at the Madison Root Beer stand, Bobby was surprised by the power of the convertible's V8 engine as he spun out of the gravel driveway, throwing stones all over the place. He noticed he'd caught the attention of the girls. Starting to feel comfortable behind the wheel, Bobby began to test the car's limits to show off around his peers. Accelerating up to 60 mph in low gear, he shifted to drive gear which caused the tires to squall. Bobby called this "getting rubber." In my day, we called it "peeling rubber." My brother took his friends on joy rides to show them just how fast that 200 horsepower engine could go and how well he could handle it. As a result of Bobby's temerity, he tore out the transmission one weekend, but never said a word to Dad.

The following Monday morning, after a weekend of reckless driving, Bobby scooted into the car with Mom, Dad, Phyllis, and me as we departed for The Question Shop for a day's work. Dad started the engine, put the car in reverse, and stepped on the gas. Instead of backing up, the Buick lunged forward and almost ran through the front of the garage. Bobby knew exactly what was wrong, although no words left his pursed lips. Dad drove to Gallatin in reverse gear. When we finally arrived at Baker Motor Company in Gallatin where Dad had originally purchased the Century, the person who repaired the transmission told Dad, "Somebody's been dogging your car." Dad never said a word to Bobby.

Bobby didn't learn his lesson. He was still irresponsible behind the wheel and continued testing his limits. One weekend while pushing the car to discover its capacity, he pulled out of Larkin Springs Road onto Old Hickory Boulevard. Gunning the engine, Bobby lost control of Dad's gorgeous Buick, veered across Old Hickory Boulevard, and careened into a ditch. The Buick nosedived into a tree and bent the right front fender. Bobby went to Betty, while she was working at the drive-in theater, seeking advice.

"Look what I've done!" Bobby cried.

Betty took one look at the car and said, "Daddy's going to kill you!"
Dad did nothing except fix the car. He didn't fuss. He didn't ask questions. He just walked away in silence. What a strange reaction from the man who had beaten Bobby on that fateful Christmas morning when he was assembling the new train track! *Had Jesse Neal's death softened his edge?* Even after all of Bobby's shenanigans, Dad continued to allow him to drive his Buick Century.

THE AUTUMN MOON burned bright in October 1956, when 16-year-old Bobby drove to Gallatin's "Teen Town" where he not only showed off Dad's cool convertible, but also his swing moves on the dance floor. Fascinated with high speed, Bobby continued to have a lead foot and drove 100 miles an hour on the 21-mile trip back from Gallatin to Madison. The next day, he bragged at school that he had made the trip on the two-lane highway at midnight in just eight minutes. A teacher at Madison High overheard Bobby gloating, pulled him aside, and told him how dangerous his reckless behavior had been. Bobby remembers the teacher's counsel, but it did little to change his behavior.

Hearing these stories about Bobby's spirited youth and Dad's response baffled me. I began to see a dichotomy between the angry father I knew and a more understanding, forgiving father. But, there was more to the story.

I distinctly remember coming home from The Question Shop on summer afternoons when Dad would start his tirade about Bobby. I don't remember hearing Dad fuss about Bobby's driving. *That would've made too much sense.* Dad was upset because Bobby had not pulled enough Bermuda grass. Although I never saw Dad work in the yard, he'd instructed Bobby to pull Bermuda grass from the front lawn. Dad considered Bermuda grass to be a weed.

It was late afternoon on that hot, humid Thursday when we pulled into the driveway. We could see Bobby in the front yard lying on his back with his friend, Patsy Marsh, up in the air, riding on Bobby's legs and feet. This infuriated my father.

Bobby must have instructed Patsy to go home because she left immediately before the verbal abuse began. Bobby had pulled some grass but not as much as Dad had expected. My father criticized Bobby for being lazy and not following his dictates. For some unknown reason, Dad looked the other way when Bobby drove recklessly, but he would fly off the handle when Bobby had not pulled enough Bermuda grass to suit him.

Bobby recalls that in 1957 when he was 17, he was tired of living in the daily household human drama. He couldn't remember a particular episode that precipitated the event - only that he'd taken all he could stand from Dad. He remembers thinking, *I'm getting out of here and I'm not coming back!* Bobby decided to go to Florida at age 17, to lie about his age, and join the Navy. He borrowed $30 from his friend, PeeWee, and bought a bus ticket to Daytona. When the Floridian recruiter asked how old he was, Bobby reported he was 18. The recruiter asked for a birth certificate. Bobby fabricated a story that the Panamanian hospital where he was born had burned and there were no records of his birth. The recruiter handed him a stack of papers to fill out. After Bobby completed the paperwork, he read a statement at the end of the document verifying the veracity of his comments. Perjury could land him five years in jail and a $25,000 fine. Without a word, Bobby left the unsigned document on the table and hitchhiked back to Nashville. When Bobby arrived in East Nashville, he went to the home of a friend, who offered to let Bobby live with them.

Phyllis, Jill, and Coco in front of Billy Buick

As soon as Betty discovered that Bobby was back in town, she shared the news with Mother. Mama called Bobby and asked him to come home. She sounded pitiful and he didn't know what to tell her. After a short pause, he told Mother that he would come home if Dad would buy him a car. Mother agreed. Bobby came home hoping to find a similar car to the hard-top convertible with a V8 engine. Instead, he was given a putrid green 1950, slow-moving Buick Super that would belong to both him and Betty. An embarrassing step down from Dad's Century, it wasn't as pretty or as powerful as the car he was accustomed to driving. Betty named the car "Billy Buick."

As with Dad's car, Bobby kept Billy Buick cleaned and polished. Because Bobby was disgusted with the car's ugly green exterior, he painted the rim of the tires red to spruce it up. Betty was more interested in socialization than aesthetics. One early school morning, Bobby hopped in the Buick to find the headliner badly torn. It was hanging down in shreds.

Bobby asked Betty, "What the hell happened here?"

Betty said, "Oh! All these boys put firecrackers in there and they went off."

On another occasion, Betty was out with her friends at Hendersonville lake. Bobby got in the car the next morning and the car wouldn't start.

Bobby asked Betty, "What did you do to the car? It won't start!"

Betty retorted, "I don't know. I filled it up with gas!"

"What gas station?" asked Bobby.

"At the boat dock," she replied.

Bobby inquired, "What kind of gas did you use?"

Betty responded, "I don't know."

Bobby discovered that Betty had put diesel fuel in the car. Bobby had to drain all the fuel out of the tank and fill it with gasoline. After it choked and smoked, it finally broke into a somewhat smooth hum.

Betty wasn't always truthful with Bobby about her escapades. One day after spending time with her seemingly wild friends, Betty brought Billy Buick home with the front of the hood all bashed in. Betty claimed that when she'd slammed on the brakes, the hood slipped off the car, and slid down the highway. However, there were no skid marks on the hood. The rest of the hood was ok. The front fender was fine. Damages ran about a foot wide and a foot long at the nose of the hood. Bobby believes that Betty ran under a truck or trailer and crushed the hood. Betty told Dad her story, and he paid to have the hood fixed. Betty and Bobby never knew how Dad would react. Sometimes he just turned away without a word, and other times he reacted violently over seemingly nothing.

Because Bobby played football, Mother kept a large quart of Welch's concentrated grape juice in the refrigerator. My mouth watered when I saw the pristine glass bottle cooling on the refrigerator shelf. I started to help myself to a glass when Mother stopped me. "No, no, no! That's for Bobby! He plays football and he needs that extra nourishment." Still today, I find Welch's grape juice in a bottle titillating.

When Bobby was in high school, he received enough lunch money for one meal a week. Perhaps it didn't occur to my parents that the price of lunches increased each year. However, Mom packed Bobby's lunches each day, which consisted of tomato and mayonnaise sandwiches or banana and mayo. Sometimes he got a treat with peanut butter and mayo. By lunchtime, the tomato sandwich was soggy, so Bobby tossed it. Brown bananas turned Bobby's stomach - another entry into the garbage can. The rare sandwich that found its way into Bobby's stomach was peanut butter and mayo.

Since he didn't have money for lunch, Bobby went to the gym to play ping pong with some of the other guys who were also skipping lunch. Bobby never complained about the soggy or brown banana sandwiches; therefore, Mother didn't know that Bobby went most days without lunch. Playing ping-pong with Jarrett Harlan became a time Bobby anticipated with pleasure. Jarrett later introduced Bobby to his future wife, Anne Gayle Farley. If Bobby had eaten lunch in the cafeteria with his peers, he may never have met Anne Gayle, who has been the love of his life for over 60 years. Those soggy tomato sandwiches became a blessing - another ruby in the rubble.

Under the harsh childhood my brother endured, he became a rare stone. Rubies are created under the earth's surface when specific minerals, including corundum, are combined together and undergo extreme heat and pressure.* The "extreme heat and pressure" of Bobby's pain and abuse throughout his life had transformed him into a high-quality jewel, even more precious than a diamond, and he was *my* brother! He'd been here for me; I'd learned something about self-respect from his tender guidance during simple, nonchalant conversations. Even though my heart opened during those precious moments, it wasn't until later when I fully understood just how impactful those discussions had been.

Bobby was eight years and eight months my senior. I cherished any moment I could spend with my brother. He was everything Daddy wasn't. He was kind, loved Mother dearly, spoke softly, and let his kid sister hang out with him sometimes.

Just as Bobby liked driving a nice car, he also dressed sharply. Mother inserted wire stretchers inside the freshly laundered pant legs of his blue jeans so they would

Bobby's shoe-shine box

fit just right on his slim, muscular body. In preparation for a date, Bobby washed and shined Billy Buick. I hung out with him when he washed his car as he gave non-solicited guidance on the serial order of the art of washing cars. I hung onto each word and can still hear his gentle, guiding voice in my head when I wash my car today. After washing his car, he sat down on his bed with the shoeshine box he'd constructed out of scraps of wood he found when the house on Coggin Pass was initially built. I sat next to him as he spit-shined his penny loafers. I don't remember asking a lot of questions, but I remember him speaking gently to me, almost as though he was just thinking out loud. He recalled that on a

---

* https:/sciencing.com/rubies-form-4963260.html

date with a previous friend, he could see her bra hanging on the doorknob from the other room. He did not approve of seeing a girl's underwear displayed in the sight of a visitor. I must have been eight, but never forgot that story and never hung my bra on the doorknob, always remembering the disapproving expression on Bobby's face as he relayed the event. I didn't realize it then, but he was teaching me to be a lady.

Bobby spoke to me with a voice as soft as silk, as if I was coming of age, so I felt important to him even though he'd never said those words to me. He didn't have to. His actions spoke volumes. As he prepared for a date with his high school sweetheart, Anne Gayle Farley, Bobby dressed in a gray Herringbone tweed car coat, red shirt with a gold stripe, Levi's, and penny loafers. As was often the case, I slept in his bed until he got home from his date, at which time he carried me to bed, and I got to see him once again before the next day. Bobby was my surrogate father - my ruby. With each interaction, this ruby shined brighter.

My kind brother went on to become a phenomenal husband and father to his two boys, both Eagle Scouts and eventually engineers. Mother often called on him when she needed a repair or the house needed to be painted. He was always there for her.

Mother and Bobby continued to have an impact on my life. This was just the beginning of noticing that from the rubble, just beneath the surface, come beautiful, rare jewels. I continued finding and polishing the rubies, not knowing the rubble that awaited me.

I had a brother who was my savior, made my childhood bearable.[17]
~ Maurice Sendak

Chapter 13:

Please Don't Go

Wᴴᴱɴ I THINK OF THE DAY Bobby turned 18, the scene comes back to me clearly. All I knew was that my brother was leaving and the whole house was upset. No one more than I! *How could I survive without him? Who would teach me about life? Who would carry me to bed at night?* Mother cried huge, desperate tears. Daddy carried on with his usual preaching discourse about what a mistake Bobby was making. After he ranted and raved, pacing back and forth, he went back to his bedroom; within 30 minutes he emerged and continued his sermon while Mother quietly peeled the potatoes. "And another thing . . . ," he said as he resumed his tirade and repeated his concerns. "Naw, I'll tell ya . . . ," he said as he paced the room. Mother's tears dried up as she fell into silence when Dad told her he had talked with the Marine recruiter. Sergeant Sweat was willing to come to the house that evening. Even though Bobby had already been sworn in, the sergeant was willing to let him out of his commitment if he wanted to change his mind.

Hearing Bobby's perspective of his recruitment into the Marines years later shed more light on the event. During his senior year, an acquaintance, George, showed up at Madison High School in his dress blue Marine uniform. Since Bobby had been a young boy, he'd been impressed with military attire. While Daddy was in the war, Mother stitched three-year-old Bobby a uniform of his own. She showed Bobby pictures of his father in his officer's regalia and talked about how wonderful it would be to see his dad again. Bobby wanted to be like his daddy before he actually knew the old man. My brother was enamored when he saw George in his dress blues, and it sparked his desire to enlist.

Another friend at MHS was also interested in enlisting. Bobby and Sam made a plan. On Bobby's birthday, February 19th, they skipped school and hitchhiked 13 miles to the Nashville recruiting center. The recruiter took them right in, swore them in, and then completed a physical exam. The boys left with a meal ticket. Bobby recalls thinking, "Man! We're in business now!" The recruiter called Mom and Dad to inform them that Bobby had enlisted. That's when the crying started. When Bobby got home that afternoon, he was faced with Dad's interrogation and Mom's tears, followed by a visit from Sergent Sweat.

What a tense visit that was! We were all in the living room together. Phyllis and I sat on the piano stool. Mom and Dad sat on the tan sofa. The recruiter sat in the green armchair, and Bobby sat in the rocking chair. Even as a ten-year-old, I was impressed by the uniform Sergeant Sweat donned. The Marine Corps is the only branch of the service with uniform colors designated to represent the American flag. The red, white, and blue colors were striking. His uniform featured a form-fitting midnight blue coat with red trim and blue trousers with a red stripe. A stand collar and white belt made the uniform even more impressive.

The recruiter spoke with Bobby in front of the family, offering to let him continue his education for three months to gain his high school diploma before entering the service. Bobby refused. He had endured enough of Dad's red-faced rages. He was finished! Nothing was more important to him than escaping his father's jurisdiction! Mother's eyes were swollen with worry and exhaustion. The defeated look on her face left her gaunt and hollow. She sat quietly as tears welled up and overflowed onto her cheeks. Dad's expression was stiff. The rest of the night was garbled, but I recall hearing the voice of my father's lectures. Not only did his discourse wear us all out; he wore himself out. We were all in bed by 9:00 p.m.

Early the next morning, Mom, Dad, Phyllis, and I all took Bobby to Union Station in Nashville to catch the train for Parris Island, South Carolina. It was one of the saddest days of my youth. *When would I see my only brother again?* He promised to write. Dad's guilt was all-consuming. As the whistle blew and the train left the depot, Dad was so overcome with emotion, he had to run to the bathroom to throw up. It felt like a death in the family.

That was the longest, coldest February night in my memory. I wanted to scream when Bobby left, but instead, I jumped into his bed, wrapped my arms around my knees, and hoped my heart wouldn't leap from my chest as it beat to the cadence of a marching band. I struggled to imagine what my life would be without him. Mother told me I could have Bobby's room. I had so many good memories of conversations and sitting beside him while he spit-shined his shoes. Being in the energy of his room was comforting, but the loss was deep and devastating. I slept in Bobby's bed, sinking deep into his mattress as I watched the last light of the day disappear into the night.

Chapter 14:

Graveyard of the Past

ODETTE CONTINUED TO CALL DAD FOR YEARS even after I was born. On one occasion in 1954, Mother answered the phone and reminded Odette that Dad had a wife and children who loved him; Mom asked Odette to please stop calling. That was the last time Mom or Dad heard directly from Odette. Friends later told Dad that Odette had remarried her first husband, Justin.

In 1958, Congress enacted legislation for retired personnel, promoting all retirees who had completed 30 years of active or retired service to their highest rank held during the war. Finally, Dad was promoted and paid as a major.

Seven years later in 1965, Dad received a call from the adjutant general saying he had questions about Dad's promotion relating to the legislation in 1958. According to the Army, the military had confused Dad's records with another Smith who was in the Air Force. Realizing their mistake brought the events of Dad's affair to the forefront; the Army demanded reparation. Dad was demoted to captain and required to repay over $7,000 plus interest. My father could not afford an attorney, nor did he have $7,000 at his disposal. His military pay was $3,000 a year, and he was losing money at The Question Shop. The equivalent of $7,000 in 1965 compared to today's purchasing power is $57,883. The cumulative price increase is 727%. Phyllis and I were both in parochial schools costing $400 a year. Looking back, it's understandable why we often ate beans and cornbread for dinner. Not one time did Mom or Dad share their money problems with me. Not one time did they consider taking me out of the Catholic high school I was attending, despite financial constraints. As I peruse Dad's letters and military records, I'm touched and appreciative that I didn't have to leave St Cecilia Academy, where I was excelling, because of the hardships my parents were enduring. Mother always watched her pennies, but I was unaware of the seriousness of their situation.

In May of 1966, Dad wrote the inspector general (IG) in Washington to answer allegations Odette and her husband had made after Dad had left Germany and returned to Tennessee - presumably to be with his family. Odette's accusations occurred after Dad left the European Theatre Operations around Jan 18, 1947. As I read the letters, I wondered if Odette's husband had demanded she make the accusations to gain re-entrance into her marriage.

Dad continued to maintain his innocence all the while accusations of misconduct of a wartime soldier were being made by his previous lover and her husband. *How did Dad feel? Was he angry? Was he heartbroken?* Nothing in that box of letters and records answered my question.

In 1967, Dad wrote to Yvonne Gosselin in Paris. Yvonne's husband, Raymond, was Odette's cousin. During the war, Dad and Odette shared time with them and they developed a close friendship. Dad wrote:

As you know the statement [Odette] *made to the Army after I left Germany caused me to be demoted from major to captain on the retired list, resulting in about $7,000 loss of pay so far. If she would sign this document I have enclosed, I would have a chance to get the money back and be promoted to Major on the retired list. I sincerely hope that you can get her to sign it for me. If she does, I will pay you well for your trouble.*

Gosselin's response to Dad's request:
Translation read as follows:

12ᵗʰ of April 1967

Dear Friend,

I have received your letter. After you left France, we didn't have any more contact with Odette's parents. Moreover, we knew that Odette remarried Justin.

As much as I would like to help you, I can't give you any information about what you are asking me. Since I became a widow, I work at the factory and I don't see anybody from Raymond's family anymore. Believe me, I wish I could help you and make you happy. I hope this letter will find you well.

I leave you, dear friend, wishing you all the best and with the good memories I had with you and our good friendship.

Y. Gosselin

~~

Even though Yvonne's initial reply indicated she couldn't help Dad, I found a letter she'd written May 8, 1967 in support of my father. Her letter reads:

8 Rue Du Pole Nord

75 Paris 8, France (18e),
8 May 1967
To whom it may concern:

So far as my knowledge and belief, the following is a true and correct statement; Mme Odette Iehl, formerly Odette Roger, is a cousin of my late husband, who died 10 May 1955.

I am personally acquainted with Robert L. Smith, who was with the United States Army during 1944 and 1945 in Paris. Mr. Smith was a major in the Army and visited with my husband and me in our home during the time that he was in Paris. He was always very correct while in our home.

It is my knowledge that Mme Iehl left Paris on the 1st of December 1945 and went to Darmstadt and Mannheim, Germany where Major Smith had been transferred and informed me she was working in Germany as his secretary. She visited Paris in January 1946. My husband and I talked with her at Hotel St. Anne in Paris while she was here. She seemed very happy with her employment and returned to Germany and corresponded with me while there. She never mentioned being unhappy or wanting to return to Paris.

It is my personal opinion that she went to Germany of her own accord and was not coerced by the Major who was always sober and courteous when in our presence.
Mademoiselle Yvonne Gosselin

Even though Yvonne had written the letter and testified for Dad, it didn't yield the results he desired. Dad believed he hadn't received a fair hearing. Although an inspector general investigation had been held in 1947, Dad said that he had not been informed of the occurrence. He wrote to various elected officials who, according to Dad, also gave him the run-a-round.

Dad tenaciously tried to get his records corrected for over 40 years after he retired. He wrote to Representatives Al Gore, Sr. and Al Gore, Jr. multiple times starting in 1977. With persistence, he corresponded with Congressman Richard Fulton and Senator Howard Baker, Jr. Dad never gave up on his efforts for the Army to correct his record. Even two years before his death, Dad wrote to President Ronald Reagan in May of 1985 requesting support to revisit the false accusations made by Odette and her husband. Dad's records were never amended, even as steadfast as he'd been to rectify them. Although Dad received responses from Army commanders and elected officials, their answers were always the same. The investigation had been exhausted; conclusions were clear. There was nothing more that could be done.

Chapter 15:

Eunice: "Shiney Bye Dodee"

AS I LOOKED BACK ON MY PARENTS' LIFE, I'd assumed we were always poor. After hearing Bobby talk about the years before I was born, I realized there was a time when our parents had plenty of money, since Dad purchased a new car every two to four years.

Even though Dad had money, Mother still lived like a pauper all of her life. She was born during the first World War and lived through the Great Depression and WWII. I suspect that being raised on the farm, her life was hard economically, but I don't think the children were aware. The kids were happy; they worked hard, but they also played hard. Mom was close to all her siblings and very close to Grandma Redman.

Mother and Grandma Redman

My mother was called "Shine" by her siblings. As a six-year-old, hearing my mother addressed as Shine, my facial expression demonstrated surprise. Uncle Pete told me the story of how Mom was given that name. As a result, Phyllis and I wrote a song entitled, "Shiny Bye Dodee." It goes like this:

They called her Shiny Bye Dodee
Suck a thumb; suck a thumb,
Tee-ny head.
They called her Shiny Bye Dodee
Suck a thumb; suck a thumb,
Tee-ny head.
They named her that when she was only three.
She was just as cute as she could be.
Her hair was just as straight as a bobby pin,
And it shined like a roll of tin.

When Mom was with her siblings, she seemed to turn young again. I loved watching her transform. She laughed and even giggled with her brothers and sisters as they reminisced about life on the farm.

Even as a young girl, Mother had a reputation of outworking her brothers while picking cotton. Grandma Redman cultivated a strong commitment to family in her children. From both home and school, Mother was taught the importance of patriotism and family loyalty. Nothing was more important than family. The five girls' education ended at the sixth grade, so they could work the fields and support their six brothers' college education. Grandma's children continued to help her even after they were married. When Mom married Dad during the Great Depression, she sent money to Grandma as often as possible.

After Mom married Dad, before having children, she seemed to live the life of a princess compared to her work on the farm. Mother socialized with friends, had nice clothes, and even attended formal parties.

My sister-in-law, Anne Gayle, took my mom's formal evening gown, gloves, and embroidered bag to a Daughters of the Revolution (DAR) meeting and shared this information with the group.

"My mother-in-law's party dress dates from 1930. The fabric appears to be silk brocade. There is a label, but the dress was obviously hand-made to order for her. There is a side opening, consisting of hook and eye hardware, and tiny snaps.

Mother's party dress purchased in Panama in 1938

Zipper closures were rare in the 1930s, and side openings were common on women's dresses until the '40s and '50s when center back openings with zippers became the norm. The bodice is quilted. The waist measurement is 24 inches!

My mother-in-law, Eunice, was a pretty, petite woman, who'd spent a hard life working on her family's farm in North Carolina. Eunice and her husband, Robert, were stationed in the Panama Canal Zone and came to enjoy a serious social life as Robert advanced in rank to become an Army officer. These

Mom's gloves and bag

were happy years for them - until WWII, and his return from the war. Their five children knew their father as an oppressor and abusive man. They were enormously surprised after their mother's death to find this beautiful dress, packed away with these white kid gloves, and a bundle of love letters, tied with a red ribbon."

I remember Dad buying Mother a few presents during her lifetime. One was a Mouton Coat. It made Mother angry. She thought it was a waste of money to purchase such an extravagant coat when she didn't even have a dress to wear with it. To my knowledge, Mother never wore the coat. Sometimes I think Dad was clueless! I wish he had known that helping out in the kitchen or the yard would have been much more appreciated than such a useless, extravagant gift. I wonder if he was yearning for days-gone-by before the children were born when Mom dressed up and they lived high on the hog.

Bobby reminded me that before I was born, Dad bought Mother a watch with rubies and diamonds. Again, Mother was furious. After having children Mother didn't give herself the luxury of new clothes. She would rather have a hand-me-down than a new dress. Money was needed for the family and she worked for the family - not to adorn herself. I don't remember ever seeing the watch. When Phyllis and I were in our teens working at Shoney's restaurant, we went in together to buy her an oak rocking chair for $25.00. Mother loved the chair! It was useful and complemented their home.

I now see how my mother's philosophy about money impacted me. During my first marriage, my husband, Rodney, often wanted to buy me flowers. I encouraged him not to waste our money on such a thing. When I was 47, I met my second husband, Dan, who sent me flowers for my birthday. It was the first time in my life to receive flowers. I loved them! Finally, I was departing from my mother's philosophy about money; however, spending money is still difficult for me. I have to overcome the inner voice that beckons me to be careful and not extravagant.

Betty and Bobby remember that as children, they had only one pair of shoes each, even when Dad was buying a new car every two years. They wore their shoes until they were too tight or had holes in the bottoms. Bobby recalls a time when his soles were flopping loose before another pair of shoes was purchased. It wasn't that our parents didn't have money, but Mom had learned to be conservative living on the farm. Living through the Depression cemented that mindset.

It is nothing short of a miracle that modern methods of instruction
have not yet entirely strangled the holy curiosity of inquiry.[3]
~ Albert Einstein

Chapter 16:

School Daze

Perhaps we didn't have money to purchase winter coats.
I don't know. Perhaps Mother just thought that she could save a few dollars by making them herself. I remember the day we drove out in the country to a textile mill to buy at least one bolt of black and brown weave wool for Mother to make winter coats for Phyllis and me. Mom stayed up all night stitching my winter coat. When I crawled out of bed the next morning, Mother presented me with my new coat. It didn't have the lining yet but I loved it!

Time, again, moved us forward; years grew us taller. We were now old enough to help Mom with yard work. Keeping the one-acre lawn manicured was left to Mother, Phyllis, and me. With all three of us taking turns, we could knock out the tedious task in about two hours if we didn't slow down. Mother worked at break-neck speed and taught me to do the same. We never stopped to take a break. We stopped only when the job was finished. When I mowed, Mother kept me hydrated by bringing out water to drink. I drank a glass of water down in one tilt of the head and resumed my track. When it was Mom's time to take the mower, I returned the favor. We wrapped our heads in turbans with sweatbands, put cold wet towels around our necks, and worked hard until the job was finished. Dad never took a turn. The routine was constant during the scorching, humid summer months. After I left home, I suspect Mother did it by herself. To my knowledge, she never paid anyone to mow the grass.

Due to the family business in Gallatin, Tennessee, Phyllis and I went to Sumner County Schools, which were 20 miles from our Madison home. Betty and Bobby were old enough to drive. They attended Madison High School (MHS), which included grades 7-10 and was less than five miles from our home. Seeing my older siblings' friends come by to hang out in the yard or pick them up for a gathering, I knew even as early as the third grade that I was missing out on something important. During my entire educational career, sadly, I never attended my neighborhood schools. Consequently, I barely knew the neighborhood kids.

Because Mother kept a watchful eye on Dad to ensure he focused on work and wasn't hitting the bottle, she accompanied him to work each day and served as his office manager. She kept the books, answered the phone, and paid bills. To keep the lights on and food on the table, Mother took the lion's share of the responsibility for keeping the office and home in order. Dad repaired televisions and radios at The Question Shop, while mom managed the office and home finances. Mother never requested or received a paycheck for her work at Dad's business.

Phyllis & Jill in 1952

IN 1954, I COULD HARDLY WAIT for my sixth birthday to begin first grade, but I soon became disillusioned. My low self-esteem was inevitable, given the many years of ridicule from Dad. Although I desperately wanted to make friends, it was difficult and awkward. School was not the fun place I'd anticipated; school was hard! After long days at school, where I wasn't allowed to talk or play with my peers except during the short time allocated for lunch or recess, I walked to my father's TV repair shop to hear him repeat his daily mantra. *What's wrong with her? Is she stupid?* Distressed, I decided I didn't like school, and I didn't like reading. By midyear, my teacher recommended glasses to correct my nearsightedness. The glasses helped me see, but they did little for my self-image or belief in my intelligence.

In third grade, school personnel referred me for speech lessons by a speech-language pathologist, because I had not mastered the pronunciation of the "r" sound by the end of second grade. I couldn't say *rabbit*. It sounded like *wabbit*. "R" is typically one of the last sounds mastered by young children. In many cases, time takes care of the problem; but often, support is needed by a speech therapist.

In Mrs. Richard's small classroom space, I was accepted for who I was, even with my imperfections. She kindly and skillfully assisted in smoothing out my rough spots. I don't remember how often I met Mrs. Richard individually for speech class, perhaps once or twice a week, but it wasn't long enough for me. She was pretty, kind, gentle, and loving, which I craved. She taught me how to hold my mouth, where to place my tongue, and before long, I learned to correctly pronounce the "r" sound.

Even at that age, I must have feared this positive teaching experience would soon be over if she knew I had achieved the desired goal, so I hid my new skill from her for as long as possible. An astute teacher, Mrs. Richard was not easily fooled, and my time with her was soon over. I felt like a different person with Mrs. Richard. My shoulders relaxed from around my ears. I found myself smiling and actually enjoying school. I now realize that this teacher had planted the seed for me to later consider entering the education field.

MOTHER WAS THE ACTIVELY INVOLVED PARENT in my life. In her attempt to offer Phyllis and me a summer reprieve from endless hours of watching TV at The Question Shop, Mom found activities for us. Due to Jesse Neal's drowning, Mother enrolled Phyllis and me in swim classes each summer.

After swim lessons at 9:00 in the mornings, Phyllis and I spent our days at the Gallatin swimming pool. If it wasn't raining, we were at the pool. We also found a Friendship Club for kids our ages and were able to hang out with them when we grew tired of swimming. Even though we weren't in our own neighborhood, summers offered a certain amount of freedom. We needed time to develop relationships with peers, have opportunities to make decisions, and learn from our mistakes.

Spending so much time at the pool, I admired kids who jumped off the high diving board. I watched as they gracefully climbed the steps, walked out to the end, held their noses, and jumped with confidence. It looked like fun. Curiosity prompted me to take action. I was drawn to the new experience.

This was the day I was going to do it! I climbed 10 feet to reach the top. Looking out, I was instantly repelled by the whole idea. *What had I done?* I couldn't breathe. Then I realized that I had just been holding my breath. Without my glasses, I couldn't see the people below. My breathing became labored and audible. Hot air, caught in my throat, escaped through my mouth. I panicked. There was no way I was going to walk out to the end of that board. As long as I was standing near the steps, I could grip the rails. I tried to convince myself I could do it. I told myself I *had* to do it, but my fear paralyzed the wobbly legs under me. I was convinced I could not walk out to the end of the board without rails to steady my quivering body. I started to back down the ladder. A whistle blew. It was the lifeguard telling me I couldn't go back down the steps. I had no choice. I'd gotten myself up there, and now there was only one way down. I had to go off the board. I took a deep breath. I prayed. But I couldn't do it. The lifeguard kept watching me pointing to the end of the board. A line was forming of brave souls who had mastered heights and wanted their turn. I remember the other kids taunting me, "Jump! Jump!" as I white-knuckled the hand-rail. After 20 minutes, the lifeguard relented and let me back down the ladder. I never ascended the steps of a high dive again for the rest of my life.

On rainy days, Phyllis and I spent time at Dad's shop. I'd watched Mom write checks while hanging out at The Question Shop, so I decided to give it a try at age eight. I enrolled Phyllis to be a part of my scheme to write a check for one dollar and cash it at the nearby grocery store. With check in hand, we proudly strolled next door to study our options for purchase. In 1956, you could buy a sack full of candy for one dollar. With mouths watering, we watched Mr. Lacy fill a paper bag with delicious penny candy. Some purchases were two candies for one cent. By the time we walked 100 feet back to Dad's business, we found Dad on the phone with Mr. Lacy, who was disclosing our recent transaction. Although I remember a bit of a wringing out from Dad, there was no physical punishment. It didn't dampen my pride that I had successfully written a check and made a purchase all by my little self.

By fifth grade, school and home frustrations wreaked havoc on my health. My teacher, Mrs. Spurlock, was a fastidious thirty-year-old who was quick to criticize me in front of the entire class. She expected me to understand and complete the work without actually teaching the materials. Lying in bed at night, I dreaded having to face another day with her. Every morning when my parents dropped me off in front of Guild Elementary, I got out of the car and instantly lost my breakfast. It didn't matter if I threw up right there in front of the car line; I was still expected to go through those doors and spend another day with a teacher who thought as highly of me as my own father.

SOMETHING NOTEWORTHY HAPPENED during that atrocious year of 1958. My father noticed that Mrs. Spurlock had marked a math answer wrong that was correct. Dad marched up to Guild Elementary to confront her. He pointed out her mistake. Mrs. Spurlock would not accept the possibility that she could have made a mistake, but rather suggested that I may have erased the original answer and corrected it myself. My father argued that no erasure marks were present. This was the dad I'd always wanted! Someone who would defend me, champion me, protect me. Having Dad in my corner felt miraculously odd. It felt like love. It felt like respect. Impervious to Mrs. Spurlock's suggestion that I could have erased my original answer, Dad trusted me. He didn't even ask if I had corrected the answer myself. Looking back on this seemingly miraculous event, I wonder if Dad was defending me or his pride in front of this teacher and wife of a prominent business owner in Gallatin.

It didn't matter at the time, because it was one of the few times in my life when I felt important and supported by my dad.

Although I stood a couple of inches taller that day, by April I was informed that I would fail the fifth grade. "Failure is a feeling long before it becomes a reality."[20] The old familiar tape played again in my ear. But now it wasn't my father's voice; it was my own voice. *What's wrong with me? Am I stupid?*

Little did I understand the pressures endured while cultivating a precious jewel. I was too young to grasp the following quote:

> "Success is not built on success. It's built on failure, frustration, and sometimes catastrophe. It's what you do with failure that builds success. Confidence is necessary to ultimately prevail."[21]

Did I have the confidence to break out of the mold my mother had endured? How would I develop the necessary confidence to fill the void and transform this embarrassing failure into a polished ruby?

Failure is the condiment that gives success its flavor.[22]
~ Truman Capote

Chapter 17:

The Paradox of Failure

NOT WANTING TO FACE THE HUMILIATION of returning to the same school with my peers who had moved on to sixth grade, I was relieved when my father transferred Phyllis and me to St. John Vianney Parochial School. Although I wasn't sure he had noticed, my father seemed to understand the strain I was under. On this occasion, Dad acted with certainty to spare me further shame. Sometimes I look back over my life and can't remember a single time my father supported me; however, acknowledging Dad's support when he transferred me from public to parochial school was a stepping stone that offered a fresh start. This laid the foundation for my fledgling confidence. Understanding firsthand how grade retention can negatively impact a student's self-image and promote fear of ridicule was a lesson that would stay with me throughout my lifetime.

My second year in fifth grade was very different from what I'd experienced with Mrs. Spurlock. I'd learned to tolerate cruelty better than the kindness I was experiencing at St. John Vianney. At first, I choked on the sisters' benevolence. When Sister Mary Jerome said, "I can't believe you're repeating the fifth grade. You already know this!" I was shocked. *What was she saying?* Her words didn't compute. I must have looked frozen, even quizzical. While I desired to have the mind of a scholar, I believed I had the mind of a moronic misfit. Immersed in an environment of acceptance and respect, I began to flourish.

Every violent and degrading moment in my life seemed to soften in the presence of the sisters' compassion. At St. John Vianney, I thrived in an environment with teachers who seemed to think I was intelligent, worthwhile, and worthy of respect. The sisters consistently treated me with dignity, without intermittent mixed messages, and I began to embrace the idea of the possibility of my value and self-worth. The acceptance I'd felt from my speech teacher in second grade was punctuated in this new environment. But rather than a couple of hours a week, I now lived in perpetual love and acceptance at school.

Thinking back, it wasn't as if I'd never attended church before St. John Vianney. In my earlier days, Mother took Phyllis and me to the Baptist Church. After she enrolled us in classes and helped us get acquainted with the layout of the building, she began to drop us off at church while she cooked and cleaned at home. After she picked us up, we sat down for a special Sunday dinner. I was interested in getting baptized, but something was said to upset me, although I don't remember the details. Consequently, I didn't want to go back to *that* church.

Mother started taking us to another Baptist Church on Gallatin Road. At one point, I wasn't happy there and talked Phyllis into leaving with me to walk three miles home. I was probably 10 years old. I knew it was a long way home, but I desperately wanted to get away from the Sunday school teacher who'd made me feel unwelcomed. After walking a mile and a half, which felt like freedom, a car slowed down presumably to offer us a lift. I warned Phyllis, "No, we can't ride in a car with strangers." Phyllis recognized the driver as a friend of Bobby's. Mother was shocked to see us walk through the door after PeeWee brought us home. Knowing her two young daughters had taken off on their own to walk three miles on a busy street with no sidewalks was enough to stop church-going for a while.

Dad had developed a friendship with a Catholic priest while he was stationed in Southern France in early 1944. Chaplain McGohan often visited Dad's room to listen to news updates on his radio during WWII. At that time, radios were the exception rather than the norm. Catholicism had interested Dad for almost 15 years, but Mother had heard false tales that Catholics worship idols. Reluctantly, Mom joined the family studying Catholicism with Father George W. Rohling at St. Joseph Church, in Madison.

Our home life began to improve. For the first time in my life, we attended church together each Sunday. I can hear Dad joyfully singing in the bathroom as he readied himself to attend Mass and sell books, medals, and rosaries at the religious-goods counter. Betty and Bobby had already moved out and started their own families, but Mom, Dad, Phyllis, and I experienced harmony we had never known before. Mother, Phyllis, and I volunteered to work in the nursery. After church, we picked up Krystal hamburgers or an occasional real treat - Shoney's Big Boy burgers. Sometimes we even went bowling together after a morning at church. Perhaps my rotten year of 1958, when I failed the fifth grade, had been necessary to bring my family to a better place. At age 11, I began to glimpse what a family could be. Both Betty and Bobby were so impressed with the transformation our family experienced through this new religion, they both began to study Catholicism, and our entire family became Catholics. We were all so proud of Dad for his abstinence from alcohol.

Dad frequently came out of his bedroom to announce some event that had happened 40 years ago, while everyone went about their chores and school work as dishes clanged in preparations for supper. We mostly ignored his running commentary. After supper each night, we all gathered in the living room to recite the rosary as a family.

Not only did I continue to struggle with my feeling of inadequacy and stupidity, but my father was also dealing with his demons. One particular night was different and illustrated a lapse in the ideal family I thought we'd created through Catholicism. Exactly what I did blurs in my memory, but what is vivid to me is the shift that came over Dad. His pious demeanor reciting the rosary transmuted to anger. His face grew tense and rigid as a vein popped out on his neck. The next thing I knew, the rosary beads were smacked across my face. I'm sure I'd done something to bring it on, but I had no idea what had just happened. I continued saying the rosary - praying he would die.

Even after a night of altercations with Dad, participating in the school's ritual of morning Mass brought me a renewed sense of hope. I loved attending Mass, experiencing the quiet, contemplative time, and hearing the uplifting Gregorian chants. Even though fifty students surrounded me, I felt the intimacy of oneness with God and experienced peace.

ST. JOHN VIANNEY was a three-classroom school encompassing grades 1-8, taught by three Dominican Sisters. Grades 1-3 were in one classroom, grades 4 and 5 were in a second classroom, and grades 6-8 were in the third. From 1959-1961, I attended fifth through seventh grade in this three-room schoolhouse. Although I'd often felt small and insignificant, the respect and encouragement I received here changed the trajectory of my life. The intimacy of small classes helped me find my voice. I didn't have to hide; there was no place to hide and no reason to hide. Excelling felt great! Vigilantly, I worked hard, always did my homework without being cajoled, and earned good grades.

Two boys and three girls comprised the five students in my fifth-grade class. Mood swings during adolescence may be the reason girls are often wishy-washy. In the three-girl triangle, we often shifted alliances and took turns being the outcast. It seemed it was always two against one. Since I didn't live in the same city as my classmates, I didn't get invited to birthday parties. When Henry Daughtry, a cute boy in 6th grade, seemed to show me favor, one girl liked me, and the other was distant.

Despite these dynamics, music would bring us all together again. A short, little, round retired piano teacher occasionally taught music and helped us prepare for an afternoon tea with parents or a Christmas holiday event. My love of music flourished there and continued throughout my life. Music was another avenue that connected me to the Divine.

All students attended daily Mass at St. John Vianney. My parents joined the ritual. During this time of reflection, intimacy with my Creator continued to blossom. Because the sisters were accustomed to seeing Mom and Dad each morning, they began to call on my parents to help them when needed.

Although the sisters lived above the school, their motherhouse was in Nashville, an hour's drive from Gallatin. During certain holidays and Holy Days, our family transported the three sisters to their motherhouse on Eighth Avenue. Having this personal time with them was my first time socializing with adults. On those trips to Nashville, I marveled at the night sky in the big city, a sight I'd never experienced - picturesque skyline views reflected in the Cumberland River that borders the city. The glimmering lights reflected in the water as we crossed the bridge. My eleven-year-old self was awestruck.

The sisters appreciated their transportation to Nashville. In return, they invited Phyllis and me to come to the convent above the school on Saturday mornings to help run the sweeper, dust the furniture, and then join them in baking homemade, mouth-watering, cinnamon rolls. The aroma of rich, browned butter, caramelized brown sugar, and yeast filled the air and reminded me of the delicious homemade rolls and biscuits Ma Neal had made. Spending time with the sisters on Saturday mornings while my parents worked at The Question Shop was a cherished reprieve away from the concrete building and the loud TV noise.

My fifth-grade failure had transformed my family life and ignited a joy of learning in me, proving that grief and resilience can live together.[23] Another ruby was surfacing from the rubble.

Chapter 18:

The Carter Family

WHILE GOING TO SCHOOL IN GALLATIN, I didn't realize the opportunities for socialization I'd missed by not attending my neighborhood school. However, the boys next door became part of our extended family and impacted my life in ways I couldn't have predicted.

Danny Jones, Phyllis Smith, David & Kenny Jones

Our backdoor neighbor, Helen Carter Jones, was the sister of the country music icon, June Carter Cash. Helen, June, and Anita were the daughters of the legendary Mother Maybelle. A.P. Carter, his wife Sarah, and sister-in-law, Maybelle, were country music's pioneers during the 1920s and 1930s and became known for such songs as, "Will the Circle be Unbroken." After the original group disbanded in the 1940s, Maybelle and her daughters continued the family's legacy featuring the all-female country and folk music group. Helen had four boys. I'd often dreamed of how life would've been if Jesse Neal had lived. What would it have been like to have had a brother closer to my age? Danny and Kenny Jones were the neighbors closest to my age. Although I was a bit older than Kenny, I often thought of him as my surrogate brother, and I loved him.

Helen Carter's singing career required her to travel for various performances. Her husband, Glen Jones, an inventor and pilot, also traveled frequently; therefore, Helen and Glen hired live-in babysitters who sometimes relied on my mom for support. Living next door to the Jones allowed me to feel like I had a larger family with more brothers. I spent a lot of time with Kenny, who taught Phyllis and me how to play the guitar. He not only taught us chords but also how to strum and pick.

In 1968 when Johnny Cash married Helen's sister, June Carter Cash, we kids would all pile into the back of Johnny's Lincoln Continental to go swimming in his pool overlooking the lake in Hendersonville, Tennessee. The boys next door had a lot of freedom unlike the sheltered life my sister and I led. They knew all the neigh-borhood kids and gladly included us in their music-making adventures. Danny and Kenny were our childhood playmates: building snowmen, singing together, record-ing our songs on a reel-to-reel. Phyllis and I never took guitar lessons but went on to perform publicly, including on the local TV morning wake-up show with Ralph Emery. This was partly due to our relationships with the boys next door.

A SEMINAL MOMENT stands out in my memory relating to Helen Carter. Mother had taken Phyllis and me to a teenage dance called Teen Town at Father Ryan High School. Rather than traveling back to Madison, she used the time in downtown Nashville to purchase a book I needed for a reading assignment at school.

Mother wasn't aware that it could be dangerous to walk downtown alone. A man stepped out from behind a building, put a gun to my mother's back, and demanded her purse. She immediately complied, and the villain fled with her mon-ey and keys. So shaken from the feelings of a narrow escape from death, Mother's energy drained from her body. With wobbling legs, she walked back to Father Ryan. Mother located a telephone and tried to call my father. The television was likely too loud at home; Dad probably didn't hear the phone ring. Feeling desperate and alone, Mother called Helen next door. Helen banged on Dad's back door until he finally emerged. Dad gave Helen an extra set of car keys, which she brought to Mother at Father Ryan. We were so thankful that she was in town and willing to go out of her way for us.

Helen was a good neighbor. Our families helped each other on numerous occasions; however, Dad was competitive with the Jones family. If they bought a new window air conditioner, Dad went out and bought one a bit bigger than theirs. Dad's bragging didn't alter Helen's willingness to help us. When my sister, Phyllis, was only 14, she wrote the lyrics and music to a song she entitled, "Joey Joey." After she sang it to Helen, our sweet neighbor scheduled a recording session with backup musicians so she could have a vinyl recording of her teenage love song. Helen never asked for a dime for offering such an adventure. Instead, she helped negotiate a contract with a recording studio for Phyllis' song. We were too young and inexperienced to know how to proceed; nevertheless, her signed contract is a treasured keepsake.

In 1962, my father moved his long-time business from Gallatin to Madison, which allowed me the opportunity to attend eighth grade at St. Joseph Elementary. For the first time in my life, I attended school in Madison. Even though it wasn't a neighborhood school, at least I was in the same town.

I WAS QUITE A PRUDE. I wore big, thick glasses due to my nearsightedness and was very studious. I was able to make a few friends through singing in the choir. At St. John Vianney School, I'd developed close relationships with the sisters, so I was inclined to establish a relationship with my eighth-grade teacher, Sister Mary Margaret.

Attending daily Mass and developing close bonds with the sisters, I wondered if I had a calling from the Divine to dedicate my life to God and become a nun. I spoke with the sisters about the possibility of a vocation to serve God after high school. They began to foster that vocation in me. Sister Mary Margaret noticed how dedicated and sincere I was about my studies. She suggested I attend an all-girls preparatory high school in Nashville, St. Cecilia Academy. I knew we couldn't afford the tuition, but Sister Mary Margaret would not let money deter me. With her help, I was honored with a partial academic scholarship so I could attend the college preparatory academy. My parents agreed. Mother and I began to plan the logistics for my freshman year in 1963.

My home life was sweeter since Phyllis and I were old enough to stay home alone while Mom and Dad worked together at The Question Shop. I don't know if Dad had mellowed or if I just wasn't around enough to witness further confrontations. I continued to come out of my shell bit by bit.

Chapter 19:

St. Cecilia Academy

Sт. CECILIA ACADEMY IS LOCATED in West Nashville, 21 miles from my home. I had never visited, nor did I know anything about West Nashville. South Nashville was somewhat familiar because of a handful of previous trips taking the St. John Vianney Sisters to their Motherhouse on 8th Avenue South. However, that route didn't help us navigate the new location of St. Cecilia Academy (SCA) on Harding Place in West Nashville.

A week before school started, my mother and I caught the city bus on Gallatin Road in Madison as she prepared me for this new odyssey. The voyage included taking two city buses and involved a downtown transfer. It took an hour to travel 21 miles, stopping every few blocks as others boarded and exited. Mom demonstrated the route through tall buildings downtown and a maze of church steeples, monuments, and long-established buildings on West End. It was a new frontier for both of us. Looking back, it must have taken a lot of preparation for Mom to plan the hour-long voyage, but it didn't occur to me then. As we drew closer to the school, Mother pointed out different landmarks so I would know where to exit the bus to walk a quarter-mile up a hill to my new high school.

I had to work daily to ground myself at SCA since I was in new territory, knew no one, and didn't have many social skills. I'd gained some self-confidence at St. John Vianney, but I still felt shy and backward. Other students were wealthy and more confident than I; they had already established cliques with friends from their elementary schools who were now attending SCA. Some students talked about things foreign to me like extensive travel requiring a passport. Their parents were doctors, lawyers, and business owners. None of my previous classmates from St. Joseph or St. John Vianney chose to attend St. Cecilia. I forged ahead appreciative of this tremendous opportunity.

During my freshman year, my father purchased contact lenses for me after a recommendation from the ophthalmologist due to my severe nearsightedness. In 1964 at the age of 15, I was shocked to discover the color of my eyes was green. How had that fact escaped me or my family's awareness? In my younger days, I remember relating to the children's story about the ugly duckling. I had internalized that I was unattractive, as indicated by my aunts who praised my sister's beauty without noticing mine. Without the heavy, thick glasses, I began to discover new aspects about myself, and my confidence grew.

At St. Cecilia, I had a choice of an academic path or a homemaker path. I chose the academic path. I couldn't bring myself to spend time on anything but academics in order to achieve my dream of becoming an educator. Part of the SCA junior year course of study required me to write a term paper. To offset my anxiety, I enrolled in a summer typing class at Madison High School. This simple move not only helped me type and retype my term paper, but these skills have served me well throughout my life.

I was determined and persistent to fit into this new environment, but it was painfully slow. My experience at St. John Vianney had been limited to small classrooms of five to seven students. At SCA, if I thought someone was superior to me, either in looks, intelligence, or wealth, I avoided them like the plague; therefore, I only had a few close friends during my four years at SCA. I hid behind my "not-good-enough" belief. Through the years, I had lots of acquaintances but didn't let anyone get too close. Only one girlfriend spent the night with me during my entire time in high school. Sheryl seemed to be from a similar socio-economic background, and she was shy like me.

From watching my mother cook, clean, and work with Dad, I developed a strong work ethic. Perhaps from being raised by a military father, I learned unforgiving punctuality. I learned the importance of planning at SCA. I needed to plan sufficiently before class to feel relaxed as I walked in the door, because I never knew when another run-in with Dad would interrupt my flow and ability to concentrate.

My need for security required me to complete assignments early so I could make last-minute changes if necessary. I found that nailing down every detail helped me relax and stay in control so I could fulfill my ambition for success. I asked my mother to quiz me before tests, even though she couldn't pronounce many of the words. My self-confidence and self-respect increased as I found success in keeping up with the rich kids at SCA.

I REMEMBER ONE WARM FALL AFTERNOON when I was attempting to solve a trigonometry problem, I complained to Mom about my difficulty. Without my request or permission, she brought Dad in, thinking he could help. My father was not a patient man. His rationale and explanation made no sense to me. I couldn't follow his line of thinking, and that infuriated him. He started again with his demeaning comments:

"I just told you . . . (blah, blah, blah)."

"How many times do I have to tell ya?"

"What's wrong with you? Can't you think?"

Later, I made Mother promise never to go to Dad again on my behalf. I wanted to say to her, *Can't you see this is not helpful?* but the words caught in my throat before they escaped my lips. It would have sounded too much like Dad. Over time, I learned to get up, walk away, and put my mind on something else. When I returned to the problem, I could see it with different eyes. Taking a temporary break created an aperture in my brain that allowed me to gain access to the information needed to solve the equation. This became my new strategy, and 50 years later, the same strategy still works well.

Summers were sprinkled with jobs Mother found for us. Once we delivered four to five-inch telephone books for pennies on the book. The job was so immense, she finally enrolled Bobby to help during his days off at the Metro Fire Department. Another time, she signed us up to take inventory at K-Mart. At the time I thought it was because we desperately needed money, but looking back, I realized I learned a lot during those work projects. I think she was trying to teach us responsibility, work ethic, and the importance of working together for the family.

Completely inexperienced in cosmetic application, I relied on Phyllis to teach me some tricks of the trade. I'd never seen my mother wear make-up, except an occasional lipstick application. Even as I watched her apply her lip color, she cautioned that utilization of such fake color would take away from the natural beauty of my lips.

Although I was not prissy, wearing contact lenses gave me the impetus to join my fellow students and apply make-up when boys from the nearby all-male Father Ryan High School or Montgomery Bell Academy came to visit. I even attended the junior and senior proms at SCA and Father Ryan. When I was a child, my father told me that I would never get married. He said I would be an old maid like his sister, Liz, and I would live with him and Mama and take care of them in their old age. However, I was beginning to see that I might have other options.

There is nothing more meaningful than being true to yourself and finding your own voice.
Follow your heart and don't let anyone discourage you.[26]
~ Jane Fulton Alt

Chapter 20:

Finding My Voice

Anytime I planned to go out with my friends, I shared my intentions with Mother. Her response was always, "Ask your father." Reluctantly, I went into Dad's bedroom seeking permission. Dad's response was always, "No!"

As I grew older, I wrote to Bobby about my dilemma while he was stationed in Okinawa. Bobby said he never asked Dad's permission. He avoided Dad. He either told Mom he was going someplace, or he just left. Once I got that straight in my mind, my life became somewhat easier.

Instead of asking, I began *telling* Dad. "I'm going out with Sarah on Saturday." Dad would say, "No you're not." I'd turn and walk away, and it seemed he'd forgotten all about it by Saturday night. When it was time to leave on Saturday, Mother asked me to let Dad know I was leaving.

His response was, "Where are you going?"

I'd tell him and he'd say, "No, You're not. You didn't ask me."

I reminded him I'd talked with him about it several days earlier. I learned to walk away and just leave, attempting to settle my nerves as I drove out of the driveway. He didn't pursue me or an extended conversation. The new strategy worked well.

Phyllis and I played guitars and sang together with sisterly harmonic voices. Dad was proud of our talent and began to relax a bit when we left the house. Although we entered many talent contests around the Madison area, we never won a title or award. At one event, Jim Glaser, the country music group, from Tompall and the Glaser Brothers heard us perform, took us under his wing, and became our manager. Jim encouraged us to join the musicians' union, which resulted in receiving a small stipend for performances at various venues around town. Earning a few bucks was just icing on the cake; our true love was singing together. We appreciated Jim's support and guidance and went anyplace he sent us to perform. Phyllis and I sang at a lot of gigs during my junior and senior years in high school. Dad was proud of our singing, and he calmed down about our requests for going out.

Jim booked us on the WSMV Noon Show and the Ralph Emery television shows several times during the late '60s and early '70s. Ralph Emery was known for giving attention to aspiring singers and performers. His WSM-TV show was the highest-rated television program in the U.S for many years during the 1970s. Each time we performed on his show, we had to wake up at 3:30 a.m. and leave the house by 4:30 to arrive at the studio by 5:00. We were required to be there early in order

Jill & Phyllis preparing to sing together in 1967

for the makeup artist to prepare us for the cameras. Accustomed to singing together accompanied only by the guitars we played, it was a thrill to rehearse with the band before the show. As they asked us to name the key in which we played the particular popular song, they were quick to transpose our use of capos to the correct key for their accompaniment. We had no interaction with Ralph Emery until he introduced us in his affable manner as the cameras were rolling. There was usually a sentence or two of introduction followed by a welcoming statement. Occasionally he asked us a question. Each time we left the studio, we looked forward to getting home to hear Mom and Dad shower us with accolades.

Once we opened for Skeeter Davis at the Centennial Park Band Shelter. It was a warm Sunday afternoon in July and the only time we opened for a big country star. I don't recall actually meeting Ms. Davis as we stood behind the band shelter awaiting our time on stage. What stands out in my memory is the closeness I felt to my sister, the beauty of the tall green trees blowing in the wind, and the hundreds of people gathered to hear Skeeter Davis entertain them for an hour. Phyllis and I were teenagers with a busy, summer life and activities planned for the afternoon. After we performed, we skipped out to continue our lives.

Once Phyllis and I sang at the unwed mothers' home in Nashville. Attempting to be cognizant of these women's tender hearts, we avoided love songs as we planned our repertoire. Yet, we were surprised that during the time we accepted requests from the audience, it was love songs they wanted to hear. The backup band provided by the musicians' union, heightened our experience. We were on a roll. In 1967, the *Tennessean* newspaper named us the "Discovery Act of the Year."

Mᵧ LEADERSHIP ABILITY THUS FAR had gone untapped; however, toward the end of my junior year, my peers elected me President of the Sodality of the Blessed Mother. This religious organization holds the mother of Jesus as the highest ideal for women. Running for the position, I prepared and delivered my first speech in front of what I considered to be a large student body consisting of fewer than one hundred girls. I steered my enthusiastic spirit with certainty. When I heard the applause, I knew I had it. This was my first elected position. I was becoming a leader and a lady at this prestigious preparatory high school. I felt confident and began to see myself as smart, logical, and analytical, and I began to trust that God had a plan for me. The only thing I had to do was to be aware and open to taking the next step coming into my awareness. I was becoming an intrepid follower of my heart.

ST. CECILIA
ACADEMY

Jill at SCA graduation

As President of the Sodality, I had the honor of crowning the Blessed Mother as Queen of Heaven in a full-house gymnasium on a bright, hot Sunday afternoon in May. We didn't have the money to purchase a new dress for the occasion, so we borrowed one from a friend. We looked at several dresses before we settled on the most modest choice. The long white gown had a high neckline with an open back. It didn't occur to us that the sisters would consider the dress indecent. They were appalled when they saw me walk in and noticed my naked, exposed back. The sisters immediately began to scurry around trying to find a white sweater to cover my indecent back. I realized I'd made a horrid mistake due to my naivety. Eventually someone located a sweater, which saved the day!

As I prepared for high school graduation at St. Cecilia Academy, my classmates bestowed on me the superlative of "most-sincere." I had made friends along the way even though no one knew about my home life or my insecurities. Only Mother and Phyllis attended my graduation ceremony. Dad didn't attend again. He had few social skills and could have been an embarrassment. Even though I was glad he wasn't there, it hurt that he hadn't come.

Mᵧ NEIGHBOR, KENNY JONES WAS A TALENTED MUSICIAN. He started writing songs as early as age 14 and was under contract with Monument Records when he died tragically at age 16. I was out of town when I heard the news on the radio: "The son of Helen Carter, Kenny Jones, has been involved in a horrific, fiery automobile accident."

Time stood still; I felt crippled. I immediately called my mom. In her attempt to save me distress, she had not informed me of Kenny's accident. I immediately came home but found that the hospital was not allowing visitors due to severe burns on Kenny's legs and chest, which had resulted in pneumonia. Kenny's father and brothers held a vigil at the hospital. I later learned the details about this accident. A 25-year-old neighbor took the four teens on a joy ride in his Corvette. Four lanes on the newly constructed Briley Parkway had just opened. According to an officer at the scene, the driver was traveling at high rates of speed when a wheel came off, caus-

Kenny Jones

ing the vehicle to leave the road. The Corvette went off into a ditch and then back onto the highway where it overturned and burst into flames. The driver was thrown out of the car when it hit the ditch. He rushed to the burning vehicle and attempted to put out a fire on one of the young girls with his bare hands. Within a week, all the teenagers had died from extensive burns. The driver was the only one to survive.

Kenny had taught me to play and sing songs he had written that were published posthumously. "Sing a Travelin Song"[27] was introduced by Johnny Cash on his first network television show in 1970 and quickly sold a million copies. The Carter Family recorded the "2001 Ballad to the Future."[27] Some have noted the lyrics as eerily prophetic of the 9/11 attacks on the United States, which took place more than thirty years after the song was written. Kenny is still with me today, especially when I play my favorite song he wrote, "Two Satin Pillows," which to my knowledge, was never recorded. Thinking back, I realize Kenny Jones, my surrogate brother and my young guitar teacher, played a major role in my singing opportunities.

Meanwhile, Jim Glaser offered us a two-week gig to sing out of state. I found myself at a crossroads. *Should I continue a path in the music industry, which I found exuberating, or hold fast to my dream of college?* Remembering how much my neighbor, Helen Carter, traveled and the fact that a live-in babysitter was often with her kids, I decided to go to college as my mom had hoped and for which she'd helped me prepare. I didn't want to be an absent parent; I wanted to raise my own children. I gravitated toward the stabilizing, seemingly bland normalcy of wife, mother, and teacher rather than the prospect of a glamorous life as a singer/performer. I wanted to balance work life with home life with the goal that neither would suppress the other.

Chapter 21:

Gateway

I WAS THE FIRST IN MY IMMEDIATE FAMILY to choose to attend college right after high school. As I look back, I credit my mother for her tenacity, believing in my ability, and supporting me through the various seasons of my life. I believe the Holy Spirit led me through my failure in the fifth grade to an academic high school, and now college. Even though I still carried embarrassment and shame about this seeming loss of an entire year, I felt that at some point I would look back on my life, and it would all become clear. *Was it really a loss of a year, or was there a higher purpose to that experience?* After all, it's what you do with failure that builds success.

In the 1960s many women didn't consider college an option. A technical career or learning homemaking skills such as cooking and sewing were often impressed upon young females as more valuable choices. In 1967, some women went to college to find a husband. I wanted to be independent and secure without a husband. Watching Mom struggle with Dad gave me all the evidence I needed to vie for a college education. Mom did all she could to support me. *How could we afford it?* Because of Dad's reduction in pay from the military, our family was indigent. Although we ate a lot of beans and cornbread, I loved beans and cornbread, so the lack of household funds was only now beginning to affect me directly. During my senior year in high school, Mom and I began to write grants and complete loan applications. The grants came through first, so there was less need to borrow substantial amounts of money. During my lifetime, Mother had never worked outside the home other than with Dad. As was her way, Mother was concerned about the money I might need in daily college life, including the need for clothes, so she found outside employment to help fulfill our desire for me to attain a college degree. She wanted me to have a chance at a different life than the one she'd endured.

Mother took a job as part of the cleaning staff at a local hospital. Her small salary was used to help pay for my college tuition and living expenses. With only one car in the family, Mom could walk to work without interfering with Dad's schedule.

Mother made friends with some of the ladies with whom she worked. On Sundays, they sometimes would go to the mall together, sit on a bench, talk, and watch people walk by. Mother enjoyed time with her female friends. Dad wanted to know where she was going and when she would be back, even though he slept Sunday afternoons away. Eventually, Dad got a job at the same hospital, doing the same work, and arranged his schedule to coincide with Mom's shift so he could keep an eye on her. Perhaps he was scared she would find another man and leave him cold. I bet it irritated Mother that he followed her like a puppy, but she never said a word. Maybe she was just glad he was working and not drinking. I later discovered from Bobby that Mom and Dad worked together as a pair to clean the hospital rooms; however, Dad spent a lot of his time talking to patients rather than doing the actual work. Again, Mother carried the load.

Orientation and registration for college was another milestone similar to my first experience riding the city bus to SCA. Mother and I drove 44 miles to Murfreesboro, Tennessee to register for classes at Middle Tennessee State University (MTSU)*. The gymnasium was packed with over a hundred tables and throngs of freshmen; the noise level was over 90 decibels. Big screens and charts were posted to help students navigate through the process of choosing classes, days, and time periods. I remember getting all my classes scheduled, but before I could turn in the paperwork to the registrar, at least one of the classes had filled and I had to go back to the drawing board. It took hours! It might have been the blind leading the blind, but Mom and I made it through the confusing and messy process of freshmen registration before the convenience of the World-Wide-Web.

College registration
1967, MTSU *

The bright Sunday afternoon when I moved into my dorm at MTSU, my father announced he was going to accompany Mom and me. *I couldn't believe it!* He hadn't bothered to come to the hospital when I was born. He didn't attend my high school graduation, but now he wanted to be a part of this big day in my life. Irritated and unhappy, I sat in the back seat of the car as we made the 45-minute trek to Murfreesboro. Looking back, I realize that even though my father never told me he was proud of me, his desire to be with me now evidenced his approval of my decision. He seemed to recognize I was an adult, and perhaps he was even a bit proud of me. I'm sure he knew how to convey that message. I later learned that he called seven of his siblings to brag that his daughter was in college.

---

*Image provided by the Middle Tennessee State University, News and Public Affairs Photograph Collection, University Archives, Albert Gore Research Center, NPA 285

Life at the university was like a fast-moving comet! I constructed my path carefully with a robust work ethic. I was reluctant to ask questions in front of the class for fear others might think I was stupid. My Dad's mantra had become a defining moment in my life as his words still rang in my ear. I was fighting my demons that told me I wasn't smart enough, and I was determined to prove those voices wrong.

Devoted to punctuality, I power-walked even when it wasn't necessary. I used social skills learned at SCA to look everyone in the eye and say "Good morning!" as I walked across campus. It was good to be away from home - to have independence. Combating a continuous flow of papers, assignments, tests, and timelines, I was good at living by my to-do lists, and I never procrastinated.

I was from one world but now partially lived in another. My father wouldn't allow me to spend weekends on campus. It might have been my choice to come home, but I resented that I had to be under his rule each and every weekend. Staying on campus might have encouraged me to find weekend activities to engage my attention and opportunities to meet and socialize with other students. Since Dad demanded that I come home every weekend, I complied. It wasn't worth a fight and I'm sure I wanted to see my Mother. Although as a young child, I had fought my father at every turn, it didn't occur to me to fight him now. Looking back, I can see that losing Jesse Neal had impacted him, and Dad wanted to keep his children close. Even though he didn't engage in conversations with me, knowing I was home brought him peace.

Although many college freshmen haven't settled on their vocations in life, they are required to declare a major for their coursework. In 1967, I proclaimed a major in social work. Attending a sociology class opened my eyes to acknowledge my family's dysfunction. Without conscious adulation or altruism, I began to consider changing my major to education with the intentional goal to balance the dream of raising my own children while maintaining a career. However, after reminiscing about my childhood experiences through a sociology class, I began to wonder if I could use those experiences to impact other children's education in a positive way.

For 19 years, I'd been called " stupid" by my father or through my own self-talk. Reflecting on my feelings of defeat and the contrast of how success and achievement in parochial schools had lifted my spirits, I became aware that I wanted to utilize my negative childhood experiences to help children who had endured similar home environments and similar negative teachers. I wanted to make an impact on education. I changed my major to education! I wanted to continue singing for enjoyment, but education felt like the path to begin to make sense of my trauma. I wanted to turn this thing around! My avenue to healing and transforming my childhood pain led me to a passion to change the world of education.

All journeys have secret destinations of which the traveler is unaware.[29]
~ Martin Buber

Chapter 22:

Balancing Act

THROUGHOUT MY FOUR YEARS AT MTSU, I focused on achievement. Although I was short on life experiences, I was emboldened by the skills I'd developed at St. John Vianney and SCA to tackle any academic problem and perform well. At SCA I'd learned to write efficiently and think critically. As a result, I blossomed at MTSU.

Although I dated a few boys in high school, I only dated Rodney in college. He was a friend of Phyllis' boyfriend so we double-dated on weekends. I came to realize that MTSU was known as a suitcase college. Most kids went home for the weekends. Rodney was still in high school while I was a big college freshman. It was fun being with Phyllis, and my relationship with Rodney continued out of convenience. He wrote beautiful letters to me during my freshman year, and my heart began to open to him. Rodney joined me at MTSU the next year, and we continued to spend time together. He had a gorgeous head of thick curly hair and a muscular build. He was smart, enjoyed my singing, and seemed to genuinely love me. Looking back, I realize I had adopted the unconscious beliefs my father had instilled in me: *I would be an old maid, taking care of him and Mama in their old age.* Rodney professed his love for me for three years before I was willing to accept his marriage proposal. Unconsciously, I was fearful no other man would ever come along with the same profession of love; I'd better accept Rodney's proposal. *Was this the way my mother felt when she married Dad at 16? Or was this part of the reason she stayed with him for all those years? Did she think she couldn't do better, as I did?* I'd put him off long enough, and he was growing tired of the rejection.

"Will you marry me?" Rodney continued to ask.

"Someday," I replied.

"This is the last time I'm going to ask!" Rodney retorted.

I married Rodney in the spring of my junior year in college. The announcement of my marriage sent my mother into a state of disbelief, disappointment, and depression. She had assiduously prepared for my college graduation, and now she feared it was in question.

Rodney was a good man. He was generous and would give someone the shirt off his back; however, we were both immature. I loved being loved - feeling loved. Without a good role model, I knew little about marriage, and I fell into some of the same patterns as my mother. Years later when Rodney wanted to buy a house for investment in a poor section of town, I sensed that it was an ill-conceived idea; however, I felt guilty saying "no" to him. I relented and eventually gave in to his request. It was a bad business deal. It would take years for me to learn to trust myself and stand by my inner guidance.

At the beginning of my junior year, after finishing all prerequisites, it was time to qualify for entrance into the education program. I don't remember a lot about it except for one particular interview. After one member of the interview team, Mr. Hansen, asked a few questions, he stated that he didn't think I had the "voice" to become a teacher.

Shocked, I rebutted, "I earned an A in my speech class!"

"You did? Who was your teacher?" he asked as though he didn't believe me.

He left the room, made a phone call to my speech teacher, and returned with the recognition that I had been truthful. Then I shared that I had sung on the Ralph Emery show on WSM-TV with my sister on numerous occasions. He was familiar with the show and seemed to trust me now. I explained that when I'm nervous my voice becomes somewhat gruff; my nervousness was what he was hearing. I had lived by the code of effort, expecting results and achievement. *Surely it wasn't going to end here.* After my initial fear of not being admitted to the education program, Mr. Hanson signed my paperwork and I was in.

As a DEVOUT CATHOLIC, I complied with the church's stance on the use of artificial birth control. Rodney and I married in March of 1969. Lori was born in June of the next year, short of my 22nd birthday. She had a head full of dark curly hair, and she never outgrew those beautiful blue eyes. After only a few months, Lori slept through the night. Before my sophomore year, I had changed my major to education, partly to be able to balance a career and family. With Lori's birth on June 14th, I had the summer to recuperate from childbirth, spend precious time with my daughter, and continue my senior year in the fall. My mother was ready and available to help care for Lori when classes resumed.

Lori: six months old

Time pushed us forward. My senior year flew by with assignments, student teaching, and coming home to my daughter each afternoon. I was soaring! I had it all! A sweet marriage, a beautiful daughter, and a college education close to completion. As I walked across the stage to receive my Bachelor of Science diploma in Education, I saw my future flash in front of me. I wanted to give my daughter a better life than the one I'd had. I wanted to impact education so that other children could be spared some of my scars. I wanted to bring the joy of learning, the exhilaration of success, and the tools to cultivate self-appreciation and self-respect into my daughter's life and public education. Facing and embracing my childhood pain ignited a passion in me that continues today.

To avoid the draft of the Vietnam war, Rodney joined the Air Force for a four-year tour. During his last three years, we were stationed in Albuquerque, New Mexico, where I taught kindergarten in the mornings while Lori went to the base nursery. I was able to collect Lori by noon, feed, and read to her before her afternoon nap. I didn't want Lori to grow up as an only child, because I'd found so much comfort, companionship, and closeness with my younger sister, Phyllis. The research I'd read indicated that three to four years' difference in age was ideal - close enough to form an affectionate relationship but not feel competitive. Three years later, I discovered I was finally pregnant. I wrote in my journal that I had yearned for Phaedra for a long time before her conception. She came into my life at the perfect time. I'd learned so much from my firstborn that I felt like somewhat of an expert. When I gave birth to Lori, it had been a hard, long delivery so I decided to give Phaedra a natural childbirth, free from pain medication. I wanted Phaedra's entry into this world to be a welcoming, clear-headed experience. I didn't want to do anything that might dull her senses. Natural childbirth was a wonderful, yet scary experience. Rodney and I had completed Lamaze classes to help prepare me to relax during the pain. When we got into the depths of labor, I was ready to pull out, but Rodney got right in my face and helped me breathe through my contractions. Having a natural childbirth cut my labor in half from when Lori was born. The Holy Spirit continued to be with me and seemed to fulfill all my wildest dreams.

So far away from home in Albuquerque, Rodney and I were on our own. Rodney's mother had crocheted a beautiful green and white blanket before Lori's birth, so I decided to crochet a pink, blue, and white blanket for the new life developing inside my body. During the early 1970s, before the days of ultrasound, parents learned the gender of their child at birth - not before. The variety of colors in the blanket would be suitable for the unknown sex of my child.

I wrote this letter to Phaedra when she was 5 years old. Each year on her birthday I relive the day of her birth, and I wanted to write it down so I could share it with her one day in the future.

November 5th

My Dearest Phaedra,

Every year at this time, my thoughts go back to the days immediately preceding your birth. What a wonderful time of life for me. I'd wanted another child so badly! When I finally discovered my pregnancy, I was ecstatic! Our time in the military was almost complete, and I knew God had sent you to me just in time. Having you inside me felt like a miracle, and I treasured being pregnant - even thinking I was absolutely beautiful. I could feel your heart, your aliveness, and your energy. I got so big that your dad had to help me wash my hair.

I loved tickling your tootsies and feeling you scooch your foot over just a tad bit, as if to say, guess where I am now? Your little personality was already beginning to take shape.

I wanted to give you the best - the very best! I didn't want you to come into this world sedated from pain meds so I decided to give you a natural childbirth. After some convincing, your dad agreed, and we began Lamaze classes where they taught me to breathe and concentrate on something other than the pain. With Rodney's assistance, I began to experience that when I focused on another part of my body, the pain lessened. It reminded me of my mother's counsel to get my mind on something other than the problem at hand. I began to experience circumventing the pain, hurt, and fear by controlling my mind's attention.

On Halloween evening, I dressed Lori in her ghost costume. I was too big and swollen to go far myself, but our little family of three all went down the street trick-or-treating before Lori accompanied our neighbor and her kids to continue the fun. I knew you would be born soon - maybe tomorrow. My bags were packed and ready to go. After much deliberation, we had chosen male and female names.

On Sunday, November 4th, I started having cramps and thought the time was close. I woke up early on the 5th thinking this was it. Your dad took me to school where I was teaching kindergarten, so I could turn in my key. I told them it was probably a false alarm and I would probably return later that morning. We dropped Lori off at the base nursery and were at the base clinic by 7 that morning. The doctor reported that I'd dilated to three centimeters, and they admitted me to the hospital.

I was scared. Could I do it? Your father stayed with me all day. I don't even remember him leaving me to go to the bathroom. He never left to eat. The Lamaze instructors had trained us to pack crackers and snacks. Rodney helped me remember my breathing exercises and concentrate on relaxing. At one point, I began to lose faith in my ability to proceed without medication. The pain had grown worse, and I had difficulty relaxing into the discomfort. I cried out saying, "I just can't do this!" Rather than your dad saying, "Ok. Let's give her an epidural," he nudged me to stay with it. He had faith in me when my faith had dwindled as he assured me I wasn't alone.

Right before you were born at 8:05 that evening, the nurse instructed your dad to leave in order to put on a hospital shirt, so he could accompany me into the delivery room. While they were moving me into the delivery room, I had an epic contraction. Because your dad wasn't there to help me breathe through it, I grabbed this little medic and demanded, "Breathe with me." I pulled him to my face. I think I scared the bejeebers our of him!

You were born in a matter of minutes. They said "push" and you came out in a burst of energy. How good it felt to give birth to you. You were so beautiful lying there on my tummy. Thank you for choosing me to be your mom.
I love you,
Mom

~~

Phaedra had blonde hair and big, gorgeous, deep, almost black eyes. Once again, Spirit's timing had been impeccable, giving me two full months to be home with my girls while only missing six weeks from my kindergarten students. My mother and father came to Albuquerque to help me through the first two weeks.

Phaedra: six months old

By the time I'd healed from childbirth and established a routine, Rodney received orders for an early-out departure from the military. Phaedra was only six months old. Lori was almost four.

After returning home to Tennessee with my diploma framed and hung on the wall, I found it challenging to secure a teaching position in public education, so I taught in parochial schools for two years, which yielded only about half of a Metro teacher's salary. Because few demands were placed on me as a private school teacher, I was able to spend quality time at home with my family. However, I continued to dream of joining the ranks of Metro Nashville Public School (MNPS) teachers.

Newly hired Metro teachers advised me that the best way to gain employment in the saturated field of educators was to become a substitute teacher, so I could get acquainted with principals throughout the district. I quit my job teaching in a pa-

Lori: 4 years old

rochial school and worked as a substitute teacher for two years. If I needed a day off with my girls, it was easily available.

Substitute teachers were in high demand. Every day I was offered work and consequently met many principals across the district. If I was impressed with the school, I asked the principal to keep me in mind for future openings. Although I later learned that Metro Schools' Personnel Office advised prospective teachers to call weekly, I missed that advice. Rather, I listened to information from a newly hired teacher who suggested I contact the Personnel Director, Mr. Whitman, daily to let him know just how enthusiastic I was about employment in Metro schools. I took my friend at her word and called many days asking for a job. What a mistake! Consequently, Mr. Whitman surmised that I had poor judgment and made the decision not to hire me.

Did I get this tenacity, or perhaps lack of judgment from my father? Referencing the letters Dad wrote Mom during the war, I recalled that Dad had written his supervisor "every day" requesting an assignment stateside. *Had I inherited this drive from my father? Was it a blessing or a curse?*

One day on the phone Mr. Whitman exclaimed, "I'm not going to hire you because nothing is outstanding in your employment file!" Even though his words devastated me, I didn't believe him. Three principals had shared with me that their requests for me to fill particular positions had been overlooked; I contacted the teachers' union to help with my dilemma. Dr. Bob Bogen, the union representative, suggested we set up an appointment with personnel to review my work file. Sitting in the personnel office with Dr. Bogen, we perused principal feedback forms from a two-inch-thick folder relating to my work as a substitute teacher from across a district that spanned over 500 square miles with approximately 50,000 students. Many principals had rated me "outstanding!" Some rated me "average." None rated me "below average."

Dr. Bogen was ready to go to bat for me with Mr. Whitman and believed personnel would have to offer me a position, but I felt dejected and deceived by Mr. Whitman. I questioned if I even wanted to work for Metro Schools. Reminiscent of my childhood, I felt disrespected and unappreciated, and I wanted nothing more to do with MNPS.

Meanwhile, I saw an ad in the paper from the American Red Cross for a Coordinator position for Services to the Aging. Funded by a short-term grant, the position would only last for 18 months. Looking back, I can see how Spirit provided blessings to my family and me for what was to come.

Grief can be the garden of compassion. If you keep your heart open through everything, your pain can become your greatest ally in your life's search for love and wisdom.[30]

~ Rumi

Chapter 23:

Loss

I WAS TETHERED TO MY MOTHER. She was my salvation, unwavering in her love for me. She had lived to watch me graduate from college as the first person in our immediate family to earn a degree.

Mom had been diagnosed with breast cancer seven years earlier. Historically, she'd received her care from the military hospital at Ft. Campbell, Kentucky. After her mastectomy, Mother underwent chemotherapy and radiation. Finally, there was good news that the cancer was in remission, but by 1976, the breast cancer came back with a vengeance. By 1978, she was in and out of the hospital, and her time was drawing near.

The Red Cross policy for employees allowed me to spend time away from work when a family member was hospitalized. This gave me the time and flexibility I needed to be with my mother. Her condition was deteriorating, and I wanted to hold on to each moment.

Sitting at the hospital, waiting to see my mom for 10-15 minutes an hour in Intensive Care, I kept a journal to write my most intimate thoughts and prayers throughout the day. When I was a child, the fear that would bring me to my knees was losing my mama. How could I ever survive without her? When I was eight, I wrote a poem entitled, *Today - Tomorrow.*

> *What will happen tomorrow?*
> *I pray it won't be like today.*
> *My mother died.*
> *I am all alone.*
>
> *When I was joyful,*
> *She rejoiced with me.*

When I was depressed,
She comforted me.

But now-
-now-
I am all alone.

My classmates asked if I'd lost my mom.

"No," I replied. "She's still here."

Just the fear remained. But 22 years later, the time was close for that poem to become a dreaded reality. The months between March and August were probably the most agonizing in my life.

It was a cool, crisp morning in early March when I arrived at Vanderbilt Hospital. Mother had been taken by ambulance the evening before with a 102-degree fever. She must have lost consciousness because she couldn't remember much and didn't even know she was in Intensive Care.

According to my journal entry, "They are giving her morphine and she's feeling good right now. I think she's ready to go skipping down the hallway."

I saw Mother that morning at 11:00 in the Medical Intensive Care Unit, and she was worried about money. Mother asked, "Do you know it costs a dime to make an outgoing call? How will this sickness be listed on the insurance forms?"

Before coming to the hospital, Mom had already written checks and addressed envelopes to pay bills. She asked me to make a list of things that needed to be completed. I jotted down her requests in my journal as she enumerated the things that needed attention:

1. Be sure to put the checks in the mail.

2. Deposit the U.S.A. pension and Social Security checks.

3. Get Daddy some milk.

Mom was still taking care of Daddy and the household chores. I wrote in my journal, "My mom is slipping away from me. She's only 63."

"I just fed Mother lunch. She ate a hamburger and really enjoyed it. Her mouth was watering for the orange. I started to peel it for her, but she suggested I cut a hole in it and let her suck the juice out like a baby sucking a bottle, as she had taught me when I was a kid. The plastic knife was too flimsy so I peeled the orange and fed it to her piece by piece. I told her that the chemotherapy had damaged her heart." Mother said, "I'll be with y'all as long as I can."

She turned the subject to the family. Mom wanted Lori to have a pair of boot skates and remembered how much Bobby loved his first pair. Then she talked about the time a girl kissed Bobby when he was in elementary school. Apparently, Bobby had told Mother about the experience, and she remembered that she'd burst into tears. Mother laughed as she told the story and wondered if Bobby remembered.

Then she grew pensive. With resignation in her voice, she said,

"You know, Jill, I don't have long to live."

"Why do you say that, Mama?"

Mother's friend, Alice, had breast cancer. After her mastectomy, Alice began to go in and out of the hospital, but when her tummy got big, the doctors began to draw fluid off, and Alice died soon after that. Mother could see the writing on the wall. I begged Mother not to die. "Please don't leave me, Mama!" *How could I live without her?*

A week later when Mother was in the hospital again, I talked with her on the telephone before visiting. Mother must have had a room on an inexpensive floor because there was no TV. She was uncomfortable. It was too hot. When I arrived, Mom was talking to Dad on the phone. He'd called to tell her about the television program he'd just watched, *Little House on the Prairie.* As we visited, I welled up in tears several times. Mother complimented me and expressed her love and respect. She talked about what fine kids she had. She voiced concern that when families go through this type of trauma, stress can cause feelings to get hurt. She hoped her children would not do that. We talked freely about death. She said Father Rohling had heard her first confession, and she wanted him to hear her last. Three days later I wrote in my journal, "It's Sunday. Mom's home but sick again. The ambulance has been called. I go down to her house at 11:30 a.m. while Rodney finishes cooking breakfast for the girls. Mom's crying! The ambulance passes the house. I run out the door, flail my arms wildly to retrieve it. While riding in the ambulance with Mom, my eyes are glued to her face. Her pain and frail body are heart-wrenching to observe. She squeezes my hand as we exit the ambulance."

After some tests, the doctors determined that Mom's potassium level was too high. The heart medicine was poisoning her by adversely affecting her kidneys. They instructed her to stop taking the prescribed heart medication. I kept the family informed during the afternoon and evening. That night, Rodney picked us up at the hospital and brought us home.

After I cooked dinner for my family, I usually took Mom and Dad a meal. The next day, Dad called me to tell me that Mom thought she could eat a Wendy's hamburger. I took the hamburgers on my nightly visit. Mother had been on a low-salt diet, but she had stuck to the diet so well that now the doctor said she needed more salt. Mother was irritated that the doctors didn't seem to know how to help her. They'd previously put her on a fluid pill but then attributed her problems to the effects of the fluid pill.

When I got home that evening, I found Phaedra playing outside with the neighborhood kids. Although she didn't mention it at the time, she had woken up in the middle of the night with pain in her right arm. The next morning I took Phaedra to the doctor and discovered she had a broken arm. After setting her arm in a cast, we went to see Mother. She looked so much better, and her voice was much stronger.

By Saturday morning Mom was back in the hospital. I'd been running back and forth to visit her every day either at home or in the hospital. Betty called me Saturday morning and woke me up to ask me if I would take Dad to see Mom at the hospital. I was exhausted and furious that Betty had disturbed my rest on the only morning I could sleep late. Clearly, she didn't know how much I was doing on my own. I told her "No!" and she hung up on me. I called her back, and she hung up on me again. I suspected Dad had called Betty to ask if she would take him to the hospital. I remember what Mother had said. "Times like this are hard on the family." My sisters were spending time visiting Mother, too; we were all upset that our time with her was slipping away. Betty called later that day to apologize. "I don't want to fight with you, Jill. I love you. These are hard times for all of us."

Mother laid in the bed looking poorly for the next three weeks until I admitted her to the hospital on July 10th. Her tummy was so big, she teased the doctors that she felt she was delivering a 10-pound baby. Mother had delivered five children; none of them were 10-pound babies. Two staff doctors had been with her until after midnight. Mom's siblings were calling and planning to come to Tennessee to say their "goodbyes."

The next day I saw Mom before lunch. She was supposed to get the results of her EKG, X-ray, liver scan, and electrolytes. Mom's oncologist, Dr. Furr told her they'd done all they could. "Now it's time to make you comfortable," he told Mom.

The oncology volunteer came in at noon. Mom shared with her some of what the doctors had said earlier that morning. The volunteer said, "OK, I think I hear what you're saying and what you're not saying."

The volunteer disclosed that she had lost her husband to cancer. After the doctors had done all they could, they sent her husband home to die. It happened around Christmas time. The children all came in, and they got all their business settled together. The volunteer described this time as one of the happiest with her family.

Mom asked her about death. The volunteer said she personally believed in life after death, but if there was nothing, she really hadn't lost anything because she'd had a good life and tried to be a good person. Mom was afraid she would not make it to heaven because she was not a good person. She said she had committed an unforgivable sin. *It was hard to hear my mother describe herself as "not a good person." I had always thought of her as a saint. She'd put up with so much and still kept love in her heart. How much better can a person be?* The volunteer said she believed God accepts us all and understands our nature. The conversation with the oncology volunteer helped Mom. I was glad I'd been there to witness how talking about death had helped my mom.

Bobby came in, and Mom told him what the doctor had said. Bobby looked so sad for a few seconds, I thought he was going to cry. His modus operandi is to make a joke. To alleviate the tension, Bobby said, "Now, Mama, you've been in and out of this hospital claiming to be dying and haven't yet. I don't believe it. Cry wolf too many times and no one believes you." We all laughed.

Whether by miracle or magic, my work with the American Red Cross offered an opportunity to help Mother and me heal when I heard Dr. Elizabeth Kubler-Ross[31] speak at a conference. A renowned Swiss-American psychiatrist, known for her book, *On Death and Dying*, Dr. Ross spoke about her research with terminally-ill patients through interviews with the dying. At the conference, Dr. Ross shared how a loved one could linger in an attempt to help those who would be left behind. I realized I'd been selfishly holding Mother hostage to her body and that the best gift I could give her was to let her go. After spending a day with Dr. Kubler-Ross, I went back to the hospital, told my mother I loved her and that I would be okay. I gave her permission to die. She listened and nodded her head, saying very little.

Dr. Furr was one of the kindest, most caring doctors at Vanderbilt University Hospital. He knew how hard Mom's passing would be on her children. He'd watched us closely for two years. He told Mom about some new experimental drugs that he would consider for her. When he left, I followed him and Dr. Porter into the hall. I told them that Mom was ready to die. Dr. Furr became very solemn as Dr. Porter spoke. "Your Mother is right. She's in her last stage of cancer. She's suffering. It's time to take her home and let her die in peace surrounded by her family." The doctors ordered hospice. Our family had made a shift. We all started helping Mom and Dad prepare for the inevitable. Betty called Mom at the hospital. She cried for an hour telling Mother she wished she'd done more to help her and from that time on, she did do more.

When I lived in Albuquerque for three years, it was rare to have a babysitter. The base nursery was available so I could teach a half-day, but we rarely used them at night. Once we came home to Tennessee, my mother welcomed opportunities to be with her grandchildren, so I often left them with her. I hadn't realized how sick she'd been in the early days of her cancer, and she wasn't one to complain. I felt bad that I had left my girls too often after I later discovered how sick Mom had been. I apologized for this. Mother just told me how much she loved her granddaughters and how sorry she was that she didn't feel well enough to continue to help.

Mother's brothers and sisters began to come for short visits from out of state. Although Mother was close to all her siblings, she was especially close to Fann, as they'd had a double wedding in 1930. Fann and her family also lived in the same Royal Oaks Subdivision with Mom and Dad in Kannapolis, North Carolina, Mom asked Fann if she would come to help her through this period. Fann immediately packed her bags and hopped on a plane.

Betty called me to ask me if I would take Mom's brother, Foster, to eat and then bring him back to the hospital. I told her, "No." I was doing all I could, but I wasn't calling my siblings to ask them to take the load off me. I needed some time with my family. Then Betty told Phyllis that I had hurt Mother's feelings. I never refused my mother anything, but it was easier to refuse my siblings and claim some space for my family and myself. Looking back, I wish I hadn't been so abrupt with Betty. Bobby was studying chemistry 20 hours a week working toward a college degree. We all had children. Life was busy, yet we all wanted to be there for our mother.

My supervisor, Hazel, and other friends from my work at the Red Cross began to bring food to my house. I took the baked hen, a jar of green beans, cornbread muffins, and potato salad to Mom's house. Betty and her family were there. That little hen fed nine people. Mom enjoyed eating with us so much Sunday and Monday that she invited us again on Tuesday, but my daughters begged to eat at home. We did stay home on Tuesday and enjoyed some normalcy. On Wednesday after feeding my family, I took supper to Mother in bed. She'd had nothing to eat all day except one egg and a tomato.

Father Rohling came to see Mom the next day at 2:30 p.m. He spoke to Mom about heaven. He made it sound so good, I was ready to jump in her bed and launch off to paradise alongside her. Father Rohling said that in heaven, if you want to be someplace, you just think about it and you're there. I chuckled to myself thinking, *Sure would beat all this traveling I'm doing.*

When I saw mom the next day, her eyes were watering. Her feet were larger than on Monday when we saw the doctor. Her tummy was huge! Life was leaking out of her.

I called Dr. Furr the next morning. He said, "There's not much we can do."

He could double her fluid pills. He was not concerned about nutrition because she wouldn't live long enough to become malnourished. He said the tumor could be causing the fluid to build up; the tumor may have been pressing on her blood vessel. He also said they could radiate the liver, but that would cause liver damage, and she would not live long after that. Dr. Furr gave me his home telephone number so I could call him day or night. "I love this man," I recorded in my journal.

On August 1st, I threw a surprise birthday party for Mom. It was the first she'd ever had in 64 years. A couple of mom's siblings and all her children were there to celebrate. I brought homemade cake and regular pizzas. It was past the time for low salt. It was good to see Mother eat; she clearly relished the salted food. Only a few days later, Mom was mostly in bed. I went down and gave Mother a sponge bath.

On Saturday, August 5th, I went to see Mom twice and then again at 10:30 p.m. to spend the night by her bed. She asked me to say the Lord's Prayer with her. I was so honored to do so. When I told her I was going to spend the night, she told me that it wasn't necessary, and I told her I wanted to. She said, "If you are, sleep in my bed." But I had brought a cot. Throughout the night Mama sipped on ice water, and I could tell my presence had been useful; however each time we spoke, she was concerned about my comfort. I slept beside my mother's bed for several nights, thinking it would be her last night, and I wanted to be with her when she drew her last breath.

On August 15th, hospice delivered a hospital bed, oxygen, and a bedside potty chair. I took Friday, the 18th, off to be with Mother and took Aunt Fann shopping. Mom rang her bell when she needed something. She ate pretty well - mostly fresh tomatoes and cucumbers.

On Sunday, the 20th, I gave Mom a sponge bath before attending 9:00 Mass. Then I called Bobby to inform him of Mom's condition. He immediately got the doctor on the phone. Dr Greco recommended that Mom go to the hospital by ambulance, to drain the fluid from her tummy. Fann rode in the ambulance with her. Because Vanderbilt is a teaching hospital, various interns asked Mother a thousand questions even though she could hardly speak.

At last, Bobby said to the nurse, "Don't let another doctor ask my mother any more questions. If they want to know something, let them talk with her oncologist, Dr. Greco." I love the way my brother got right to the heart of things and advocated for our mother.

I don't remember why my siblings had to leave, but they were gone for hours. The doctors explained the dangerous procedure to me. She could hemorrhage internally and go into shock. If that happened, they would do nothing to stop her bleeding or put her on a respirator. Meanwhile, nurses tried to get Mom to take her medication. So unlike my mother, she said, "Just go away and let me die!" This upset Fann and me.

As the doctors left, they patted me on the shoulder and said they were sorry. *Was this the moment I would lose my mama?* I had to sign for the procedure. Although I hated to have that responsibility solely on my shoulders, I knew it was the only way Mom could get relief. I called Dad before the procedure and explained what the doctors were planning to do. He sobbed. Dad had transformed from lecturer to observer, from angry to subdued. I could feel Dad's divergence, but I didn't know where to place it, given my litany of complaints against him. Pensive in tone, he began to pray for her, fearful she would die in the hospital.

They completed the procedure at 11:30 that morning. Although one doctor told me to leave, Dr. Greco intervened and gave his permission for me to stay. The fluid was like bloody water - a half gallon was withdrawn.

The family returned, and the doctor talked to us at length in a room down the hall. In essence, Dr. Greco said we could put Mom through this time and time again or we could allow her to die. He also explained that the pain could get much worse. In the end, he might have to cut a nerve to the brain to relieve her pain.

I went back to Mom's room. I had been close to tears all morning with very little sleep over the weekend. All the family entered Mom's room. I was sitting in a hardback chair. My eyes were swollen. I found it difficult to blink. I said I was going home. With a half-smile on my face, I looked at my siblings and said, "Don't call me!" My brother, whom I love tremendously, said, "Jill needs to get her priorities in order." As I look back, I believe he was saying that he thought I was spending too much time away from my family to care for Mother. He knew how much I had been with her, and he was trying to help me. However, at that moment, I wanted to scream, "If y'all would do more, I could do less," but those words never left my lips. Furiously, I said, "When you figure out how my priorities should be, just let me know." Phyllis was shushing me as I ran out of the room. Betty rushed after me. I was bawling as tears burned my eyes. Betty hugged me while I surrendered to desperate sobs.

I drove directly to my mother-in-law's house a few miles away. Rodney's mother fed me, but I never stopped blubbering the whole time I ate. As I was heading out her front door to go home to my family, Rodney's mother stopped me. She made me lie down and get myself together before driving 20 miles to Madison. I was not always close to Mrs. Waddell, but I sure appreciated her that night.

Mrs. Waddell called the doctor, and he ordered some nerve pills. I left to pick up my girls. As I prepared supper, Bobby called to apologize. Although he'd only wanted to be helpful, he admitted saying the wrong thing at the wrong time. He knew how I'd driven myself into this state of exhaustion and rattled nerves by my over-commitment to Mother. As was Bobby's way, he'd been joking to try to relieve pressure in the room, but at that moment I was so full of emotion, I reacted with intensity.

Mother went home by ambulance. My siblings and I followed. We wanted to help her get settled and talk with Dad. Betty told Dad how proud she was of him. He'd taken a bath. Mom had told him the girls wanted him to clean up, and he complied. As a child on the farm in Jackson County, Tennessee, my father didn't have the luxury of bathing frequently. As Dad grew older, his desire to get in the bathtub waned even more. This was his first full bath in over a year, although he'd "washed up" occasionally. I think getting in the tub scared him.

We all came to see Mom every day now. When Betty and her husband, Tommy, spent the night with her on the 22nd, she was making a gurgling sound. The next night when I saw Mom, I'm not sure she recognized me. She smiled at Lori and Phaedra. Aunt Fann checked her watch and said Mom needed to sit up. I helped Fann get Mom out of bed to sit her in a rocking chair. Although sitting up was difficult for Mom, her breathing greatly improved.

On the 24th, Betty called at 3:00 p.m. and told me to get to Mom's house. At 3:00, when Dad gave Mom her pills, she said, "Something's wrong. Call Emergency." Betty was ready to call the ambulance, but Dad called the nurse. The nurse called Dr. Greco. When I arrived, Bobby was calling the priest. Mother was hot and wanted to be fanned. Her gurgling was much louder. Lori, Phaedra, and Rodney came in. My sisters were concerned that Phaedra was too young to see her grandmother in this shape. I was not opposed to Phaedra seeing her dying grandmother, and I allowed her to stay.

Father Rohling came, as well as a nurse, Carol Showalter. She had a prescription for morphine. Dr. Greco told the nurse that Mother was dying and that the morphine would knock her out so she wouldn't be afraid, and she would be out of pain. Bobby and Carol had difficulty getting a pharmacy to fill the prescription. Neither Madison Hospital nor Memorial Hospital would fill it, and most of the pharmacies didn't carry intravenous morphine.

Carol told the pharmacist at Madison Hospital that she would bring her nurse's license. She invited him to call Dr. Greco to verify the prescription. She pleaded with the pharmacist that her patient was dying and might not live for 30 minutes, to no avail. He said, "No."

She said, "I'm in no mood to put up with this today. My patient is dying. Please will you honor this prescription?"

"No," was the answer.

Finally, after extensive telephone endeavors, Carol found the morphine at a pharmacy across from Memorial Hospital. Bobby and Carol set out to get it. All of this time, Aunt Fann stayed in the den sitting in the tan chair. She and the adults were drinking Falstaff beer. I didn't think I liked Falstaff, but the benefits of relaxing outweighed the odd taste.

Father David Perkins arrived and said to Mom, "Eunice, let's say the Lord's Prayer together." We all prayed. Mother tried, but we couldn't hear her weak voice. Even Carol joined in the prayer. We were all crying - tears dripping from our faces.

Bobby was sitting next to me, holding Mom's hand. He asked if she wanted to be fanned. Mom said something to him. He didn't understand, reached over, and leaned down where she could speak into his ear. Mother's words weren't audible to any of us. I'd never seen my brother cry, but he cried out, "Oh, God!" and began to weep loudly. With tears streaming from his eyes he asked, "Do you want Pop?"

We all made room for Dad to sit by Mama. Dad was despondent. I'd never seen him so helpless and hopeless. They exchanged words of love as Dad wept holding Mom's hand. Mom glanced at me as she gasped for breath. When I leaned over to her, she whispered, "I love you!" The feelings of loss streamed through my psyche. *This was it. This was goodbye.* Tears welled and slid from my eyes. At 30, I was too young to lose my mama!

Bobby was crying so hard, he went into the bathroom. Betty followed. I followed her. We wanted to know what Mother had said to him. She'd said, "Goodbye, Darling!" Betty and I clung to each other in unfiltered heartache.

As Carol was preparing to leave, she taught Bobby to give an injection by practicing on Carol's arm first. Bobby then gave Mom the morphine injections on a specific schedule throughout the evening and night. After Carol left at 6:30 that night, Rodney went out and brought supper back for everyone.

At 4:00 the next morning, I received a call from Bobby saying Mama had died. I went right over and helped Bobby make the necessary calls. The undertaker was already there. Mom looked so peaceful. Bobby had set his clock to give Mother another shot of morphine at 3:30 a.m. The alarm didn't go off. When Bobby woke up at 4:00 a.m., Mom had passed. I called Father Rohling. He said, "Your mother is in heaven this morning." Bobby flushed the rest of the morphine down the toilet.

I had wanted to be with my mother when she took her last breath. It must have been her wish to slip away alone in the silence of the night while the house was full of loved ones. I have such great appreciation for my siblings and all the family and friends who came to visit Mother and brought food and gifts. I've never forgotten how important those acts of kindness were.

Even though Mom's passing was not a surprise, I still experienced all the stages of grief. I found comfort studying old photographs, remembering the contours of her body and the lines in her face, but I grieved the loss of hearing her voice. My father was experiencing the same grief when he found a cassette recording of Mother talking. He and I listened to the audio together as we allowed our tears to flow.

Time progressed. Betty became the heart of our family. Not only did she open her home for family gatherings, but she also continued to look after her two younger sisters with special care even though we were adults. If we needed anything, Betty was there. As Betty grew older, Bobby, Phyllis, and I began alternating our homes for family celebrations - a tradition set by my mom, carried by Betty, and embraced by us all.

Grief is selfish and stole valuable time from my children. The grant for my Red Cross position soon terminated, and I was out of work again, which provided needed time to mourn my sweet mama, regain my strength, and spend quality time with my family. Rodney and I agreed I needed a hiatus to stay home with Phaedra the year before she started kindergarten; it was fundamental to parent myself and my children with the care I was unable to provide while spending so much time with my mom during her last year on earth.

The loss is immeasurable but so is the love left behind.[32]
~ Unknown

Part II

First the pain, then the waiting, then the rising.[33]
~ Glennon Doyle

Chapter 24:

Healing

MY CHILDREN NEEDED ME. Phaedra was devoted to the blanket I'd crocheted for her before her birth. She held her "blankie" between her ring finger and her thumb while sucking her index finger. She couldn't go to sleep without her blanket. Phaedra faithfully held and rubbed that frayed covering even through her teenage years. I offered to make another one, but she only wanted the one that felt just right, smelled just right, and supplied the comfort that was - just right.

To earn a little money, I loaded scrap floor pieces from Bruce's Hardwood Flooring mill in Nashville with five-year-old Phaedra in tow. She was right beside me as I parked the truck under the wood chute and watched the bed fill with scrap lumber. Hard, dried wood provides excellent kindling and leaves a nice bed of coals for those who heat their homes with wood. I ran an ad in the paper and found the kindling to be in high demand. I earned $30 a truckload in 1976 and brought in about $90 a week, just enough to provide money for groceries. I cherished my time with Phaedra, reading books, watching Sesame Street together, singing songs, and playing outside.

I learned more about parenting from my work as an educator than from the example of my parents. I discovered that some parents brought treats to school to celebrate their children's birthdays. I learned that some parents volunteered to participate in special events. With Phaedra in tow, I was able to volunteer at Chadwell Elementary, bring treats for special holiday events, and lead choral singing in Lori's third-grade classroom while I played the guitar.

After nesting at home with Phaedra for nine months and being available to take Lori to and from school, I began to feel a nudge to get back into teaching. Here I was - making $90 a week with a college education, as compared to working in Metro Schools where my salary would have more than doubled. I lived in a constant state of calibration, tweaking one area to balance another. My children and I had healed somewhat from losing my mom. Now it was time to bring my work back into balance. Was there a way to use my college education and continue to be available to spend time with my girls?

Shortly after I felt the urge to get back into education, I saw an ad in the paper for a Director of La Petite Academy, a daycare and after-school program. This position complimented my need to return to education while maintaining my voracious appetite to be with my girls. I applied, interviewed, and began work the next week, my children beside me. We opened the center in Hendersonville, Tennessee. Although we were a one-car family, La Petite provided a van, not only to transport students to and from school but also for my own transportation to and from work, a 15-minute drive from home.

La Petite provided palpable relief for my family's needs until Lori developed spinal meningitis at age 11. Even though I'd never taken a day off from work for the entire year, when Lori was ill, my supervisor complained when I needed one day off. That was it! I was not going to let work take priority over my daughters! I was not going to apologize or listen to any flak for taking care of my children. My priorities were ironclad. I turned in my notice.

Still aspiring to get into public education, I began to reconsider Metro Schools. However, just thinking about my previous experience with Mr. Whitman left me feeling demoralized, so I decided to apply for a teaching position in surrounding Sumner County. When I interviewed in Gallatin, the interviewer asked if I had attempted to work in Metro Schools. I explained that in my zeal to get a placement, I'd tried too hard and angered the personnel director by calling too often. The interviewer appreciated my honesty and hired me on the spot.

I'd finally secured a teaching position as a public school kindergarten teacher at Bethpage Elementary. There were only two problems: I had to drive 45 minutes one way, and I had to commit to four years at this location before I could request a transfer. Although the money was not as good as teaching in Metro Schools, the salary was a big improvement over my previous jobs.

For an entire four years, I hurled myself out of bed at 4:30 a.m, drove 45 minutes to arrive at school by 6:45, and started class at 7. Because of my colossal need to be with my children, I enrolled them at Bethpage Elementary, 35 miles from our home in Madison. Traveling from the town of Madison in Davidson County through the city of Gallatin in Sumner County and on to the rural, tobacco-farming community of Bethpage felt like going through The Twilight Zone.

Traveling to Bethpage felt like going back in time. The cities disappeared into a wide-open country with friendly people who knew everybody's business. As a child,

I'd made the trek to Gallatin each day to accompany my parents to Dad's work at The Question Shop. Now I found myself going back in time as I made a similar trip.

The principal at Bethpage Elementary taught eighth grade half a day. During the tobacco season, the eighth-grade boys often stayed home to help in the fields. Their absences were expected and understood. Harvesting seasons gave the principal more opportunities to govern with fewer students to teach.

Lori was in fifth grade; Phaedra Dianne was in first grade. Even though my girls were thrilled to come to school with their mama, it was difficult for them to rise and shine at 5:00 a.m. and leave the house by 5:45.

Spending time with my daughters on these daily commutes was both heart-warming and entertaining. On these long voyages, I sometimes asked the one sitting in the passenger seat to take the wheel for a few seconds while I applied lipstick. Lori was totally opposed to this request so she relegated herself to the backseat for the remainder of the year. Phaedra took the front seat, as she was open to taking the wheel if I needed to place my hands elsewhere. Phaedra was self-confident and easy-go-lucky, while Lori was hard working and more easily stressed. Both my girls were funny without trying to be. Humor came easily to them; they kept each other and me in stitches. I was proud of both my girls for who they were and for the self-respect each of them displayed.

For these long daily trips, we bought a used Volkswagen Bug. Although driving the 10-year-old VW was good on gas, it was not always dependable, and we often broke down on the way to school. Rodney was in a position where he could help us when we broke down on the road.

The teachers at Bethpage Elementary dressed well and wore three-inch heels to school. Kindergarten teachers customarily don't wear high heels because we spend a large part of the day on the floor with our students or bent over paint jars in art projects. Because I wanted to fit in, I occasionally dressed up and wore three-inch heels. It seemed like every time I wore those heels, the car broke down on the way to school. There were no cell phones in 1979, so we had to walk to the nearest telephone to call for help. Rodney quickly came to our rescue. My girls began to call my three-inch heels my "bad-luck" shoes. When they crawled into the Volkswagen in the mornings and saw those heels, they presumed car trouble would ensue; a walk to the nearest telephone and help from Dad were imminent.

At MTSU I'd decided to go into education because I thought it would provide balance in my life. I wanted to become a good parent and offer my children a better homelife than I'd had, and I wanted to become a powerful educator like Mrs. Richards and the sisters at St. John Vianney. The two seemed to go hand-in-hand. I anticipated efficiency and effectiveness in both important roles. Teaching in the same school where my daughters attended was the fruition of my dreams. I loved any time I could glimpse them in the context of their own lives. Seeing them in the lunchroom, the hall, or on the playground were precious moments. When Phaedra was not feeling well, the office sent her to my classroom. Phaedra fell asleep in a carpeted corner until it was time to go home at 2:05. Although I loved being close to my daughters, being available when they were sick was invaluable, given my experience at La Petite. Although the trek and the early mornings were difficult, teaching in Bethpage was an awesome experience.

Phaedra Dianne
in first grade

One of the blessings for teachers is having a few weeks off during the summer. Having that time with my daughters was priceless. By May, we'd begun to plan our summer schedule. We joined the Sun Valley pool in Madison and left the house each morning by 10:00 a.m. I packed a cooler of sandwiches and drinks. We swam from 10-2:00 Monday through Friday but arrived home in time to watch *The Guiding Light* on TV. The kids either took naps or talked on the phone while I began preparations for supper. When Rodney returned from work at 4:40, we ate dinner together as a family. By this time I was exhausted!

SUMMER FADED INTO FALL AND IT WAS TIME TO GET BACK TO WORK. Thirty-five children were enrolled in my kindergarten class. We were housed in the only portable classroom at the K-8 elementary school. The administration demonstrated neither the willingness to transport another portable or to hire another teacher; therefore, a parent was assigned to work with me as an aide. Now there were 37 bodies in my 700-square-foot portable classroom. A typical elementary classroom is 900 square feet for 20 children. Even so, all my students learned their letters and sounds in that small space. I attributed that success to body movements I created that correlated with the alphabet song as well as other songs we learned. While singing the letter names, we moved our arms in the shape of the upper case letters. When the body moves, the mind works at higher efficiency. I had already begun to learn from my students.

Peer relationships are an important factor in the educational experience of children. Lori and Phaedra were often invited to sleepovers with their friends on

Friday nights, but it became arduous to consistently drive 90 miles round trip on weekdays and then make the trek again on Saturday to retrieve my daughters. I soon realized I was repeating a pattern from my childhood. When I attended elementary school in the town where my father worked rather than my neighborhood school, I felt I was missing opportunities to make friends with those who lived near me. Now I was depriving my own children of that same opportunity. This scenario was not working for my family; a new plan had to be created. I wanted my girls to attend school in our neighborhood and develop long-term friendships with their peers. I decided to withdraw them from Bethpage Elementary at the end of the year and enroll them in their neighborhood school in Madison.

The new plan was ideal. Holy Spirit helped work out details to find a family down the street who transported my girls to school in the mornings. Because Bethpage Elementary was dismissed at 2:05 p.m., I was able to make the drive to Madison, pick up my girls at 3:00, and transport them to their after-school activities. I wanted to give my daughters the gifts I had failed to receive as a child, such as tap dancing, baton twirling, gymnastics, softball, and cheerleading. Life was full, and my girls were happy. Seeing them satisfied fulfilled my innermost sentiment for a balance of work and family. It wasn't always easy to establish equilibrium because of my drive to succeed, but snow days and time off during the summer helped to bring me back into harmony.

I suspect all teachers and students love snow days. My sister, Phyllis, had to work, so she brought her son, Andy, to spend the unexpected holidays with us. During the 1970s and 1980s, we had at least 10 snow days a year. As a teacher, I could stay home with my girls. We played in the snow, built snowmen, sledded, and ate snow cream together. There was not a boring moment when Andy was in the house.

The more a teacher teaches, the more experienced and capable the teacher becomes.
Students benefit from improved teaching and from the additional time teachers spend with them.[34]
The Development of the Better Schools Program in Tennessee from 1981 to 1986
Daris A. Gose, 1994

Chapter 25:

Career Ladder

AFTER TEACHING AT BETHPAGE ELEMENTARY for four years, I received a transfer to Lakeside Park in Hendersonville, only 20 minutes from home. My girls had attended their neighborhood schools for three years, and now I asked Phaedra if she would like to spend her 5th and 6th grade years with me in Hendersonville. She eagerly accepted my invitation. Rodney and I noticed a major change in Phaedra's personality when she started at Lakeside Park. She was much happier. We had been together when she was in first grade, and now we were finally together again. Traveling to and from school gave us uninterrupted quality time. Phaedra never complained when school responsibilities required me to arrive early or stay late. She enjoyed hanging out with her friends and quickly became known as the teachers'

helper. Our school was like a community and Phaedra was happy. Each night in my journal, I wrote how much I appreciated my life, my teaching, my husband, and my children. Lori and Phaedra were good students, attentive, and responsible for their work. My daughters' nine-week average grades were typical: Lori achieved a 100% average in Latin, 98% in Algebra, 96% in English, and 80% in Physical Education. Phaedra made Bs in Math, a B+ in English, and a B+ in Reading.

Phaedra in sixth grade
playfull carrying Jill

Lakeside Park Elementary was in a middle to upper-middle-class neighborhood. One parent volunteer who helped publish books in my classroom was concerned that I allowed kindergarten students to make mistakes in their daily writings without correcting their errors. She didnt speak to me about this but sent her husband, Ron, a college professor at nearby Volunteer State Community College (Vol State), to come to the parent-teacher conference to advise me on this matter. After

Ron shared his wife's concerns, I explained to him, "As children begin to speak, we accept their approximations, attend to their needs, and over time, they learn the correct pronunciations of words; however, if we begin to correct too early, children will be more reluctant to try new things and express their needs. The same is true when students begin putting pen to paper. If we accept students' attempts, support them by teaching sound-to-symbol correlations at the right time, and in the right way, kindergarten students continue to become risk-takers, try new things, and learn how to spell correctly as they are exposed to accurately spelled words in their published books. Kids want to do it right. They want to use conventional spellings; however, as I have learned, when writers begin a new piece, they don't stop to correct errors but value the process of letting ideas flow, keeping the inspiration going and getting the message down in print. Editing comes later."

Ron, understood my words and became a supporter of my teaching style. Years later, I taught a writing class at this same college where he was now the head of the department. He apologized to the group of adjunct professor attendees that night saying, "I'm a bit nervous tonight. My daughter's previous kindergarten teacher is here. She's a great teacher. I've been in awe of her so please overlook my nervousness." Ron had become a comrade.

While I was teaching kindergarten at Lakeside Park in 1984, then-Governor of Tennessee Lamar Alexander created a plan to evaluate teachers and financially reward those who scored highest on the secretive Career Ladder evaluation program. Because it was the first year of implementation, much of the information and expectations were purposefully obscure. Nevertheless, I jumped right in with both feet. If successful, I could potentially add $7,000 to my yearly salary, which would significantly impact my family. Like my dad, I was accustomed to evaluations, and I welcomed them with ease, knowing I would learn a lot in the process.

During the same month I signed up for the Career Ladder year-long evaluation, I learned that Tennessee State University (TSU) offered a pathway to a master's degree in reading at the Vol State campus, primarily for teachers in Sumner County. The timeframe and location fit perfectly into my schedule. This was an opportunity I couldn't pass up. *Would starting graduate school take too much time away from my family?* Rodney supported my goal.

Tenacity, determination, and ambition were the traits mirrored in my dad's Army career. I recognized those same rubies were prevalent within me. I knew I had the right skills and plenty of passion that would carry me through. As it turned out, each process fit together like a hand in glove, each complementing the other. It must have been Spirit opening a new door. As each entry opened, I walked through.

Having a husband who pitched in to prepare supper when I attended evening classes once a week from 4-7 p.m. made it easier for me to proceed. I had a lot going on raising two daughters who were both into sports, dance, and cheerleading. Nevertheless, I simultaneously pursued both the Career Ladder Evaluation and a master's degree program. My work was both interesting and rewarding, but I always had to be attentive to maintain a balance between motherhood and career.

When Lori started her first year at Father Ryan High School, she decided, right out of the gate, to run for president of the freshman class. It was a lofty goal, but I encouraged her to go for it. Lori had worked hard on her speech, and her commentary was powerful and engaging. I was able to leave Bethpage and arrive at Father Ryan in time to take a spot outside the auditorium under the shade of tall oak trees within earshot of the freshmen assembly. It was the kind of day that made me breathe deeply, thinking anything was possible. I was thankful to be alive, alert, and active in the lives of my children.

Finally, it was time for the candidates to present their platforms to over 300 fourteen-year-old students. I took my place at the back of the auditorium, appreciating my invisible stance. Lori wore a dress as white as a dogwood blossom. Shafts of light from the stage flooded through her hair and made her appear saintly. She spoke eloquently with poise and passion. Her competition was a well-known football player who was not nearly as eloquent as she; however, when I heard the applause the jock received, my face burned with fever. I immediately ordered flowers for Lori, hoping to soften the blow of her likely defeat. Even though Lori lost her election, she was strong and took her defeat in stride. She had taken a step out of her comfort zone. Around the dinner table that evening, Lori expressed how receiving the flowers had lifted her spirit and helped her walk away from school that day refreshed with even a sense of relief.

Rodney did most of the cooking, grocery shopping, and running kids around at night while I prepared for Career Ladder evaluations and class assignments for TSU. After I tucked my girls in bed at night, I read and completed assignments for my coursework. Going to bed, I had to turn off my mind as I was absorbed in thinking about what needed to be done the next day. As my eyes opened in the mornings, my mind was already preparing a checklist for the day. I privately praised myself for being a good mom who was able to keep many balls in the air and simultaneously prioritize time with my girls.

During the year-long Career Ladder evaluation process, three different evaluators from across the state visited my classroom to observe me teach. Two visits were scheduled; the last was unscheduled. My first two observations which occurred between November and February went well, but the looming surprise visit seemed to create the eternal now. Spring came early in March as I planned and anticipated this would be the day for the pop-in visit. I'd spent hours each night working on portfolios and interview questions required for Career Ladder evaluations, as well as papers required for my graduate classes. In my journal, I wrote that I was looking forward to a Mother-Daughter Tea on Sunday afternoon at Father Ryan with Lori.

THE REDBUDS WERE BLOOMING on the cool, crisp morning of April 11th, 1985. Phae and I arrived at school an hour early. My colleague, Nancy, and I were the only two teachers at Lakeside Park going through the evaluation process, but the entire staff was cheering us on, providing moral support. From my principal, Opal Poe, to our custodian, they were all rooting for our success. Although I'd been expecting visit number three for weeks, my colleagues seemed to have formed a consensus that this Thursday was the day for my last visit from the third evaluator. My colleagues said they could feel it in their bones. My students were creating concept maps during our unit on plants. We'd even drawn and labeled a beautiful mural together as they wrote stories about the growth observed on various plants around the classroom. I wrote in my journal, "Another dynamite lesson and still no evaluator."

Liz Castleman, my third Career Ladder evaluator, finally came the next day. It was a marvelous experience! My lessons were superb, as my students engaged easily with their continued reading and writing processes. Our scheduled 20-minute interview lasted 90 minutes because Liz wanted to hear more. The interview felt more like two friends talking rather than an evaluation. Liz told me that after spending the day with me, she couldn't wait to return to her classroom in August, as she had learned so much from spending the day with us. As soon as Phaedra and I left school that Friday afternoon, we celebrated with a large Dairy Queen ice cream before supper. With only one month left in the school year and the year-long evaluations completed, I breathed long, exasperated sighs of relief as I let go of the tension from the past seven months. My weekend was characterized by the release of anxiety and worry, unbridled joy, and deep sleep.

Learning to write is learning to think.
You don't know anything clearly unless you can state it in writing.[35]
~ S. I. Hayakawa

Chapter 26:

The Creative Process of Writing

PROFESSORS FROM MY GRADUATE PROGRAM were teaching me to hone my skills, follow the child rather than an arbitrary curriculum, and become the educator I longed to be. So often a boxed curriculum assumes students are at a certain level. Lessons are presented based on that assumption. However, in the schools where I'd taught, children displayed a variety of achievement levels within the classroom. It was incumbent on me to know my students intimately: their skill levels, their interests, and their motivation. This information helped me to craft a curriculum that met the needs of each individual student.

Marissa writes. "We don't have no neighbors. Get out!"

As visitors and parents entered my classroom, they didn't find a typical kindergarten environment. They found an active classroom where children were moving about, busy at the tasks of reading, writing, and illustrating their stories. Multiple projects were going on simultaneously as students were working independently or with peers to complete their projects. Everyone was on task. I knew which skills needed to be taught, and I allowed my students to lead me in the process. Observing them closely, I was able to build my instruction on their strengths and interests while weaving in state and district required skills. Early in the year, students drew pictures as a pre-writing activity and then attempted to translate sounds to letters as they created a story to go with their illustrations. After only a month in kindergarten, Marissa writes, "We don't have no neighbors. Get out!"

She was writing from personal experience. A stranger had knocked on her door at home. Her dad told them to go away.

When students had questions, they could ask a friend or me for help. Students were free to get up, move around and talk to one another; but they were all on task! When a student had trouble choosing a writing topic, watching the gerbils play or nurse their babies could be counted on to provide interest. Because children like to tattle, I channeled their inner motivation by providing an Antics Book where they could register their complaints. It became so popular I had to enact rules about how many students could stand in line to submit their side of the story.

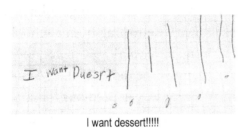

I want dessert!!!!!

Students enjoyed writing to express their desires. Marissa wrote this message at home. It reads, "I want dessert!!!!!!" She demonstrated knowledge of the correct spelling of "I" and "want." She uses invented spellings to write the word "Duesrt" (dessert). By this incorrect representation of "dessert," Marissa demonstrated knowledge of initial, interior, and ending consonants as well as a correct vowel. So much to praise! She capitalized the word "I," demonstrated spacing between words, and also used exclamation marks to express strong emotion.

Thanks to my graduate classes, I was learning the importance of daily process writing even at the kindergarten level. Writing became an integral part of each day's schedule. Kindergarten students had the freedom and responsibility to choose topics for their writings. When parent volunteers came to help, the children enjoyed writing letters to them, as illustrated by Scott:

Scott writes a letter to parent volunteer Mrs. Jones

> *Dear Mrs. Jones,* *
>
> *I like you very much. I hope you like me too. You are a good person.*
>
> *Scott*

I could determine a great deal about students' skill levels through their compositions. For example, Scott understood the basic mechanics of writing a letter with the salutation followed by a comma. Scott closed his letter with his signature. He spelled "you" correctly and consistently. In the body of his letter, the spacing between words was sporadic and periods were omitted. He may have thought "are a good person" was one word. Scott could hear dominant consonants and vowels within a word. Most invented spellings retained the initial and last sound of the word. Scott had good letter formation with a variety of upper and lower case letters within the text. This kindergarten student was well on his way to becoming literate. As his teacher, I could praise him for a variety of skills he demonstrated in this piece of writing. The rainbow and flower illustrations were gifts for Mrs. Jones.

When I was a young child, I yearned for praise. While pointing out strengths, rather than errors in children's writings, I observed their self-concepts improve as their zeal for writing blossomed.

One morning Chad burst through the classroom door exclaiming, "I know what I'm going to write about today! My bus broke down." Returning from a school assembly, Antwan inquired, "We haven't missed writing, have we?"

Due to a consistent daily schedule, children planned the topics of their compositions even before they entered the classroom. Writing was not tedious for students. I watched in amazement as they owned the process. Their piece of writing with an accompanying illustration was their work, their art, their thinking. Students were proud of it and eager to learn more as they saw themselves blossoming into literate members of our classroom.

I had two great professors from TSU at Vol State: Dr. Carole Stice and Dr. Marino Alvarez. Dr. Stice ignited a passion in me for children's literature and the writing process. Dr. Alvarez taught me the importance of building on students' prior knowledge, interests, and experiences. He even came to my kindergarten classroom, and together we conducted science experiments with my students. As I learned more about hands-on activities, I found students' motivation increased proportionately to my increased knowledge and excitement watching them learn. Plotting and labeling their addresses on a classroom map spurred more opportunities for discussion, making connections, and more writing.

Kindergarten students plot and label their addresses on a classroom map.

Dr. Alvarez taught my students and me about concept maps, which are visual representations of information in the form of flow charts. These pictorial images are useful for visual learners, but they can benefit any type of learner. In preparation for learning to use flow charts to organize their thinking, I read several books about different animals to the children. Each student chose an animal. As a prewriting activity into expository writing, children drew concept maps and included as much information as they could about their animal. Through perusing the maps, I could immediately identify any misconceptions. Amie had written that birds like to eat grass. Although it's natural to assume that birds eat grass, given that we often see birds pecking at the ground, I asked Amie, "Do birds eat grass?" She responded, "I don't know." I asked, "How can we find out?" Amie responded, "Go to the library."

Our librarian, Judy Bryant, willingly allowed students to come to her resource center when they were in pursuit of knowledge on a particular topic. Mrs.

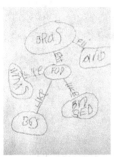

Bryant pointed them in the right direction even when she was working with other classes. Judy believed that libraries should be accessible to students at times other than just their scheduled library period. After Amie's trip to the school library, she returned to class equipped with a broader understanding of what birds eat, but even more importantly, she learned how to search for information. Amie read her map, "Birds fly around. Birds eat food like bird seed. Birds eat food like bugs. Birds eat food like worms."

Kindergarten student's concept map on birds

It might have been more expedient to have just told Amie what birds eat, but I would've robbed her of the experience of actively searching for information, interacting with another adult, learning her way around the library, and making decisions about what she wanted to include or exclude in her map and subsequent descriptive writing.

More students began to request individual library time to further their quest for information as they augmented their concept maps. The walls of our classroom had extended as their knowledge expanded. At the tender age of five, my students

demonstrated their ability to think, organize ideas, seek additional information, monitor assumptions, test hypotheses, and draw conclusions. These kindergarten students were not only readers and writers; they had become researchers!

It was hard to believe what these five-year-old students were accomplishing due to the environment we had created with the help of my professors. The children's enthusiasm for school was palpable. One would have thought students were at play

First-grade student reads to her peers as they closely observe.

rather than learning to read and write because they were so fully engaged, moving into each activity with excitement and confidence. Science experiments were thrilling to my little ones, and the books I read in class enhanced their eagerness. Children naturally want to learn. Because of the impact of my professors, my classroom came alive with the joy of learning.

One day as I was preparing for a scheduled interview with a Career Ladder evaluator, I noticed Nicholas looking out the window prior to writing his story.

I instructed, "Nicholas, Get busy!"

He replied, "I'm thinking!"

Although I feared that an evaluator might code looking out the window as off-task behavior, Nicholas was clearly *on* task. I wondered if I had made a mistake to think my graduate classes and Career Ladder would align.

Time would prove that, once again, I could trust Spirit. I did what I thought was best, put one foot in front of the other, and moved forward with confidence. Confidence was the void my mother and I shared, but now I could see it growing strong within me.

First-grade students illustrating their published books

Students worked in pairs to read classroom stories, charts, and even the wall where I hung stories illustrated by them.

By basing my instruction on students' prior knowledge and interests, I found I was able to effectively teach them and at the same time fulfill state and district requirements. It was too scary to ask for permission to deviate from the curriculum because I didn't completely trust myself or the process. I took a step forward and assessed, paying close attention to my students and discussing outcomes with my professors.

Students read a Thanksgiving story as they take turns pointing to the words.

Teaching became an art for me. It was exhilarating to teach by following the children in front of me, rather than by following a scripted curriculum written by a group of people across the country who didn't even know my students. Rather than perceiving the curriculum as the expert, I became the expert in integrating the knowledge of my students while respecting state and local mandates. I knew my students intimately through their writings, both academically and emotionally. As I embraced this role, I continued to develop my expertise.

On a trip to Toronto to attend a reading conference, I sat next to Dr. Helen Brown who was the Executive Director of Teaching and Learning with Metro Schools. I don't know what came over me, but I took a leap. I shared that rather than assessing students using the arbitrary skills-based testing packet created by the district, I appraised all reading skills through portfolios of my students' reading and writing products. I said to Helen, "I hope you won't fire me for this." Dr. Brown

First-grade students writing in their journals

chuckled and said, "Jill, that's the way the skills were intended to be assessed, but we felt the need to develop the testing packet for teachers who were not secure in their teaching." Dr. Brown assured me that I was not required to use the testing packet, given my system for demonstration of mastery of skills through authentic reading and writing classroom experiences. Sadly, it appeared to be more expedient to create pre-packaged tests rather than train educators to become experts in their field.

As I witnessed the power of authentic engagement, my students thrived. Teaching was exhilarating. Each day I read powerful children's literature to the class. As a result of hearing stories that piqued their interests, students wrote daily, often using the content or the author's voice as a guide to their own productions. I served as their editor, fixed their mistakes, and published students' writings into books, as I transformed invented spellings into a typed, corrected version. Parents helped with the publishing process.

The delight on the children's faces was observable as they saw their original story edited, typed, and published in a brightly wrapped, hardbound book. Since students were the authors of their original stories, they were able to read the corrected version, and over time I noticed them using more conventional spellings, punctuation, and grammar in initial drafts. Previously-published books and stories displayed around the room became resources for students as they referenced them for correct spellings in their new writings. Our classroom was actually littered with literature. The students knew how to access information contained on the walls, bulletin boards, and within our library of books. Students actively used the available resources to locate conventional spellings - either in their own published books or in some favorite poem or verse displayed in the room or in one of the language experience stories we'd written together. I fell in love with the process because mistakes were not seen as problematic.

When I was a student in school, mistakes were marked in red. This reinforced Dad's message that I was stupid. Now mistakes were honored as part of the learning process. Children were praised and rewarded for their near-attempts at perfection. My belief that success is a result of confidence which stems from learning from errors became even more concrete in my mind and my teaching. Student-published books were read and reread. Since we wrote stories every day, I could see spellings improve. The publishing process provided the impetus for students to continue writing.

We write to communicate our experiences, thoughts,

Student signs up to share his work from the Author's Chair.

desires, and needs and to allow creative juices to flow. The higher octane of communication is communion. A writer's soul can make an impression on a reader he has never met, revealing himself in some way. Both the reader and the writer are transformed by the content and experience of the words and, in the process, discover something about themselves.

Communication gels when the student author shares his writings in various stages of the production and receives feedback from his peers. One component of

our writing process was for five students to sign up daily to share from the Author's Chair. During this time, the author sat in a big chair in front of a large carpet. The students and I were the audience and sat on the carpet together. After the author read his story to the class, those who wanted to make comments raised their hands and were recognized by the author. Students were taught to respond to the author's piece of writing by offering positive comments before they asked questions or provided suggestions for revisions. Often a question arose that helped the author make clarifying alterations. Particular experiences shared from the Author's Chair often stimulated memories about which others decided to write. Each student made his own decision about when he was ready to share his story with peers. As I observed

Student shares his draft from the Author's Chair as his peers listen and respond.

students share from the Author's Chair, I saw relationships develop more deeply as students' interests expanded. Even the most reluctant readers and writers eventually signed up once they experienced the risk-taking environment and peer support our community of learners had created.

Because children saw themselves as published authors, the five-year-olds suggested they write to various authors to share their feedback about particular stories and books I'd read in class. Several students chose to write to Eric Carle. One day my students and I received a response from the author of *The Very Hungry Caterpillar*.[36]

The children were overjoyed when the colorful card came in the mail. They passed it around and read it to each other. Eric Carle's letter to my students was written in invented spellings. His letter reads,

Letter to students from Eric Carle written in invented spellings

Dear Mrs. Waddell, Dear Friends,

Thank you for your letters and pictures, and pupil materials. I like your approach to teaching. I wish I'd had a teacher like you. My teacher didn't let me make mistakes. But now I have a wonderful editor. She corrects my mistakes. I am lucky. Keep up the good work!
With admiration,
Eric Carle   ~~

Children learn to read in much the same way as they learn to speak. Infants' babblings are praised by their parents with smiles and words of endearment. When a young child wants a drink, he may point to the container and say, "Ink." Parents are excited that the child has come this far with their pronunciations and attempts to communicate. Isn't it ironic that parents would not dare correct their toddlers when they make this type of error, yet later criticize them for errors in their writing attempts? As students' approximations are accepted in writing, their needs are met, and they enjoy the process of feeling like a valued, published author. This reminds me of the way I'd felt at St. John Vianney my second year in fifth grade. Teaching with this philosophy gave me great pleasure and propelled me to learn more to support my students. I was thirsty for knowledge!

Since I was the new teacher on the block, I hadn't sought permission to deviate from the curriculum; nor did I share what I was doing with my colleagues or principal. I closed my door, taught the way I was learning in graduate school, and watched my students thrive. Living by the motto, "It's easier to get forgiveness than permission" had served me well. *Would it continue to do so, or bring angst into my life?*

The children treasured their published books. We created a classroom library using a card catalog index file system much like those used by the school and public libraries at that time. Kindergarten students monitored and supervised the process. If borrowers did not return student-authored books in a timely fashion, the author was reluctant to grant permission for him/her to check out their book again. Students learned leadership and management skills, not because I was actively teaching those charac-

First graders proudly displaying their published books

teristics, but because we had created a community of learners where cooperation and responsibility were the fabric of our daily lives.

My students taught me to learn from them. By watching them closely and being observant when they began to doubt their intelligence and abilities, I adjusted my responses to them and thus became a better teacher.

Case in point: In early kindergarten, KK illustrated a story and wrote some letters to attempt to put her words into print. I asked her to read her story to me that consisted of only the initial consonants of a four-word sentence. I transcribed her words in small print at the bottom of the picture so I could remember her exact story and later analyze it for progress. When I walked by her workstation a few minutes later, I noticed she'd marked out her letters with big Xs and rewritten my letters and words. I felt like a failure. I feared my attempt to remember her story had left her feeling less than adequate. I often shared with students that it was ok to make mistakes because that's how we learn. After that, I transcribed stories on the back of the piece of writing rather than on the front of the paper.

When she transformed into a butterfly, the caterpillars spoke not of her beauty, but of her weirdness.
They wanted her to change back into what she had always been. But she had wings.[37]
~ Dean Jackson

Chapter 27:

Transformation

DURING MY TRANSFORMATION AS A TEACHER, my soul also went through a metamorphosis. A new mantra was taking shape in my heart rather than the old "I must be stupid" slogan that had resounded in my head for three decades. I began to hear a still, quiet voice: "Trust the process, trust the children." Perhaps the inner voice came from my readings or my association with my college professors, but something more was happening. A whisper from deep within began to swell up within my consciousness, guiding me to trust myself. I began to feel confident that everything was going to be alright. Spirit was with me, leading me in a direction that not only impacted my students, but also my daughters and my life. I began to trust and respect that inner voice.

As I continued to examine the events of my childhood, I heard about a program for Adult Children of Alcoholic Parents (ACOA), so I started attending meetings at the Methodist Church on Elliston Place in Nashville. At the weekly meetings, attended by hundreds of people, I was introduced to books on codependency. I became passionate to learn more. Looking back, I see how ACOA taught me to be more independent. Even though I'd always thought of my mother as my savior, I learned that she had failed to protect her children. Even so, I couldn't be angry with her, as I was filled with love and compassion for her life with Dad.

As I studied more about alcoholism, I realized that although Rodney had been a great husband in many respects, his drinking had become problematic. I became increasingly aware that his Dr. Jekyll and Mr. Hyde's personality was, most likely, due to drinking liquor and tequila. When I asked him to stop drinking, our problems exacerbated. I began to see my mother's pattern repeating in my own marriage and realized I had not set healthy boundaries. I'd focused so much on the good times while ignoring the problems until they became too significant to overlook. My focus had been on pleasing my husband and keeping the peace.

But now I was learning to face the prevailing issues that I believed stemmed from his alcoholism. I learned to claim my space and requested an alcohol-free home. I learned to say "no" or "maybe" within social or school gatherings. I finally learned my first responsibility was to myself. For the first time in my life, I began to consider myself and think carefully before responding to others' requests. Being a people-pleaser had caused anxiety and high blood pressure. I finally began to realize how to take better care of myself in order to meet the needs of my children and my students.

As I continued to run a race with time, the day arrived for me to take my comprehensive exam for my master's degree in reading. Alone in the house, I leisurely dressed in preparation for the 30-mile drive. I had plenty of time and had enjoyed the solitude of the afternoon, as my children were with friends for summer fun. Preparing to apply my make-up, I took my eyeliner pencil and used the mirror on the back of the bathroom door to guide this delicate art when I accidentally pushed the bathroom door closed. *Oh No!* The door had been stuck several times before, but someone had always been at home to rescue the one trapped in the bathroom.

I turned the knob frantically as my body broke out into a hot sweat. *Calm down,* I thought to myself. I took a few deep breaths then tried again. Feeling imprisoned, I began twisting, turning, and shaking the door. The unrelenting door only rattled. Again I attempted to breathe slowly and deeply and called on the dear Lord to help me escape this horrific entrapment.

Thinking I had received an answer to my prayer, I found a screwdriver in the closet. As my concentrated breathing continued, I carefully took the handle off the door, hoping to be guided by my Higher Power. It soon became obvious to me I knew nothing about the mechanics of a door. Once it was off, I had nothing to hold on to - just a hole in the door.

By now my body was wet with sweat, and I began tearing off my clothes in an attempt to cool off. I considered removing the bathroom screen window, but I needed the car keys to get to class. The keys were in my purse on the other side of the locked front door.

In a fit of rage, I noticed the hinges on the door. I was successful in my attempt to remove the pins from the three-door hinges. Even then, I was still a captive of the small bathroom.

As terror overtook me, adrenaline rushed through my body and empowered me. I grabbed the hole in the door, twisted, and pulled in a wild fit of panic. Down came the door. I was free! I toweled my wet, sticky body, applied baby powder, redressed, and ran out the door.

As I drove to class, I was thankful I had 30 minutes to breathe as I attempted to relax - thankful I had escaped the confines of the small bathroom. I made it to class on time, completed the comprehensive exam in three hours, and eventually received word that I had successfully passed and earned my master's degree.

When Rodney came home that afternoon and found the bathroom door leaning against the wall in the living room, he wondered, "What the hell happened while I was at work?"

As I prepared for the commencement to receive my master's degree, I was informed I'd achieved the highest level on the Career Ladder Teacher Evaluation program. I'd earned the Title of Career Ladder III, Master Teacher. I began to reflect. These accomplishments were extraordinary for any educator, but how did a kid who hated school and believed she was stupid, achieve such accolades? I remembered my parents and grandparents. Even in her 50s, Mother moved with the vitality of a 16-year-old when she mowed the grass. Grandma Ovie gave birth in the morning and plowed the fields in the afternoon. My dad never gave up on attempting to rectify his military records. It was clear to me I'd learned diligence from my family. *Could it be that my childhood trauma was the extreme condition that propelled me into a finely tuned, artistic, master teacher?*

Right off the bat, attaining my new credential yielded $3,000 yearly and the potential for an additional $4,000 for summer work. The money allowed me to plan a real vacation with my family.

In the past, I'd continued my family's tradition of visiting out-of-state family members and labeling those as "vacations." With the money from Career Ladder, I scheduled a week's holiday at Seabrook Island in South Carolina. This was the first real vacation for my family and me! We still enjoy fond memories of that holiday in a gated community where Lori and Phaedra had full rein on the three-mile sandy beach with multiple swimming pools. This respite brought them together in a new way. Even though I thought I had planned wisely with the age difference in my girls, they were not as close as my sister Phyllis and I had been growing up. But in this environment, my daughters hung out together - swimming in the various pools, then the ocean, and wandering freely - enjoying each other's company. We even splurged on $50 sweatshirts as souvenirs. Lori wore hers until it was in threads. *My mother would have gasped at the thought of such extravagance.*

Take chances; take a lot of them. Because honestly, no matter where you land or with whom, it always ends up just the way it's supposed to be. Your mistakes make you who you are. You learn and grow with each mistake you make. Everything is worth it. Say how you feel, always. Be you and be ok with it.[38]
~ Unknown

Chapter 28:

Expectation

WITH MY NEW CREDENTIALS, I was anxious to begin a new school year. As I constructed a fresh new classroom, I could not stop thinking about a particular kindergartener who had expressed disappointment that he hadn't learned to read on

the first day of school. I was determined that each child would take home some text they could read to their parents on day one. As students continued the process of daily writing in an environment where mistakes were valued as part of the learning process, the writing pieces grew longer and more sophisticated. More words were spelled correctly. I displayed the children's published books in the school library as well as the city's library. An editor from Nashville's newspaper, the *Tennessean,*heard about my teaching and wanted to visit my classroom.

Student-published books
on display at the public library

Kindergarten students
sharing their writings with Ms. Jill

Oh no! What did this mean? What would my principal say? What about the central office administrators? Would they discover I had not followed the curriculum as dictated? I'd written my own curriculum, one that met the needs of my students, but would the central office administrators fire me?

I was beginning to trust the process of life. Everything I needed was always provided. As the reporter communicated with students, a photographer took pictures of their work-in-progress as they wrote and published books. Her story, entitled

"Teaching Method Thrills 5-Year-Olds," was published on April 28, 1985[39] on the front page of Sunday's local edition of the *Tennessean*. Carolyn Shoulders won a national award for her article. My principal, Cookie Word, was thrilled and asked how she could help support my work. The Director of Schools sent a personal, hand-written note congratulating me. Spirit had successfully guided me once again.

Other newspaper editors were interested to see my students at work. Nine articles were published in local papers over the next two years. I also wrote several articles subsequently published in educational journals and newspapers.

Enamored with all I'd learned from graduate school, I wanted to discover more, so I considered using money from my Career Ladder summer work to participate in a three-week Summer Writing Institute at the University of New Hampshire. Reading and writing are reciprocal processes of the same discipline. I'd learned that when students write daily, their reading improves; as students' reading improves, their writing also improves as they begin to utilize more conventions of print such as punctuation and capitalization. A doctorate in reading from Vanderbilt University began to materialize in my dreams. The more I learned, the more I wanted to know. Gaining knowledge had become contagious for me, and I wondered if that quest would be eternal.

With the goals of studying reading at Vanderbilt and writing in New Hampshire, I could examine the reciprocal processes of reading and writing in more depth. These goals were just dreams stirring up from within. I had no idea how to orchestrate them while continuing to be a mother and a wife. Labored with these thoughts, I finally decided to just enjoy the dream, pray for guidance, and proceed with my daily life.

I was self-aware enough to know that I needed more practical knowledge and personal experience to impact my teaching, so I made the decision to study the writing process with professionals at the University of New Hampshire. Rodney promised to bring the girls to New Hampshire halfway through my trip to visit and to take in the sights of nearby Boston.

As a young student, I had little reason to connect reading and writing. In elementary school, writing instruction consisted of lessons in penmanship; there were no opportunities to actually use phonics skills to create stories. Rather, writing was often used as punishment in such ways as write-offs. The two are contradictory. Write-offs foster the worst penmanship; the unintended consequence is that students learn to *hate* writing.

Although I didn't have meaningful writing opportunities in elementary school, I learned much about the reading/writing process from my professors at TSU and also from reading a great book by Donald Graves. I inhaled his book, *Writing: Teachers and Children at Work*.[40] I read and reread it. It became a manual for me to use when addressing issues as they arose within my classroom. I knew my work in New Hampshire was important, but I had little idea how it would alter the course of my life.

In New Hampshire, I studied with professor and publisher, Jane Hansen. The biggest part of our day was spent actually writing. We shared our compositions as we gave and received feedback from our peers, who helped us decide which piece to edit and publish. A smaller portion of the day was spent learning how to teach the writing process at our individual grade levels.

Students reading a book from our penpals from Quebec, Canada

While in New Hampshire, I connected with a first-grade Canadian teacher who agreed to begin a pen pal experience with my class. Students had the option to participate in this new adventure. Some were not interested until letters from Canada arrived at school addressed to individual students. Enthusiasm abounded, and every student wanted their own pen pal. Eventually, we made a class video to send to our Canadian friends.

Toward the end of that school year, I received my acceptance letter at Vanderbilt University to pursue my dream of attaining a doctorate degree in reading. It felt like the right time to reconsider employment with Metro Schools. Dr. Bogen from the teachers' union advised that I should not complete another advanced degree without gaining employment in Nashville. The fear was that the administration could then say I was overqualified. Once again, I set up an interview with Metro Schools' personnel office.

Spirit came to my aid, as usual; Mr. Whitman was on vacation. Standing in for him was Dr. Sue Goss, a principal who had just read the article about my student writers in the previous Sunday's edition of the *Tennessean*. This was very different from my previous experience. Dr. Goss hired me on the spot. I shared with her my prior difficulty seeking employment with Metro Schools, but she told me not to worry. My Career Ladder III status would seal the deal. After 12 years of dreaming, I was finally able to begin teaching in MNPS. My expectations and hope had finally come to fruition.

Teachers need to trust in children's learning and in their own ability to learn along with their children. When teachers believe in their own professional judgments and respect children's abilities, success occurs as part of curricular experience.[41]
~ Yetta Goodman

Chapter 29:

Trust

IN 1986, I RECEIVED MY FIRST ASSIGNMENT IN METRO SCHOOLS in a mid-income, suburban community with a high-profile principal. The principal had specifically requested me, so I was thrilled to begin teaching in Hermitage, Tennessee, just outside Nashville. I taught first grade and continued the techniques I'd learned in graduate school where I created the curriculum based on the interests and needs of my students. Since enrolling in Vanderbilt's doctoral program in reading, I agreed to mentor student teachers each semester, which helped defray the cost of tuition. Vanderbilt's pre-service teachers were enthusiastic and anxious to learn.

Ms. Jill and her student teacher confer with students on their reading and writing.

In conjunction with my doctoral studies, a fresh group of first-grade students, and a student teacher in my classroom, an additional desire began to swell within me. I wanted to conduct classroom-based research focusing on my newly-learned teaching skills. By studying the reading and writing processes of my first-grade students, I hoped to draw conclusions that would improve both my students' learning and my effectiveness as a teacher. I began a year-long case study - an in-depth investigation of one student.

From the beginning of the year, I found Trevor to be perplexing. His cumulative records presented confusing information. I discovered several files that included different last names, as well as some with his first name spelled inconsistently. After some time, I realized that each of these folders pointed to the same student. Perhaps

Trevor had lived with his grandmother for a while and assumed her last name. This hypothesis was never confirmed.

Trevor and his mom arrived two weeks after school began. Due to desegregation efforts, Metro Schools had rezoned Trevor's neighborhood, requiring him to be bused across town. Trevor's mom apologized for being late and explained they had ridden the city bus to the school, which was twenty miles from their home. She wanted to help her seven-year-old son get acquainted with the school before his first venture on the school bus. My heart melted because my mom had done the same thing for me when I started high school, yet Trevor was only in first grade. When they arrived at my classroom door, students were busy at work - drawing pictures and writing stories. I was able to step away from the class to greet them. Trevor's mom explained the situation to me and also a little bit about his past school experiences. He had failed the first grade, and she was concerned about his progress. As his mom left the classroom that day, she pleaded with me to help her son achieve.

As I welcomed Trevor into the room of engaged students, I gave him a pencil and a piece of paper and invited him to write something about himself. He wrote, "I ha a F a e fo."

I asked him to read it to me. He read, "I had a physical."

I responded in writing, "When you had the physical, did you get a shot?"

I read my response as I pointed under each word. I could tell he liked this game.

Trevor started to answer verbally, but I instructed him to write his answer.

Trevor smiled as he wrote, "Y e s a e D h e t." He read, "Yes and it didn't hurt."

I smiled and wrote, "I'm glad it didn't hurt. I don't like shots.

The walls in my classroom were full of print that children read as they went about their day.

This was the beginning of the transformation that occurred for Trevor during his second year in first grade. My case study, co-authored by Victoria J. Risko from Vanderbilt University, was published in 1989 in *Reading Horizons** and entitled, "Language in Literacy: Mediating Reading Problems in a Communicative Context."[42] Trevor became a part of our classroom of readers and writers.

---

* The author's first name was misspelled in this study. They refer to Mrs. Jill Waddell as "Jim."

First graders actively publishing their books

Trevor made friends easily. As a repeater of first grade, he knew more than most new students, and others looked up to him. No one was aware of his previous failure. Trevor was enthusiastic in his participation in all classroom activities. I reminisced about my second year in fifth grade, and I was delighted watching Trevor enjoy his fresh start. He was quick to sign up to share his writings from the Author's Chair and was the first to sign up for a pen pal from Canada. Our environment for learning was just what Trevor needed for success.

By the end of the year, Trevor had written 209 compositions. His various poetry and prose submissions were published in the classroom newspaper. Trevor's results on the Stanford Achievement Test at the end of the year yielded a six out of nine stanines in Total Reading, a staunch difference from his first year in grade one when he scored a one on his achievement test. Ninety percent of Trevor's reading errors from grade-level texts retained the meaning of the story.

Although Trevor had mastered only 40% of skills taught and tested at the end of his first year in grade one, by the end of his second year in first grade he had mastered 100% of district reading skills without the support of direct, isolated instruction or through support from worksheets, workbooks or basal reading textbooks. Trevor learned to read and write within an environment similar to homes where children learn to speak. In these surroundings, ideas were presented in meaningful contexts, and students were encouraged to decide what they found useful based on their interests and the function of the activity. Peer and teacher audiences provided a rationale for making sense of language experiences and social interactions, which occurred naturally and purposefully. Trevor and the other students became active participants in literacy acquisition by choosing topics for their daily writings. They wrote for multiple purposes and reread to revise and publish their writings within the classroom.

Looking back to my days as a young teacher, I remembered that I was not particularly interested in the discipline of reading. I preferred math over reading. However, the opportunity to achieve a master's degree in reading fell into my lap and fit into my schedule. It wasn't my desire to go into an exhaustive study of reading. I stepped through that door of opportunity because I wanted to achieve an advanced degree. Later I came to discover that it was my training in reading and writing that had impacted my students most and awakened a deep-seated passion within me. Little did I know that my graduate degree was one of the rubies I needed to impact students' learning.

After a few years of working in this middle-class neighborhood, I had an experience with an administrator which prompted me to leave. On an errand to the school office, I witnessed the executive become angry with office personnel. With one sweep of his arm, he cleared the front counter of all its belongings. Onto the floor everything went. His reputation afforded him a high status in the community, but I disapproved of this behavior. It conjured memories of my father, and I knew I had to leave his school. I filed the paperwork for a transfer.

Because this administrator had graciously supported me as I stepped away from traditional teaching practices, I wanted to be diplomatic when leaving this school. He respected my work because I'd brought accolades to the school due to publicity about my students' achievements without the need for textbooks or work sheets. I desired to work in an inner-city school and serve children who may have experienced similar trauma to my childhood wounding. My principal's daughter taught at a school located in the heart of a public-sector housing project. I explained I wanted to transfer to Kirkpatrick Elementary in the inner city and to work with his daughter to try my new teaching methods with students who lived in poverty. He signed my transfer papers. We departed as friends.

Ms. Jill reads to her class.

Transfer papers had to go through the Metro Schools Personnel department. Mr. Whitman called to say, "It is highly uncommon for a teacher to request a transfer to Kirkpatrick. Most teachers want to transfer *out* of Kirkpatrick. Are you sure you want to leave a middle-class neighborhood school?"

My transfer was approved. I was assigned to teach at Kirkpatrick in 1987. I'd never taught in a school where teachers yelled at students until I arrived at Kirkpatrick Elementary, located off Shelby Street, adjacent to the housing projects. Pandemonium often ensued in hallways or in the cafeteria. Hearing teachers' angry, elevated voices triggered anxious memories from my childhood when Dad yelled and berated me. There were moments I felt instantly paralyzed hearing harsh, angry voices of teachers yelling at students. I realized my childhood trauma had been reactivated by my unknowing colleagues.

Kirkpatrick students had it worse than I'd experienced. These students lived in the nearby James A. Cayce Homes, known for its violence, including rape and homicide. Residents didn't feel safe going out at night for fear of flying bullets or repercussions from drug dealings. Some teachers didn't understand that yelling exacerbated any problem. Students needed a haven where they could learn with a kind, loving teacher. I knew my principal, John, had his hands full, and I was so busy in my classroom that I avoided going to him to discuss these problematic practices. John trusted me and respected my work. In my classroom, I had full rein to do what I thought was right with no need to close the door or hide from him or my peers.

/ After my first year teaching at Kirkpatrick, Lamar Alexander, then-Governor of Tennessee, began offering summer writing workshops for interested teachers. One of my influential college professors from graduate school, Dr. Carole Stice, recommended me for a teaching position at the workshop entitled, Summer Institute for Teachers of Writing at the University of Tennessee in Knoxville. The information I'd learned in New Hampshire strengthened me as a writer and teacher of the writing process. I interviewed for the staff position with the director of the program, Dr. Richard Marcus. After the short interview concluded, he shared with me, "Your resume spoke for itself, but it was important to me that you had a personality. I'd already decided, 'If she doesn't laugh during the first five minutes, I won't hire her.'" *What a different experience from my attempts to be hired in Metro Schools!*

Smiling as I walked through the door seemed to put everyone at ease. The rest of the interview was filled with praise and excitement over our joint venture. As a staff member, I worked with kindergarten through second-grade teachers to share my experiences relating to the process of creating a writers' workshop environment. On the third day of the conference, I presented my case study on Trevor at a plenary session. The whole time I was on stage, Dr. Marcus wrote profusely, taking copious notes. I didn't know how to interpret it. He rarely looked up during my hour-long presentation. As it turned out, Dr. Marcus had been exuberantly taking notes because of his keen interest in my research. According to the professor, my presentation was the highlight of the conference. I taught for Dr. Marcus for the next two summers. Because teaching writing to kindergarten and first-grade students was so novel, several attendees asked if they could visit my classroom when school resumed in the fall. Hearing ideas presented was a beginning, but witnessing the process of children learning within the context of the classroom environment was a necessary step in teachers' development. Although this was a courtesy I wanted to extend, scheduling visitors from across the state, teaching high-need, inner-city students, and working with student-teachers from Vanderbilt was a lot to balance given my responsibilities as a wife and mother of two daughters.

LORI WAS A STUDIOUS SENIOR at Father Ryan High School, and Phaedra was in 8th grade at Neely's Bend Junior High. It seemed that overnight my children had grown tall and independent. Because of the unsafe neighborhood in which Kirkpatrick is located, my protective principal encouraged all teachers to leave the premises 30 minutes after school recessed. This framework provided opportunities to spend time with my girls and helped me maintain the balance I sought.

Lori and Phaedra were both heavily involved in sports. Lori played basketball and in softball, played the positions of outfielder and pitcher. Phaedra was a ferocious batter, pitcher, and outfielder on two softball leagues, as well as a volleyball champion. She would not let that ball escape her grasp. Rodney bought her extra-thick knee pads to permit her to dive even more fiercely for the volleyball. Lori was graduating from high school, and I knew my time with her was growing short. Sports and plans for college were the focus of our attention at home.

ONE BRIGHT FALL MORNING during silent sustained writing, Antwan, one of my low-performing first-grade students, wrote pages and pages in his journal. When I asked him to read his story to me, I was surprised to find he had included the word "masturbation" multiple times. He read his story to me with pride and without a wince. I took a deep breath. His face was so proud. This was, by far, his longest journal entry. I asked, "Do you mind if I take your journal home and read it to my family?" Antwan was thrilled! When I read his journal entry to my daughters that evening, they laughed and informed me that it was a song by Prince. I was already concerned that Antwan might want to publish his piece of writing. I puzzled about how I would respond to such a request. During the night it occurred to me that if his writing was a rendition of a song already published, he couldn't republish it under his name. My dilemma was solved with the help of my daughters. Antwan retained his sense of accomplishment for his writing, never knowing he had used a forbidden word in public discourse. Oh! And he never asked to publish it.

At this difficult school, I found a kindred spirit in Melanie Ladd, who became a life-long friend. Melanie taught third grade. We shared not only an interest in teaching holistically and meaningfully, but we also grappled with similar home issues and shared our experiences raising children. Melanie and I were both learning to create an environment of joy in learning to read, write, edit, and publish books, as well as engage students in meaningful hands-on math projects.

Because elementary school is a busy place for teachers with no time to socialize with peers or learn from one another, Melanie and I started exchanging writing journals, where we shared insights from the educational books we were reading and conferences we had attended. We shared stories about individual students' successes and concerns about reluctant writers, offering each other support and recommendations. Because we were gaining so much professional and personal support from each other, we decided to start a teachers' writing group which met at 6:30 one morning a week, an hour before school opened the doors to students. Six Kirkpatrick teachers joined the group, and before long they began to share their own writings with the group. This is a piece I shared.

~~

It's Hard to Say Goodbye

She drives away as I stand by the road waving. My little girl has grown up. She doesn't look different, nor does she act differently now that she has reached the legal age, but I am profoundly aware that my time with Lori is coming to an end.

I remember . . .

The two-year-old, curly-headed kid with a broken arm learning to fight the three-year-old boy next door. That was her first fight. What courage it took to knock him upside the body with that heavy cast.

Lori at 19

I remember . . .

The day we brought Phaedra home from the hospital. We presented Lori with a doll, but she didn't want to bathe and diaper that doll. She would rather stand by Phaedra's crib, talking to her as she watched her every move. I wonder what kind of mother she will be.

And oh, didn't we enjoy ball season! She'd put her weight on that back leg, swing the bat with all her might, and often hit home runs. I can taste hamburgers and popcorn as I see Lori run those bases.

No time after that, she fell in love with David, the beginning of trouble. What fights we had! Like most first loves, it ended with gallons of tears and new convictions for the future.

I remember . . .

During her early high school years, sneaking into the assembly to hear Lori make a speech to run for President of the freshman class. After hearing the applause received by the freshman jock, I ordered roses for Lori hoping to soften the inevitable defeat.

And the Senior Prom . . .

She dropped a lit cigarette in her purse as her date was helping her into his Firebird. When we saw how well John put out the fire, we relaxed - somewhat.

Lori didn't want us to come for the senior presentation but after we promised to come and go without speaking, she gave her permission. Funny, after her friends gathered around us, she was the one who spoke to us.

And now . . .

She drives away today. A diamond ring on her finger symbolizes plans for her future life. The chapter of Lori's youth ends, and a new beginning emerges. I cannot go back, but I will always remember.

~~

Lori loved my story. Thirty years later, it's still as meaningful to both of us as when I first penned it. Being part of a peer writing group provided the impetus for me to slow down and get my thoughts and experiences on paper. Knowing that I would share my work with my peers provided the catalyst to edit and polish my piece of writing.

Years later, I look back to relive captured moments in time and review precious junctures in life. My personal writings impacted my teaching. Students wrote every day but didn't publish everything they wrote. They chose which stories they wanted to refine and edit for publication. As time moved forward, students became more proficient with words and sounds; they refined their drafts according to the skills I was teaching individually and in class. If I had taught punctuation, they were responsible for deciding where to place periods. This classroom of authors continued to teach me about their lives and what they needed from me to become successful. I published five books per day so that all students were able to get one of their stories published each week. Unlike my teaching experiences at Lakeside Park, my experience at this school was very different. No parents volunteered to help us accomplish this. As indicated by the summaries in the following chapter, sometimes I was successful; other times I failed.

Educators are the only people who lose sleep over other people's children.[43]
~ Nicholas Ferroni

Chapter 30:

Motivation and Support

LINDA WAS ONE OF MY TALLEST first-grade students at Kirkpatrick. She rarely spoke except to say, "I need a hug" in her gruff voice. Even with all the success I'd achieved with other slow-to-accelerate students, I was unable to significantly impact Linda's learning progress. I felt I'd failed. The only option available to me was to refer Linda to be tested for special education. After much angst, I completed the necessary paperwork for the new support system and found she'd met the qualifications.

A few weeks into her placement, I went upstairs to visit her in her new classroom. Appalled, I found Linda sitting at a desk doing busy work while her teacher read a personal novel. This was a double failure for me. I felt I'd failed Linda by not knowing how to help her; by placing her in a special education class, she was getting far less instruction than she'd received in my classroom. I feared I had inadvertently condemned her to years of lost opportunities to learn with uninformed teachers. Linda was now marooned in a special education class - stuck with an unmotivated and possibly uncaring teacher.

I don't mean to indicate from this experience that all special education teachers lack ambition or interest. Many children with disabilities are supported through federal funding received for special education classes. I know Exceptional Education teachers in Metro Schools who go above and beyond requirements to support their special-needs students. However, the vast majority of elementary students who qualify for special education services for reading do not make accelerated progress. Most often administrators don't even expect students to make fast progress, close the achievement gap, or ever catch up with their peers. My experience has been that few, if any, students in special education will ever learn enough to no longer need the extra assistance. Most do not become proficient readers and writers or develop internal motivation or joy for reading. Special education teachers generally follow a scripted curriculum. From my perspective, most teachers have not had the high-quality professional development needed to rectify intensive reading difficulties. The status quo appears to be acceptable to the administrators. Historically, a great deal of money is infused into the special education programs, while only small gains are made in reading achievement.

I think back to Mrs. Richard who taught me to say my "r's" correctly. She was part of the special education program and successfully worked with me individually. I glow when I remember the sisters at St. John Vianney who taught me in such a way that I gained confidence. Through the process of building on my strengths, learning became easier for me.

Generally speaking, once children receive the label of special education, it follows them throughout their educational careers. Many students with reading disabilities do not significantly improve. This knowledge put the onus of responsibility on my shoulders. I had to learn how to help all students while they were in my classroom.

ROCHON had repeated kindergarten and was entering his third year of school in first grade. At Kirkpatrick, I was the new teacher on the block, so my first-grade classroom was downstairs with all the kindergarten classrooms. Other first-grade classrooms were located on the first floor.

Rochon started school a week later than other students. When he realized the school secretary was leading him downstairs, he started kicking and screaming because he thought they were taking him back to kindergarten. I can't even imagine the trauma he felt thinking he could spend three years in kindergarten. I understood his frustration and assured him I was a first-grade teacher. After a while, he calmed down.

Repeating kindergarten had not been productive for Rochon. Sometimes children are retained in a class where they didn't learn grade-level skills in hopes that something surprising will happen the second time around. This wishful thinking is often unlikely. During his third year in school, Rochon was still far behind. His promotion to first grade after two years in kindergarten was called "social promotion." Because of his small size, administrators thought retention would not negatively affect him later in life.

Although Rochon was not a strong student, he was an exceptional artist. Because of his artistic aptitude, other students respected him and asked for his help as they illustrated their writings and published books. At long last, Rochon was celebrated by his classmates for his contributions to our community of learners. His aesthetic, sophisticated drawings were recognized and coveted in a classroom where students were actively involved in writing stories and illustrating their published books. Rochon began to see himself differently; he began to come out of his shell and make friends. He began to recognize his gifts and gain confidence in himself. It was reminiscent of my experience attaining confidence.

CHAD AND OSCAR: Students read and reread their published books. Because they shared their drafts and published pieces from the Author's Chair, the children were interested in learning to read each other's books. Additionally, students wanted to borrow their friends' books to take home and read to their parents. As I listened and followed my students' lead, we'd decided to create a check-out system much like

the one created by my kindergarten students at Lakeside Park, so we could keep up with the many student-published books in our classroom. Students established their own prerequisites for checking out another's book. These books were precious commodities, not only for me but especially for the authors.

Partner Reading

Students wanted to maintain control over their published books, so they decided that the young authors would need to grant permission before classmates could check out their book. Additionally, we decided together that the student who requested permission to borrow the book was required to read it successfully to the author before the process could be completed. In amazement, I observed Oscar, one of the poorest readers in the class, teach Chad, a higher-performing reader, how to read his book. Everyone had qualities that were valued by their friends for the expertise they brought to the table. We were all equal. We all had our strengths and our needs. We were truly a community of learners, where collaboration, rather than competition, was the rule of the day.

I knew from my own life how impactful or devastating a teacher could be in a child's development. I remembered my adverse experience with Mrs. Spurlock in 5th grade, as opposed to the exhilaration I felt with the sisters at St. John Vianney. As a teacher, experiencing students' success was my success; likewise, experiencing students' struggle became my struggle. This propelled me to learn more, seek better professional development opportunities, and pursue the guidance of those who were more knowledgeable - through books, college professors, and peers like Melanie Ladd.

Although I thoroughly enjoyed my student-teachers from Vanderbilt, there were not enough hours in the day to work with my first-grade students and instruct a student-teacher to the degree I desired. To rectify the time element, I once again employed my love of writing. I purchased two journals so my student teacher and I could communicate about events that had occurred during the day.

Dawnette used her journal to jot down questions as they arose during reading and writing workshops; I used my journal to share my rationale about classroom procedures and my assessment of students' progress. Each evening, I answered questions from Dawnette's journal while she read commentary from mine, responded,

Students are busy writing as Ms. Jill monitors and gives feedback.

and posed more questions. We continued this procedure throughout our time together.

A professor at Vanderbilt University was impressed with the practice of using journals to support student-teachers. In 1988, Dawnette and I, along with Dr. Debbie Rowe at Vanderbilt University, presented "Dialogue Journals with Student Teachers" at the College Reading Association Conference in San Diego, California.

That same year, Dr. Marino Alvarez and I were invited to speak at an educational conference in Sarasota, Florida. Our presentation was called, "Using Concept Maps and Vee Diagrams in First Grade as Pre-Writing, Thinking, and Re-thinking Activities." I invited Phaedra, now 14, to accompany me to Sarasota. It was her first time on an airplane. Our hotel was right on the beach. Phaedra watched over Dr. Alvarez's son while we attended the conference. Walking with my daughter on the beach and watching the sunset after swimming in the ocean were special moments to cherish. I'm not sure which Phaedra enjoyed most, flying or the beach.

Later that same year, Lori graduated from Father Ryan High School in 1988. She and I traveled to Knoxville for registration at the University of Tennessee in August; however, she soon decided she would rather attend college closer to home. She enrolled at Volunteer State Community College. I think her boyfriend, William, played a major role in her decision. Lori married William a year later. Her marriage was beginning as my marriage of 21 years was ending.

As I CONTINUED TO ATTEND MY ACOA, codependency group, and my weekly therapy sessions, I began to recognize mistakes I'd made that mirrored my parents' relationship. I saw my mom staying in a marriage that wasn't good for her or her children. I saw a woman who lacked confidence in herself. As a result, she was afraid to stand on her own two feet. But my mom gave me the gift of an education. With that training, I was equipped to follow a new path, unlike the one Mom had endured. As I faced this awareness, my desire for change emerged. I craved a new life. I wanted to see myself as a child of God rather than a child of Eunice and Robert.

I had feared that I would be condemned to everlasting hell if I left the Catholic Church. Thankfully, a priest I'd met from ACOA helped me get past the fear of hell and pursue a new path for my spiritual fulfillment. I was eager for self-reliance, spiritual growth, and independence. Rodney and I agreed to separate, and after a few months, we both decided we wanted to divorce amicably. We realized how young and immature we'd been when we married 20 years ago. We separated in 1989, and the divorce was final in 1990. We remained close friends throughout his lifetime. I had the privilege of being with my daughters at his bedside when he died in 2005, and I spoke at his funeral along with his other friends.

My sweet sister, Phyllis, and I both divorced our husbands about the same time. We'd gone to ACOA and attended therapy sessions together as we tried to heal from our traumatic childhoods. Although Phyllis was not involved in the same nightly battles with Dad as I was, she'd suffered her own hell witnessing the family's abusive patterns. In group therapy, I noticed that when my sister spoke, she closed her eyes. With her permission, I share this poem.

The One Who Closes Her Eyes

I know the one who closes her eyes . . .
She's the little girl who hid in the corner when Daddy and I were fighting.
I know the one who closes her eyes . . .
She's the one who slept alone while Mama comforted and slept with me after Daddy and I'd completed our nightly confrontation.
I know the one who closes her eyes . . .
She's the one who pierced her ears against Daddy's wishes. It took him six months to notice. You were surprised he noticed that quickly!
I know the one who closes her eyes . . .
She's the one who ingested one adult aspirin after another from the small tin she held

My precious sister, Phyllis

in her hand, as she witnessed yelling and screaming between my father and me. Perhaps she was trying to ease her anxiety. The bitter taste matched the bitterness of the evening. Were you trying to escape this life, like Jesse Neal?

I know the one who closes her eyes . . .
She's the one who didn't tell Daddy when she got the speeding ticket. He only learned about it when the court date announcement came through the mail.

I know the one who closes her eyes . . .
She's the one who sometimes didn't want to sing around strangers. With a little acceptance, a smile of encouragement, and a lot of patience, she came around.

I know the one who closes her eyes . . .
She's the one who looks strong, feels weak, and doesn't know how to mend the discrepancy.

I know the one who closes her eyes when she speaks intimately . . .
Connecting with herself
   in the darkness
   in the aloneness
   in hope.

~~

Phyllis and I had a close relationship during most of our lives. After Bobby left home, she became my best friend. Sharing experiences from our dysfunctional family and ultimate divorces brought us even closer.

Watching Lori move forward with her marriage to William was hard for me, given my fresh perspective on life. I felt she was making a mistake, but she was determined and old enough to make the decision. Trying to talk her out of the marriage only seemed to drive us apart. I thought I understood how much my marriage hurt my mother, but Lori's marriage brought it all back. As disappointed as I was with Lori's decision to marry, I knew she had a good head on her shoulders and time would take care of any mistakes, just as it had for me. Both my girls followed their own paths; my job was to guide and support them. Within only a few months, Lori realized she'd made a mistake by choosing William, but it took several years for her to leave the marriage.

For 30 years I'd lived according to the theology of the Catholic Church. Now I was thirsty to try something different. To make a new start, I visited churches of different denominations looking for the loving God I'd found through ACOA. Through my studies of the book called *A Course in Miracles*, I found Unity of Music City Church. The theology is encapsulated by a loving God and punctuated by uplifting spiritual music. I could feel the breath of God breathing through me. I had finally found my church home.

Even though I wanted the divorce, adjusting to my new life was difficult. I cried for an entire year. To assist the healing process, I wrote affirmations for myself, recorded them onto a CD, and listened to the assurance of my own voice whenever I traveled in my car. It felt like my spiritual self was offering me guidance. Finally, I began to feel a quiet nudge for a change away from the classroom.

I responded to an invitation to apply for a Career Ladder Evaluator position. The interviewer, Nancy Simpkins, asked why I hadn't responded to any of their previous invitations over the past four years. Before this time, it hadn't occurred to me to consider leaving the classroom, as I'd found the work to be thrilling and fulfilling. Given the intensity of my work at Kirkpatrick and the emotion of starting a new life, I was ready for a fresh perspective in both my personal and my professional life. The trajectory of my life was changing once again.

Chapter 31:

Career Ladder Evaluation

THE TENNESSEE DEPARTMENT OF EDUCATION sought permission from Metro Schools to loan me to the State for a few years to work as a Career Ladder Evaluator. I still received my monthly paychecks from Metro Schools while the State paid Metro for my time. I enjoyed being on the other side of the evaluation table and found it to be a pleasant culture shock.

Away from school, the company of adults was a palpable relief from the constant demands of the classroom. Evaluators spent weeks training at the downtown Nashville Cordell Hull building. I'd been teaching young children for 18 years with little time to visit the bathroom or wolf down lunch. While in Career Ladder (CL) training, I was able to enjoy hour-long lunches in restaurants with colleagues - never a possibility in the classroom. My schedule dramatically changed. Although it's typical for teachers to work 10-hour days to prepare for the beginning of the school year, I was able to devote only eight-hours-days while in training. Once the month-long training was completed, I traveled across the state observing and evaluating kindergarten through second-grade teachers. Fieldwork was more challenging than training days because the work reflected educators' long days. But extended periods between scheduled interviews and classroom observations gave me time alone to write and study my *Course In Miracles* text. I continued to feel a calm detachment, freedom, and even luxury in life away from the daily grind of the classroom.

For two years, I traveled across Tennessee three to four days a week observing and evaluating classroom teachers. Even though fieldwork was tedious, I enjoyed the challenges each week brought. Pre-observation conferences with the teacher helped to focus my attention on what the teacher wanted me to observe, as well as to understand the scope and sequence of the lesson. Post-observation conferences provided opportunities to ask clarifying questions about the lesson. At the end of the day, I conducted an interview with the teacher on a variety of topics. On non-travel days,

I reported to the Cordell Hull Building. Office days were fun and easy, and I looked forward to time with my peers. Although making friends had been difficult as a child, the CL experience allowed me opportunities to interact with colleagues on a more personal level. Having lunches together, sharing common experiences, and hearing family stories were comforting compared to the confines of the classroom. Office work was very different and much less stressful than teaching or evaluating teachers in the field.

After two years, I began to feel a tug for another change. If things got too calm, I took it as a sign that something new was coming around the bend. I grew weary of being on the road and sleeping in hotels two to three nights a week, so I decided to return to Metro Schools. Since I had been "on loan" to the Tennessee Department of Education, I was promised a position when I returned to the district. By August, I still hadn't received notification of placement from personnel.

After experiencing freedom outside the classroom, I wasn't sure I wanted to submit myself to the classroom again; however, I interviewed with the principal and leadership team at Percy Priest Elementary School. This was an affluent school in southwest Nashville. The principal and teachers were welcoming and interested in learning more about my teaching processes. After a two-hour interview, they offered me a first-grade position. Although I would have prospered there, just thinking about going back to full-time classroom work was daunting. I had assiduously maintained an enthusiastic career for 18 years, but freedom away from the classroom appealed to me now. I had learned to trust the process of life and pay attention to the ebb and flow of my energy levels and passions.

Sometimes it amazes me how a brief interaction from the past can have such long-lasting effects on the future. Earlier, I'd met Dr. Helen Brown, Executive Director of Teaching and Learning, on a trip to Toronto to attend a reading conference. Sitting next to her on the plane, I'd fearfully shared that I could demonstrate evidence of students' skills through authentic reading and writing experiences rather than using the district testing packet. But instead of being upset, Dr. Brown honored me for my initiative and expertise. That was the only conversation I'd ever had with Dr. Brown. Six years later, she remembered our brief conversation on the plane and offered me a job teaching gifted students. *Was this another ruby in the rubble?*

This position provided the freedom I was seeking. As an educator of gifted students, I traveled across Nashville teaching seven, three-hour classes a week. Similar to the schedule I'd maintained while evaluating teachers, my schedule changed daily and provided an opportunity to work with colleagues as well as students. Working with gifted students was dramatically different from working with underprivileged children. Parents were anxious to be involved. Thrilled their child had met the criteria to enter the Encore gifted program, parents were quick to offer appreciation and abundant support. I had settled into a life of relative tameness and predictability. Trusting the process of life, I had come to realize that when God put opportunities in front of me that felt good to my heart, it always worked out in my favor. This position required me to return to school to earn a certification for teachers of gifted students. More school and more learning were always welcomed in my book.

After I attained my credential to teach students in the gifted program, my new work schedule enabled me to embark on a social life in the evenings. This was the first time in five years that I wasn't attending graduate classes after school or during summer vacations. A fellow teacher, Cheri Doubleday, invited me to accompany her to the Music City Bop Club where I began taking dance lessons.

Although I'd wanted to learn to dance for many years, Bop wasn't in style during my teenage years, and Rodney hadn't been interested in learning to dance. As a kid, I remembered seeing Betty and Bobby dance the Bop, so I visited my brother in Georgia where Bobby taught me the basic steps. This provided the impetus for me to begin formal dance lessons.

Since the DJs played a variety of music, I wasn't satisfied dancing only to one genre, so I began to learn the Sweetheart Schottische, the Cha-Cha, the Two-Step, East and West Coast Swing as well as the Waltz. I danced six nights a week. With all that exercise, my body grew lean

Brother Bobby teaching Jill to dance the Bop

and muscular. In my forties, I was in the best physical shape of my life. My kids were grown, and I began to live life to its fullest. I continued my weekly therapy and ACOA classes and then completely let it all go on the dance floor. I began to learn how to date. Ample opportunities presented themselves for me to learn how to say "no" when something didn't feel right, to put myself first, and not allow another to negotiate my needs for theirs.

Although my three years in gifted education had been fulfilling, I realized my passion for it had begun to wane. Something was missing.

Chapter 32:

Reading Recovery® Teacher Leader Training

Poster designed by
Dr. Tammy Lipsey.

I MISSED TEACHING READING AND WRITING to inner-city children. Observing students thrive in an accepting, nurturing environment while immersed in daily opportunities to read and write, fed my soul. My passion had been ignited through my work with emergent readers and writers and kindled through learning from disenfranchised students like me. I'd learned as much from them as they'd learned from me. Perhaps because many of the struggles of inner-city students reflected those of my own childhood, my heart yearned to support them.

One Friday evening, I received a call from Dr. Helen Brown. She asked if I'd heard of a professor from New Zealand, Dr. Marie Clay, who had worked with teachers to create an intervention for struggling readers called Reading Recovery®. Because of my graduate work and collaboration with colleagues, I was familiar with Dr. Clay's work. Dr. Brown asked if I would be interested in moving to Columbus, Ohio to attend a year-long training to bring Reading Recovery to Nashville. If so, I needed to complete an application and have it on her desk Monday morning. The deadline had already passed for the position, but Dr. Brown had not been impressed with the applicants. I followed her instructions and interviewed for the position with several administrators the following week.

After the interview, I called Dr. Brown at home and asked if it was okay for me to inquire about the outcome of my interview. She told me I had been selected for the job, but I would also need to be interviewed by the Reading Recovery team at The Ohio State University (OSU).

The following week, Rosemary Estes, a trainer at OSU, interviewed me via the telephone. She asked how I dealt with disequilibrium. This brought back memories of my childhood when I was constantly out of balance, but I dared not reveal my past trauma to a stranger. Rosemary explained that Reading Recovery Teacher Leader training was much like an apprenticeship. Teachers-in-training study educational theories and strategies in university classes and then implement new knowledge in daily lessons crafted for individual students based on students' idiosyncrasies. Although I had implemented ideas learned from my master's program with students in the classroom, this new training would include individual coaching from my professors while I taught students. The idea of learning to build on students' strengths to make learning easier inspired me. Through systematic observation of individual students, I would learn to tailor daily instruction to students' strengths and needs. I was being offered a rare opportunity to further my learning. Pondering the possibility of the new training offered a soothing antidote to the failure I'd felt after subjecting Linda to twelve years of uninspired instruction in special education classes.

Now, faced with an opportunity to learn Reading Recovery, the idea of becoming more of an advocate and expert reading teacher for struggling students resonated deep within me. This opportunity spoke to the reality I'd lived as a child. Rather than following a curriculum guide, I needed expert teachers who knew how to instruct me.

After the interview, Rosemary told me to start packing for a move to Ohio. I was intrigued and could see how this training spoke to my teaching vision. However, with calm detachment, I quizzed the local administration about how this move would benefit me financially; I winced at their response. The administrator for Federal Programs explained that after uprooting my life and dedicating an entire year to study Reading Recovery out of state, I would still be paid as a teacher with no additional compensation. They were willing to pay for the rental of the U-Haul. I would be responsible for my own packing and moving.

Dr. Richard Benjamin, then-Director of Schools, advocated for Reading Recovery to be implemented in Nashville. Central office administrators were following orders but lacked in-depth knowledge; they were uninformed about details and expectations for the future. It was really up to me to lead the initiative with Dr. Benjamin. With only an economy of faith in the Federal Programs administrative staff, leaping into the unknown was daunting. *Was I prepared to make this bold move?*

Bobby advised me to pass on the opportunity, knowing I would not receive a pay raise when I returned to Nashville. He said, "What company would ask you to move away for an entire year of training to bring back a new initiative and then not compensate their employee? I answered that in my head, *only education*. I thought long and hard about it. The intensive training would give me a chance to learn, grow, and improve my ability to instruct students. I believe that learning to read and write are basic human rights that can change the trajectory of a child's life. I knew this training would alter the course of my teaching. I was so drawn to it! *How could I say "no" to the possibility of learning at this intense level?*

Even though I would have a more rigid schedule than ever before, the idea continued to intrigue me. Teaching gifted students for the past three years had provided predictability, balance, and tilted more toward fun. Learning new genres and writing curricula for gifted students had met my assiduous need for knowledge, but I was not fulfilled in that role. While teaching in the classroom, I'd made an impact on at-risk students - a goal that had grown out of my difficult youth and early career. Although my previous work had been harried and demanding, it had proven to be worthwhile and fed me on some deep level.

I was at a critical juncture. *Did I want to navigate another change in my life again and go into the unknown? Did I want to move away from balance and fun into a haze of long hard days of inconsistency and vulnerability?* My philosophical stance on education insisted that when students fail academically, it's the teacher's responsibility to seek and discover ways to change the course of their academic paths. *We can't blame under-performing students and then wash our hands while taking little responsibility. Failure is not the student's fault; it's a failure of the educational system and society, resulting in the need for teachers to seek, expect, and demand high-quality professional development. I contend it's the responsibility of every teacher to learn how to empower students to accelerate their own learning.*

Planning to vacate my home for a year to receive Reading Recovery training brought up concerns about fear of intruders as well as insurance coverage for my unoccupied home. Meanwhile, Lori had decided to leave her husband. As I was moving out, Lori moved back home to seek refuge, take care of herself, and heal from her divorce. Again, it felt like Universal Energy was highlighting a path for us. I had no idea where it would take us, but I had learned to trust this inner guidance. I started preparing for my move to Columbus, Ohio.

I soon learned more about the history of Reading Recovery. A cognitive psychologist, Dr. Marie Clay, together with a team of educators, developed this intervention during the 1970s. Dr. Clay had been a teacher of young children, a special education teacher, a school psychologist, and a trainer of school psychologists. Additionally, she'd studied developmental psychology. Her research focused on the formative years of literacy learning. She studied changes in literacy behaviors of young children as they learned to read and write continuous text over time. Because Dr. Clay had great respect for elementary teachers in her homeland of New Zealand, they met often to collaborate, relating educational theory to classroom practice. Together Dr. Clay and New Zealand teachers discovered how to help struggling readers accelerate their learning to become active participants in the classroom. This work received international attention and was named Reading Recovery.

The name "recovery" conjures ideas of a 12-step program in America. Reading Recovery is not a 12-step program for kids who have been hooked on phonics. "Recovery" in New Zealand is a nautical term. The islands of New Zealand are surrounded by the Pacific Ocean and the Tasman Sea. When a ship gets off course, the navigator plots the coordinates to "recover" the ship and redirect its course. The sooner the navigator discovers the problem, the quicker he can "recover" the ship. As educators identify students who are falling behind, trained Reading Recovery teachers can plot the coordinates to "recover" them. With 30-50 hours of intensive instruction in first grade, the learning gap is often closed without the need for years of remediation, and the child's self-respect and confidence are enhanced. However, for success to continue through elementary grades, we must ensure students receive high-quality classroom literacy instruction after they leave the short-term intervention of Reading Recovery.

In the early 1980s, Ohio State professors learned of the excellent literacy work coming out of New Zealand. At that time, thirty percent of first-grade students in the Ohio Public Schools were retained in first grade. Dr. Gay Su Pinnell, a professor and researcher at OSU, wanted to assist students and teachers in the Columbus City Schools. She wrote a grant to bring Dr. Clay to the United States in 1984 to begin the first Reading Recovery training site in the country. Ten years later the opportunity to enroll in this life-changing training fell into my lap.

From my early childhood education and my previous classroom experiences, I was aware of how much latent promise sat undiscovered in struggling readers. Although I had great success with my students as a result of my graduate work, I wanted to learn how to further inspire that underlying potential. Even though my zeal to support students of poverty had driven me to develop a certain level of expertise, some children needed more than I was able to provide. I hoped this Reading Recovery intervention would be the answer to that phenomenon. And it was!

Speak up for those who cannot speak for themselves; ensure justice for those being crushed.
Yes, speak up for the poor and helpless and see that they get justice.[46]
~ Proverbs 31: 8-9

Chapter 33:

Embarrassment and Isolation

AN INTERVENTION IS DIFFERENT FROM REMEDIATION. My childhood experiences had taught me that "failure is a feeling long before it's a result."[20] Intervention occurs before failure is realized, much like I had received in second grade from my speech teacher. If students are offered high-quality support from highly trained teachers, many will not have to experience the harmful effects of failure.

I'd spent many decades of embarrassment over my failure in fifth grade even though I had a positive experience my second year with the sisters. I hid my fifth-grade failure from my friends; it was something I never discussed. I know the isolation that results from failure. But worst of all, the feeling that I was incapable of learning was the biggest travesty. It took years of success to overcome that one year of failure. The opportunity to learn Reading Recovery was personal to me. There was no randomness in my life. Even with my childhood trauma, I could see that my life was unfolding through an exquisite chain of events that I could never have dreamed possible. Here I was - the kid who had failed fifth grade, the one my father labeled "stupid" - chosen to move to Columbus Ohio to receive the best literacy training in the world. Unlike most of the professional development I'd personally financed through my meager teacher's salary, the district would cover my training and living expenses. Everything was falling together. I was learning to trust the exquisite wisdom of Universal Energy more and more. *But how was I going to maintain a balance in my life while living in Ohio?* Knowing my tendency to throw myself completely into a task, I began to plan for stress outlets.

As an educator for 20 years, built into my calendar was approximately eight weeks off during the summer. This time offered opportunities for summer fun with my girls as well as a chance for me to enroll in art classes. During such times, I learned how to cut glass and make stained glass pieces, weave a rug, shoot photos, and develop film. Hours melted into minutes in my darkroom. Pottery had become my most recent hobby. Even in pottery classes, my fear of failure and embarrassment were evident to me. The majority of the students in my class were experienced and skilled. Only a few of us were new.

My childhood phobias of failure followed me wherever I went. I wouldn't dare ask a question publicly. I stopped my work on the potter's wheel, walked up to my teacher, and asked my question privately - so fearful of embarrassment. Years of failure had taken over my body, affected my voice, and led me to hide from authority. Even as an adult, it took writing this book to be able to admit my shame of failure.

Once a child fails a grade, it takes abundant time, energy, teaching expertise, and money to remediate misconceptions and heal the damages to a child's self-confidence and self-respect. The unintended consequences of repeating a full year in the same grade are enormous. In 2020, the cost of repeating a grade in Nashville was over $10,000. Research has demonstrated that grade retention can produce harmful emotional and psychological consequences and greatly increases the likelihood that students will drop out of school. I didn't want another child to experience the childhood failures I'd endured. This goal had been foremost in my mind when I walked across the stage to receive my undergraduate degree. Combating a continuous flow of childhood criticism and giving up on myself were the hardest to overcome. I couldn't have turned my life around without my mother's guidance and belief in me.

Through my years in the classroom, I had clear evidence of how positive feedback in an accepting environment propelled my disenfranchised students to success. Reading Recovery presented me with an opportunity to become even more skilled in my teaching and to use my voice to advocate for less fortunate students and those who were simply mystified by the reading process. I knew that if educators were taught to identify students who needed support, they could learn to teach powerful strategies that empower students along a continuum of success. This would change our educational system!

Reading Recovery provides daily, 30-minute, intensive instruction by highly trained teachers for the lowest-performing first-grade students. The goal of Reading Recovery is to close the achievement gap by assisting students to accelerate their learning from the bottom of the class to function as an average student within 12-20 weeks. I could not pass up this moment. I began packing my bags. Believing this opportunity was from Spirit, I jumped in with both feet, and I never looked back.

A friend volunteered to help me move to Ohio. I knew Carl from the Music City Bop Club. He'd shown interest in getting to know me a few years before, but I was busy with other things. At a July 4th party, I met him again, and we began to spend time together. When he first offered to help me move, I politely said, "No thanks." But as we continued to hang out for the next few months, I changed my mind. I wondered, *Was this Holy Spirit opening another door for me?* A week before school started in September, Carl helped move me to Columbus, Ohio.

I knew I would need an outlet for stress, so I took my guitar, bicycle, and photo enlarger to Ohio and began to search for a pottery studio. I had enough self-knowledge to know that finding balance was imperative for me. With my enlarger in tow, I was able to set up a darkroom in my new apartment. However, at the outset, I had no vision of how important my personal writing would become to relieve stress and connect with my spiritual essence.

To become a teacher of writing, I became a writer myself. Journaling about my personal life helped me understand the problems with which my students grappled in their writing process. Although I'd been jotting down my thoughts and experiences for years, in Columbus I found myself going to the computer daily to encapsulate this new existence - including my fears. I often wrote to settle my mind, sort through concerns, and seek answers from within. Writing became a tool to relieve anxiety and loneliness. I found inspiration in my writing. It seemed sacred to me. It afforded me space to birth new insights and create clarity out of chaos. The words fell on the paper as I stated my distress, and then this other voice appeared and answered my concerns. It reminded me of my early childhood when Daddy and I fought, and Mom came in to help me settle down so I could go to sleep.

~~

NEW HOME
August 1994

The door opens to my new Ohio home.
Oh Geez! Can I be happy in this small apartment?
I don't like the smell. Open the windows. Air this place out!

Carry boxes up three flights of stairs from a car and a truck.
At first, there's spring in my step. I tire significantly after an hour and a half of
Constant climbing and descending.

Supper? We forgot to eat supper!
Breakfast at 2 a.m.
It feels good to be away, to clear my head.

Thank God I know where the sheets are so I can get to bed.
No, I promise. My back doesn't hurt too much.
It's only . . . I'm just SO tired.

A good night's rest and I'm ready to confront the boxes.
How can I get all my stuff in this little space?
It will surely take a miracle.

Yes, the TV will fit nicely between the living room and dining room.
The computer can back up to the TV.
My study is in the dining room.

My bookshelf is in the dining room.
My office supplies are in the small dining room.
My filing cabinet is under the printer table in the small dining room.

Bad? No, I think I can live with it.
A pot of fresh flowers on the table,
A window to connect me to the outside.

This will be ok.
Mail in the box already?
A card from my brother and his wife wishing me luck, promising to write,
Assuring me that time will pass quickly and I'll be home soon.

My exercise bench goes together without much difficulty and is placed in
*   the bedroom.*
The closet will be a good space for my photo enlarger.
I printed 15 pictures in the kitchen last night after dark. It works!

I'm excited!
I'm scared.
I miss my children, friends, and family.
I'm thankful for so many blessings.
I feel safe.
I'm ready for this adventure,
I think.

~~

I had an entire week to get settled while learning my way around Columbus and the OSU campus, which accommodated over 50,000 students in 1994. I found a community center where I could continue my aspiring art by throwing pots on the wheel. I moved my enlarger so I could print pictures in my utility room and could exercise on my bicycle and weight bench. My guitar was a trusted friend and provided hours of entertainment as I spent time alone. Even so, after getting everything settled in my apartment, I began wondering what to do next. Writing was my go-to when I felt lost or alone.

Without the dark, we would never see the stars.[47]
~ Stephenie Meyer.

Chapter 34:

Sacred Writings

Aʟᴛʜᴏᴜɢʜ ɪ ʜᴀᴅɴ'ᴛ ʟᴇᴀʀɴᴇᴅ ᴛʜᴇ ᴘᴏᴡᴇʀ ᴏꜰ ᴡʀɪᴛɪɴɢ during my elementary school years, it became an entity - a friend - that I loved to frequent. Giving my concerns a form of expression brought me peace as I connected with the Divine.

TIME ALONE
August, 1994

Being alone . . .
*   I don't like it*
*   Or not much of it.*
I keep thinking of places I could go, things I could do.
*   I could make a quick trip to Niagara Falls.*
I could go home for a few days and clean that mildew
*   Off the north end of my house and carport.*

But while I was busy with thoughts of could-dos,
I decide to print pictures from my family's North Carolina reunion.
Then a poem came to me, and I had to write it down at 1:00 this morning.

I awoke with another poem on my mind.
I sat down at the computer and wrote for hours.
*   For whom? For me.*
The finished product becomes like a fine piece of pottery or a print that I've dodged and burned.
It takes on my energy.
*   And I love it!*

And I want to share it with others.

Yet a voice inside calls my name and asks,
"When are you going to get busy and stop this playing?"

And then I want to sit down and write about that.
        I want to go into it.
        Who is this voice?
        What do you mean, "Stop this playing?"
        What else do I have to do?

Oh, time . . .
        How sweet it is!

~~~

Phyllis had been my closest companion, friend, and confidant since we were teenagers. My guitar sat in the corner of my apartment and provided comfort when I was lonely. As I sang, I could hear my sister's harmonic voice in my head, and I yearned to hear it in person. For my birthday, I asked her to send me a recording of her singing some of my favorite songs, so I could sing harmony to her lead voice on my way to school and work. Sometimes I heard songs on the radio that Phyllis and I had sung on television. I was so immersed in my work that finding moments away from my constant educational focus brought joy to my spirit and sometimes tears to my eyes.

THE HARMONY IS SEPARATED
September, 1994

        The sun is blaring in my eyes
        As I drive to school.
        A song comes on the oldies radio station.
        Soon I begin to sing.
        I miss you, my sweet sister!

        I call Carl to ask when he can visit.
        He says Ohio is too far to continue a relationship.
        I'm hurt; I'm angry.

I need to talk to you. I have to sort through this.
Feel it.
Dissect it.
Learn from it.
And you help me with that process.

I go days and days,
Hours and hours,
Immersed in school
Studying and talking Reading Recovery
Connecting with no one except Dr. Marie Clay.

Then I hear your voice, sweet sister.
My heart feels warm.
My body light.
My spirit is free.

I wanna hear about your husband, Lon.
I wanna hear about your job.
I wanna hear about the new hot tub.
    And sailing,
    And meditating,
    And just about what you've been thinking.

Our spirits connect.
The harmony is reborn.

~~~

For years I'd taken notes in my journals about the events of the day or a feeling that captivated me. Turning 46 was no different. I loved my forties. I was divorced, knew how to dance, my kids were happy and grown, and I was free to pursue a new life to discover who I was without a husband or children nearby. I hadn't dated much as a teenager but my involvement in the Bop Club in Nashville had allowed me to meet various men my age, interact with them, become friends, and decide if I wanted to know them better. When I began a relationship, it only lasted three to six months. It didn't take long before I knew it was time to move on. From each, I recognized the gifts and integrated them into my life. I'd learned to shoot and print pictures from

Earl; pottery, hiking, and camping from Bill. It seemed as each relationship ended, I polished the rubies left from the rubble, and I shined brighter.

TURNING 46
October, 1994

Today, I'm writing to the future me. I've been in Ohio for almost a month. Sometimes I'm so excited to be here, I throw my arms up in exultation; other times I sink in sadness and loneliness. The Reading Recovery training is stressful. It's like learning a new language with some of the best minds in the country while my "not good enough, not smart enough" complex is a constant companion. I yearn to integrate these new strategies, this new language - to collaborate with the brilliant minds around me. I take a long, slow, deep breath, settle down, and touch that inner knowing, as I let go of my worry and fear.

~~~

Phaedra called this morning, and I could hear the coos of my granddaughter in the background. Phaedra has news of a new pregnancy. Her son will be born in March while I'm still in Ohio.

~~~

At the behest of Metro Nashville Public Schools, I'd rearranged my life for Reading Recovery training. I'd only been at The Ohio State University for a month, and I was still learning my way around Columbus. The instruction was intense. Reading assignments from three different books, plus planning for daily individualized lessons for four of the lowest-performing students, engaged my time and energy. There were few opportunities for anything else.

After a full Saturday of reading and thinking, I wrote this poem.

~~

BECOMING
October 1994

Up in the trees
In this third floor apartment,
Sitting and thinking,
Pondering and reading,
Studying and learning,

Questioning and considering,
         New   Possibilities.
Strategies for learning,
         For teaching,
              For Becoming.
Transforming ever so slowly,
         Yet certainly,
                   Into a finely-tuned,
                        Highly sculptured,
                             Piece of ART.

Learning to observe,
         Where to attend,
         What to ignore,
                   How to dodge and burn my focus
                        As I support this young reader
                        Who is becoming more independent,
                        Self-confident,
                        An active processor of
                             Reading
                             And
                        Thinking.
                   ~~~

READING RECOVERY BOTH DRAINED AND FED ME at the same time. I thought I knew something about teaching reading, but I soon discovered I had a great deal to learn. Now I lived in an abstract realm of academia while engaging in intensive work with students. I gave myself to it with zeal. I was a one-woman show - responsible for the largest and smallest of operative tasks. Learning to code a running record of a student's oral reading and capture each student's behaviors such as; pauses, eyes-off-text, waiting, re-reading, asking for help, word attempts, errors, and self-corrections. I was entrenched in my learning. Reading Recovery had proven to me that progress was possible for all children; their gains were measurable.

Half of each day was spent in an inner-city school teaching hard-to-accelerate students using strategies, philosophies, and ideas we had distilled from various theorists in our extensive reading assignments. Grinding away in classes at the university entailed learning how to differentiate instruction to meet the needs of individual students. When we build on children's strengths, learning becomes easier.

Moving from the "known" to the "unknown" gives children a baseline for learning. Going from "unknown" to more "unknown" leads to defeat. My students had already experienced a year in kindergarten where learning was difficult. My job was to make learning easier and more natural. I was beginning to bridge the gulf between these extremes.

~~~

THE SATURATED TEACHER
October, 1994

Stop, stop, stop all the teaching,
    Give me time to think.
        Stop, stop, stop all the teaching,
          Give me time to breathe,
            To implement,
              To attend,
                To internalize,
                  To experience,
                    To understand.

To be so fully immersed in something
    To the point that there is NO other life.
      No other time.
      No rest.
        No break in the stress.
Another sleepless night-
Can't turn my mind off -
    I can be better.
    Not take this so seriously
    Relax in the uncertainty of my teaching.
    See "behind the glass" as an exciting experience,
    Like sleeping on a mountain top on the first day of the New Year in 20-degree
        weather.
Oral comps?
No big deal!
This group of teachers
Share and work together.
There is nothing to fear but fear itself.

I'm tired of the stress.
I'm ready to let go of grandiose ideas of perfection.
It's ok to be in this new experience.
>   *To be a learner -*
>   *To make mistakes -*
>   *To reveal my lack of knowledge and expertise with my peers and professors.*
I respect the learning process, and I will become a better teacher because of this
experience.

~~~

I often heard from Lori while she was house sitting and healing from her divorce. After she called to share her process, I headed to the computer.

~~~

DIVORCE
November, 1994

You, my sweet daughter, have been to hell and back!
The good news is that you didn't stay there too long.
Confused?
No baby. I'm not confused,
I understand the loss you refer to.
A song comes on the radio,
>   *And the tears flow.*
Grieving is a process -
And it happens one layer at a time.
Grieving the sound of one's voice,
>   *The scent of a loved one,*
>   *The aroma of one's house and one's clothes,*
>   *And one's washing powder and softener.*
Grieving the end of a marriage,
>   *Dreams that never materialized,*
>   *Lost family members,*
>   *Friendships.*
>   *Yes! That comfort level.*
My sweet love,
>   *You are wise to give yourself time to grieve.*

For in grieving, you can let go.
As you complete your grieving,
You will be given all you desire.
All you deserve!
Even more than in your wildest imaginations!
Be patient with yourself!
I love you so!
Three interesting men . . .
Isn't that fun?
Trust yourself.
Listen to your heart.
Ignore your head.
Pay the most attention to what makes Lori happy.
The place is here.
The time is now.
This is truly the Garden of Eden.
Everything you want can be yours.
Time will help you decide exactly what that is.

~~~

My sister, Phyllis, and I'd historically enjoyed a close relationship. Because of my busy schedule, I didn't call often. This was a time prior to cell phones. One day I sat down to call my sister and was surprised when I couldn't remember her number.

FORGETFUL FINGERS
November 1994

I picked up the phone to call you this morning,
And my fingers couldn't remember your number.
It's been too long, my dear sister.
Talking to you is like an easy Sunday morning.
The fog lifts; I can see clearly again.
Ah! The air smells sweet.
The blue sky makes me feel light and hopeful.
I can relax.
You help me understand myself . . .
My needs.
You help me accept my i d i o s y n c r a s i e s.
I miss you, dear sister.

RETURN OF THE BIRDS
January 1995

I walked out of my apartment this morning,
And I heard the birds singing.
I haven't heard the song of birds since October!
What a way to brighten my morning,
>*my day,*
>>*the whole world!*
What could this mean?
Spring is near.
Snow is on the ground; more expected.
Temperatures remain low.
I've have been stuck in such a funk.
>*Not happy with my life,*
>*my workload*
>*my relationship.*
And yet the birds help put a pep in my step,
>*A smile on my face.*
>*Is the sadness in my heart about to change?*
Perhaps I could go through this day with a song of celebration.
>*The birds have returned!*
Maybe this place isn't so bad after all.
Maybe I can accept it,
>*Find peace here.*
Maybe I can accept me,
>*Love me,*
>*Take responsibility for me.*
Ah! What lessons the birds teach . . .
>*To be so free,*
>*So trusting of the Universe,*
>*So joyous that they sing eternally,*
>*So playful,*
>*So sociable with one another,*
>*So free of fear,*
>*So full of love.*
Hush now while I listen . . . . The birds have much to teach me.

~~~

My beloved brother, Bobby, lived in Augusta, Georgia. When he had an aortic aneurysm that caused him to be hospitalized, I did the only thing I could. I wrote!

MY BROTHER
March, 1995

What a gift you are! You taught me gentleness when you carried me on your
shoulders that Halloween night.
I was five or six, maybe seven . . .
And sick with some childhood epizooti.
You turned my disappointment into magic
  When you helped me
  t r a n s f o r m
    From a little sick girl
     To a great big, tall, scary ghost.
I loved you so much!
  I would sleep in your bed when you were on a date,
  Knowing that when you returned, you'd carry me to bed
  And I'd get to say, "Goodnight" one last time.
And oh, how I loved sitting beside you,
  Watching you spit-shine your shoes,
  You talked to me about important things,
  Like the importance of spit on the boot,
And reminisced about things you had built with your Erector Set.
  Your soft voice, gentle spirit-
  Your silly, funny expressions-
  Made me laugh and feel important to you!
And I still love those conversations with you, my big brother,
Whether it's about the skin falling off our faces after an appointment with
  the dermatologist,
Or how much money we've lost or gained in the stock market,
  Or the myths of Joseph Campbell.
Now I don't like you being in that damn hospital.
And I don't like you being sick.
And I want you to promise to get well and never leave me.
You've made such an impact on my life.
I love you, my dear brother!

I called Bobby in the hospital and read him my poem. I teared up as I read. With a morphine button in his hand, Bobby could dispense enough to keep him out of pain but not enough to overdose. I could tell my words touched him because he replied, "What are you doing calling me down here, reading that shit to me!" Humor was his way, and I understood that about him. Being

Jill and Bobby

raised in a home with all women with no other man except our father, Bobby had to deal with a lot of emotion. He preferred comedy to sentimentality. I didn't do comedy very well, but we were able to meet in the middle and understood each other's message. Bobby healed quickly and was soon home. Anne Gayle later shared how my poem had touched him.

~~~

MY FIRST GRANDDAUGHTER, MARISSA JADE, was born in January 1994. Michael was born 14 months later. At first, I felt like I was too young and too busy for grandchildren. But when I returned from Ohio, I had time and energy. Nothing pleased me more than spending time with my daughters and my grandchildren.

MICHAEL
March, 1995

My second grandchild and first male offspring in our immediate family. Welcome, Sweet boy!

Incarnate from pure spirit. You

Came into the world while I was out of state in Reading Recovery training. Sorry I missed your birth!

Heaven sent you through your sweet mother, Phaedra Dianne.

And you are

Eternally

Loved!

~~~

THE RITE OF PASSAGE
April 1995

Time is getting close.
One week before oral comps.
Time to practice for the big test.
Kris, Mary, and I cut up questions and placed them in a pot.
> *Rehearse drawing questions.*
> *Feel the butterflies invade our bodies.*
> *Experience that awkwardness as we*
> *Trip over our words, and*
> *Attempt to speak intelligently on each*
> > *Particular topic.*
The morning of December 6th,
I drive to school without music.
A light drizzle falls around me.
My attention is on my body.

> *My chest feels heavy.*
> *My throat feels hot!*
> > *I practice breathing deeply.*
> > R e l a x i n g
I'm ready! How could I not do well?
In just a few hours this will all be behind me.
A previously trained Teacher Leader sends our
class warm wishes,

My grandchildren:
Michael & Marissa

> *And a hot tea party, New Zealand style.*
> *Her message to us is that this work,*
> > *This stress -*
> *Leaving our families and homes,*
> > *Is indeed worth it.*
To help at-risk children experience success,
Rather than failure,
And to have the mission to bring our developing expertise back to our states,
And train other teachers to become what we value . . .
Three months of intensive work has prepared us for this day.
A day of initiation.
> *The rite of passage.*

The hero's journey.
We join the ranks of Teacher Leaders in 48 states,
Four Canadian Provinces,
New Zealand,
Australia,
England,
Germany,
Japan.

We made it!

~~~

GOODBYE COLUMBUS
May 1995

The sparkling lights of your beautiful city driving in on I-71,
Your big blue sky,
Your magnificent sunset,
The green grass that peeks out from under the snow in March,
These are the things I'll miss about you, Columbus.
Living in this apartment feels like a dorm.
Driving through 50,000 pedestrians at OSU at 8:00 a.m.
Rushing from teaching school - to class on campus - to fieldwork.
The narrow focus I've had to maintain since my arrival nine months ago.
These are the things I say "Goodbye" to, Columbus.
And now I prepare to make another journey to Nashville.
The third quarter draws near as I prepare to start a Reading Recovery site in TN.
Packing has begun. Arrangements for moving back to Nashville are in process.
The snow has melted, and the birds are singing.
I'm ready for this to be over, Columbus!.
Ah! To be home with my daughters, my grandchildren, and my friends,
To have time to think, to hike, to play, to reacquaint myself with all of me.
These are the things I yearn for, Columbus.

Reading should not be presented to children as a chore, a duty; it should be offered as a gift.[48]
~ Kate DiCamillo

Chapter 35:

Reading Recovery in Nashville

ROME
June, 1995

ONE WEEK AT HOME in Tennessee after being away for a year . . . .
Took me four days to unpack and get somewhat settled.
Think I'll take the weekend off, rest.
Relax.
Refurbish my spirit.
I sleep 10 hours at night and take afternoon naps.
Will I ever get my energy back?
Tried to climb Ganier Ridge today.
Couldn't make it to the top in this 95-degree heat.
Ah! I'm out of shape.

>*Rome wasn't built in a day, sweet Jill.*

>*Give yourself time.*

I wake each morning with thoughts of the assessment training I'll be teaching in July.
Where do I begin?
Sat down today in an attempt to sort through and organize papers.
I found my assessment notes from a year ago!
I'm somewhat relieved.
The phone rings.
Phaedra's in the hospital - gallbladder surgery.
Grandma is needed - I'm on my way.
I'm SO glad to be home.
Lori's 25th birthday is tomorrow.
The cake is ordered, menu planned, shopping completed.

"Sarasota sunset" is matted and framed.
Once again I awake with thoughts -
Fears of assessment training.
> *Rome wasn't built in a day, sweet Jill.*
> *Give yourself time*
It feels wonderful to have a life again,
To be part of the world again,
Excitement of change . . .
Of a new, unknown future.
A revisited past in the present.
Dancing, dining with family and friends.
Transition of former lover to friend.
No one close -
> *Give yourself time, sweet Jill.*
> *Rome wasn't built in a day.*

~~~

After I returned from Ohio, I met a group of Contra dancers at the Music City Bop Club who invited me to learn a new dance genre. In Contra Dancing, couples face one another in groups of four. Through intricate moves announced by the caller, couples facing the front of the line - advance up the line, while couples facing the end of the line - progress down the line. Contra expanded my dancing skills, but I also found it to be a spiritual experience. After the maneuvers have been repetitively announced, the caller backs out and lets the music take over. Moving in a powerful contra line where everyone dances with everyone as they look each other square in the eye is an intimate experience. As we're all moving together in a synchronized pattern, the energy builds; it feels like belonging. I felt a oneness I'd never before experienced while dancing. I sensed a connection not only to the group but to the whole of mankind; I was hooked! Contra dancing only on Friday nights was not enough for some of us, so my close friend, Becky Forster, and I began to travel out of town to weekend dances.

As a child, I was never allowed to attend summer camp. Weekend Contra dances were often held on campgrounds. Sleeping in bunk beds or camping in tents filled that void from my childhood. Becky and I, along with a group of Contra friends, traveled out of town at least one weekend a month. Dances began on Friday nights, followed by lessons on Saturday, culminating in a big Saturday night dance complete with banjos, fiddles, keyboards, and percussion. Sunday mornings included a ritual of singing spiritual songs, followed by an afternoon of waltzing to the sounds of flutes and violins. It was always the ladies' choice, and the men never turned us down. It was not uncommon to see ladies dancing with ladies or even men dancing with men, especially when gender balance was lacking. It was a safe environment. The reasonable price of the weekend included heart-healthy food. The more I traveled, the more I fell in love with the kind, open-hearted people who loved nature and felt connected to Spirit. These were my kind of people!

I spoke with Bobby about how happy and full my life had become. Fulfilled through family, work, and dancing, I told him that I was so content, I never wanted to get married again. And then . . .

In the fall of 1996, Don, a member of our group, invited us to attend a Cajun/ Zydeco dance in North Georgia. On a cool Friday afternoon in early October, our Nashville group pitched tents inside a barn. Don had even promised to provide battery-run heaters for sleeping to entice us to travel to Split Tree Farms in Lafayette, Georgia to learn a new dance genre for a weekend of phenomenal music including fiddles, keyboard, accordion, washboard, guitar, and percussion.

After a few hours of dancing, Becky and I were ready to call it a night and head back to our tent when I felt someone's eyes on me. I looked in the direction of the energy and found Dan sitting on a sofa watching me. As soon as the waltz was over, Dan immediately came over and asked me to dance. We danced and talked into the night and then made a date to meet the next morning for a hike. I'd learned a great deal from my dating experiences and was clear what I wanted in a relationship. Although my previous relationships had been fun and stretched me to learn new things, I wanted a spiritual connection with my partner.

Between dance lessons early Saturday afternoon, Dan and I walked and talked. The sun was as bright and hot as a fire pit flame. We exchanged our own set of jokes with each other as we continued to walk and laugh together, commenting about the colorful leaves turning orange and golden brown. It was a surprise to discover that, like me, Dan attended a Unity Church - his in Atlanta, mine in Nashville. We defined our personal God and discussed our pursuit of His presence in our daily lives. The more in-depth our discussions became, the more I sensed the spiritual connection we seemed to have.

We eventually began to talk about our work. Dan worked for the elevator industry and had been a part of the team that installed all the elevators, escalators, and moving sidewalks at the Atlanta Airport. He was very interested in my work with children but especially around Reading Recovery. He asked great questions and listened attentively to my responses as he asked more clarifying questions. I was impressed with his interest in my work. I was touched when he noticed a spiritual connection between my work and my heart. As we walked around the beautiful pond filled with water lilies in full bloom, he took my hand. That afternoon we joined the group for Zydeco lessons and then a hayride over the ten acres of rolling hills.

As Becky and I prepared for the Saturday night Cajun/Zydeco dance, we realized that unbeknownst to us, Dan's tent had been pitched next to ours, so we had to be careful about how much we said. The dance hall was filled with over 150 enthusiasts from surrounding states as the musical movements brought about hand-clapping and foot-stomping in response to the accordion and washboard. After a few hours, Dan and I decided to take a break from the vigorous dance floor. In search of a snack and a place to sit, we strolled to the nearby kitchen when Dan laced his arm around my waist. Before we finished our tidbit, we heard waltz music on the wind. Dan put his plate down and offered me his hand for a waltz under the twinkling stars of the balcony. As he scooped me in his arms, I could hear my heart pounding. When the dance was over, he leaned over and kissed me softly.

We met again on Sunday morning for breakfast, spiritual singing, and then an afternoon of waltzing. After packing our bags and tents to depart from the weekend dance, Dan asked me to come over to his SUV to listen to a song on his car stereo. We were both familiar with Jana Stanfield because she sang at Unity Churches around the country. Dan played one of her songs that summed up our time together, "We've started a conversation that I never want to end." I was smitten! Before I arrived home on Sunday afternoon, Dan had already called from Atlanta. When I talked to my daughters later that week, I told them I'd met the man I was going to marry. They called each other and said, "What has happened to Mama?"

I knew that weekend that this was a special relationship, different from any I'd known before. As time moved us forward, we became friends as well as lovers. I came to realize that life with Dan promised to give me something I'd yearned for. I would be the "First Chair." I would be the most important person in his life. My childhood had been persistently traumatic. I never felt close to my father. My marriage to Rodney had been great at times and difficult at others as we were both immature. But now I had developed assurance about who I was individually and spiritually, including clarity about my interests and priorities. Within six months, Dan moved from Atlanta to Nashville; two and a half years later we were married. We've now been happily together for 25 years.

Assured of my direction in life, I taught Reading Recovery strategies to experienced educators for the next 15 years with an unshakable commitment to my work. I had so much – an intimate relationship with my creator, two wonderful and healthy

Jill & Dan on their
wedding day in 1999

adult children who were productive members of society, two healthy and happy grandchildren, a doting husband, an education, a great job, a healthy sense of self, a deep arsenal of ambition, and now a new title: I was the Reading Recovery Teacher Leader for Metro Schools. With that title came a new set of responsibilities to wrangle as I established my new identity. I'd climbed the mountain, reached the summit, staked the claim, and had arrived with grace and fortitude. I continued to credit my mother for my persistence and passion. She had stayed the course with Dad through all those years with an unwavering love for her children. Similar to my own childhood, many of my Reading Recovery students had difficult home lives. These experiences helped me better understand my students as I extended grace through accepting their approximations in their near attempts at words, sounds, and strategies in reading and writing. I found and praised students' half-right responses. I no longer lamented my struggles with my dad. I had not only reached this point in my life in spite of my difficult childhood but because of it. As a result of my strife, I'd learned to be self-reliant with a passion for helping others like myself. I was hardwired for optimism as I successfully navigated my upbringing.

For 15 years, approximately 8-12 teachers enrolled in Reading Recovery classes in Metro Schools where they could earn nine hours of graduate credit outside the school day. Teachers attended a three-hour class after school one day a week for an entire academic year. This professional development was rated as exceptional. Teachers paid for three hours of graduate credit; the district paid for six. A typical Reading Recovery teacher's day consisted of teaching four first-grade students with the lowest reading levels in individualized lessons. During the remainder of the day, teachers used their expertise to instruct groups of students. The total number of children reached in a school year amounted to between 50-70 per teacher. Historically, the lowest-performing learners made little to no progress in groups; they needed the intensive individualized instruction of Reading Recovery to make gains. In my role as Teacher Leader, I was able to offer support, feedback, and guidance for teachers with hard-to-accelerate students.

Reading Recovery training is intense. I found that if the district committed to pay for the entire nine hours of credit, some teachers dropped out after discovering the amount of work the training required. With no personal money invested, a few teachers found it easier to drop out rather than commit to the work, since they had nothing to lose. But when I changed the rule to require teachers to pay for the first three hours of graduate credit and the district would pay for the next six hours, teachers seemed to honor their commitment since they had invested their own resources.

Funding for Reading Recovery was at risk each time a new Director of Schools was hired. The biggest myth I had to fight was the misconception that Reading Recovery was too expensive. Because two and a half hours of the teachers' day are spent working individually with four of the lowest-performing, hardest-to-accelerate first-grade students, some administrators incorrectly concluded that Reading Recovery was too costly. But what were the options for the lowest-performing students? My experience with Linda had taught me that special education was not a place to expect students to accelerate their learning. I had first-hand experience with grade retention which had left me feeling embarrassed and ashamed. It's difficult to learn under those circumstances. *I believe that school districts have a moral obligation to provide high-quality professional development opportunities for teachers to ensure all students' success in school.*

If you want to save the world, start by saving just one kid.[49]
~ Gen. Colin Powell. U.S.A. (RET.)

Chapter 36:

A Voice for the Voiceless

YEARS AFTER I BECAME A READING RECOVERY TEACHER LEADER, Dr. Linda DePriest, a high-ranking administrator in Metro Schools, asked if I would work with Mark, an eighth-grade special education student. His parents had asked Metro Schools to pay tuition for a private high school placement due to the district's continuous failure to teach him to read. Even after eight years in special education classes, Mark knew few literacy skills. His mother demanded a state-certified reading specialist to work with her son. I accepted the challenge.

I began working with Mark in the spring of 2006. At almost six feet tall, he towered above me as we walked from his SpEd classroom to our work area. It was obvious that his self-concept had been greatly damaged; he wouldn't even make eye contact with me. I worked with Mark three days a week for 30-40 minutes each session. I learned that in his eight years in special education classes, Mark had not learned such basic concepts as the difference between a "word" and a "letter." He spelled "of'" as "ov." I worked with him for six weeks, totaling fewer than 18 hours. When we first began to work together, Mark tested at text reading level four, which translates to the end of kindergarten. After 12 weeks of my intervention, he performed at the beginning of second grade. It was clear that Mark could learn. Sadly, he had not received appropriate instruction.

According to 2019 estimates by the California Legislative Analyst Office (LAO), the average annual cost of educating a student with disabilities is $27,000.* This is almost triple the cost ($10,000) to educate a student without disabilities. When I was a Teacher Leader, I calculated the cost of Reading Recovery to be less than $3,000 per student. When comparing this intervention to special education, Reading Recovery is a bargain. I don't place any blame on special ed teachers when it's appar-

---

* http://lao.ca.gov/Publications/Report/4110

ent they have not received adequate or appropriate instruction on how to effectively teach children to read. Districts are too quick to advocate for scripted curricula rather than investing in valuable, in-depth professional development for educators.

First-grade classrooms generally consist of 20-25 students. Reading Recovery teachers in Nashville taught an average of 50-70 students a year. This intervention is cost-saving when compared to the alternative - retaining students at grade level for an additional year or placing them in special education for years on end.

Reading Recovery was first implemented in Nashville in 1995. In 1997, an internal research study was conducted by the Department of Research and Development. The conclusion revealed that Reading Recovery had saved the district over $330,000 in two years, in just retention savings alone. In other words, more first-grade students were being promoted to second grade after the implementation of the short-term intervention as compared to those retained before Reading Recovery was in place. As a result of the powerful intervention, classroom educators began to realize students' potential. Children in first grade were catching up to their peers in a short amount of time, able to bypass failure. The achievement gap was narrowing. I was unapologetic for prioritizing the needs of children. This was my life's work. Reading Recovery had proven to be sensible, effective, and economical. This intervention was successful. The difficult clutch of my past was being rectified in the present as I witnessed fragile k-3rd grade children make accelerated progress in reading and writing through the work of Reading Recovery teachers - circumventing the experience of failure and defeat.

As I've mentioned before, my experience with special education has not been positive. Very few children, if any, have opportunities to accelerate their learning or catch up with their peers. Many students qualify for special education after they have not learned to read in first grade, yet most fail to make rapid gains or close the achievement gap, even with *years* of SpEd classes.

Clay was in first grade when I met him in January 2005. From a middle-class family, he attended Goodpasture private school for 2.5 years. In December of first grade, the principal at Goodpasture called Clay's dad, Mike, to recommend that he be tested in Metro Schools for special education due to slow growth in learning his letter names and sounds. Clay qualified for special education and was labeled dyslexic. He transferred from Goodpasture private school to Stratton Elementary public school in Madison. Mike heard about me from a neighbor and came to my home to inquire if I would teach Clay how to read. I rearranged my schedule and began teaching him in February 2005 by traveling to Stratton Elementary each morning before I began my other responsibilities. Although Clay needed 20 full weeks of instruction

Reading Recovery
student: Clay

to become an efficient reader and writer, the school year ended before his lessons were completed. We continued his lessons at my home each weekday during the summer. When my timer went off indicating our 30 minutes were up, I asked Clay to finish reading the book at hand. He scolded me, "Miss Jill, you're cuttin' into my playtime!"

I never charged parents for the literacy support I offered before and after school or during the summer. By the end of 20 weeks, Clay was reading at grade level and no longer needed special education classes. Even though the SpEd department recognized that Clay was reading at grade level, they continued to keep him enrolled for another two years, although he didn't receive services or support from that department. Administrators explained that this was a precautionary measure in case he needed future support. After two years, Clay was removed from the roster of special education. Unlike others, he was able to escape the label.

Clay graduates from
high school standing
beside Ms. Jill

Clay recently graduated from high school. While we were together after his graduation ceremony, Clay leaned over and said, "Ms. Jill, I wouldn't be here if not for you!" His words not only touched my heart but emboldened my convictions.

In Nashville, Reading Recovery teachers provide individual lessons for 10-12 first-grade students as well as small group instruction for another 40-60 kindergarten through fourth-grade students, through three rounds of instruction. The number of students served in individualized lessons is contingent upon the number of weeks students need the intervention. Some make more rapid progress than others.

At peak efficiency one year, 90% of Reading Recovery students graduated from the intervention reading at or above grade level; 70% was more typical and reflected the national average. Our Nashville data demonstrated that all students made progress; however, some students needed more than 20 weeks to close the achievement gap. The training of special education teachers would have solved this dilemma. I offered to train their teachers in literacy development, but the administrators wouldn't bite. I was told they didn't have the funds.

All trainers of Reading Recovery teachers simultaneously work with hard-to-accelerate students. We learn most from those grappling with the same issues. Administrators and central office personnel, far removed from working directly with children, are often less effective when offering professional development for teachers. Reading Recovery provides in-depth training for leaders who are then able to provide training for their peers.

Classroom teachers recognize and value trainers with expertise, who know how to impart practical knowledge. Time is a precious commodity, not to be wasted in poorly organized, poorly staffed professional development sessions. Those missed opportunities feel like a travesty for educators who are thirsty for practical, applicable, valuable information that will impact the learning potential for their students. So often, central office personnel are not steeped in literacy knowledge. Rather, their focus is for teachers to learn how to follow a prescribed curriculum guide.

Reading Recovery offers a vastly different model of professional development. One aspect of the training is the utilization of an observation room. Educators take turns teaching their fragile learners behind a one-way mirror while their peers observe and critique the teaching and learning. Observers have access to the audio through the use of a hidden speaker. Students are not aware they are being observed. While the child only sees a mirror, observers have a bird's eye view of the student's expressions, body language, and the movement of their eyes as they problem-solve issues encountered in reading and writing. Afterward, the teacher who taught behind the glass debriefs the lesson with her teacher leader and peers. Everyone's learning is propelled forward. In each and every session, Reading Recovery teachers learn strategies that directly relate to students' abilities to think and problem solve within their literacy development.

After the initial year of training, Reading Recovery teachers receive ongoing support opportunities through monthly meetings with their teacher leader. There is always more to learn as we continue to refine our skills by working with the most challenging students.

When a struggling student receives a placement in Reading Recovery, classroom teachers' opinions of them begin to change. As a classroom teacher notices her previously low-performing students making progress, her curiosity is aroused. She desires to know about the dynamics that led to the child's success. "What did you do? How did you do it? What tools were used to help my student begin to make progress? How can I learn to do what you just did for my student?" She now wants more training and can learn from the Reading Recovery teacher on site.

When I was in fifth grade, my teacher gave up on me. Perhaps she was doing the best she could. Perhaps she just didn't know how to nurture my learning potential. Perhaps she blamed my difficulties on the fourth-grade teacher. Perhaps her sense of failure was translated into blaming me and my parents for my seemingly low aptitude.

When we blame, we relinquish responsibility. Every teacher is responsible for the children in her class. An administrator's job is to provide the necessary support for teachers so they can successfully meet that challenge.

Two of my strong Reading Recovery educators, Jo Littlejohn and Lynn Hudson, worked at a high-poverty school with mostly indigent students. When a new

Jill teaching a student behind-the-glass

principal was assigned to the school, the first change she made was to slash Reading Recovery from the budget. As the administrator of Reading Recovery, I scheduled an appointment to talk with her to see if I could offer assistance. She explained her rationale for cutting the intervention:

"Jill, I will be judged by the achievement test scores of my third and fourth graders. We have a high number of transient students who likely will not even be here by third grade. I am not going to waste my money on those kids."

Hearing her words reminded me of the Bible verse: *Speak up for those who cannot speak for themselves, for the rights of all who are destitute.* ~ Proverbs 31: 8[46] I was appalled that this principal was not willing to take responsibility for all students in her building. Thank God there are not many principals like her in our district. Over time she became an Assistant Superintendent before retiring.

In 2005, the Tennessee Education Association named me Exemplary Educator of the Year for all of Middle Tennessee. My husband, brother, sister, sister-in-law, and my daughters attended. I know my Mom was there in spirit. My dreams of becoming a powerful and impactful educator had manifested, not only through teaching children to read and write but also by providing compelling Reading Recovery professional development for educators. In my mind, the title of Exemplary Educator carried weight that the education community supported my teaching methods.

I'd learned the importance of state and local politics in my Reading Recovery work. Through the use of the observation room, I invited dignitaries and community members to view a lesson behind the one-way mirror. This room was not only utilized for training teachers but also for visitors to hear explanations of the teaching and learning without interrupting the child's learning process. While observing a lesson on the other side of the glass, politicians and visitors received a front-row account regarding the amount of learning achieved by students. It's captivating to observe a struggling reader - one identified as the lowest student in first grade, one thought by his teacher to need long-term support in special education - achieve accelerated progress, right in front of your eyes.

In 2007, I reached out to a mayoral candidate, Karl Dean, when he was the underdog for the mayoral seat in Nashville. He was appreciative of my invitation to observe Reading Recovery, and we became fast friends. He seemed to be impressed by the Reading Recovery intervention. I volunteered for and contributed to his campaign on numerous occasions. He invited me to be on a TV ad clip. As a candidate speaking at events, he often brought up Reading Recovery and how important he considered the work. He was elected Nashville's mayor that year. I stayed hopeful - convinced that some part of my vision would prevail someday, somehow, someway.

In 2009, I began to plan for retirement, but Reading Recovery would terminate if there were no Teacher Leaders in Nashville to advocate for this much-needed support. Meanwhile, I could not even get an appointment to meet with our new superintendent, Dr. Jim Roberts, so I went to Mayor Karl Dean and asked if he would help raise money to train two Teacher Leaders to continue this program. The mayor made a phone call, and the money was secured.

I selected two Reading Recovery teachers to send to The Ohio State University to be trained as Reading Recovery Teacher Leaders. To maintain the intervention in 2010, I decided to work part time for another year on a 120-day contract. For years, surrounding school districts compensated Metro Nashville Public Schools for my time when providing Reading Recovery professional development for teachers outside MNPS. I continued to train teachers outside Nashville, bringing in additional monies for the district. When the newly-trained Teacher Leaders returned to Nashville in 2011, I decided to work another 120-day contract to support them.

That year the district budget had to be cut due to a decrease in revenue. Dr. Register decided to remove the two newly-trained Teacher Leader positions in order to save less than $160K in a $674,034,800 budget. I was devastated! *How could this have happened?* I reached out to the superintendent, but he was still unwilling to meet with me. It felt as if all of my best plans had failed; I feared the intervention would not grow. One Teacher Leader was quickly snatched up by another district. The other stayed but never trained any aditional teachers. She developed health issues and eventually left the district.

After that devastating blow, I completely retired from MNPS. For 15 years, Reading Recovery had offered success for Metro students from home environments similar to the one I had experienced as a child. For 15 years, Reading Recovery had offered strong professional development for teachers like me who had yearned for high-quality training in order to impact the most vulnerable children. For 15 years, I had strong evidence that Reading Recovery changed the trajectory of children's lives. Even with all my classroom experience successes before Reading Recovery, I was convinced this intervention was the best I had ever witnessed in my 35-year educational career. I wanted to see this powerful intervention continue for the students who needed it most. I had served as a voice for the voiceless, and now it seemed justice for those students would cease.

Perhaps I took my work too seriously. In December of 2011, I endured a Transient Ischemic Attack (TIA), later deemed a mild stroke.

Part III

*The pessimist complains about the wind. The optimist expects it to change.
The leader adjusts the sails.*[50]
~ John Maxwell

Chapter 37:

Surfacing from Obscurity

ON A COOL WEDNESDAY MORNING IN MARCH OF 2012, Nancy VanReece called to inform me that school board member Jim Nordstrom was not going to seek reelection after five years of service on the Metro Nashville School Board. Jim had contacted Nancy to see if she would be interested in running for the seat to represent District 3. Nancy was not interested because she was planning to run for a Metro Council seat; however, she was willing to help by forming a committee to select a viable candidate. Nancy shared that my name had come up at the meeting; she was calling to inquire about my interest.

When I retired from Metro Schools, the thought of running for the school board hadn't occurred to me. I was as ready to get away from Metro Schools as I'd been after working with Mr. Whitman 25 years prior.

When I was a freshman in high school, I knocked on doors with my mom when she helped Senator Al Gore, Sr., with his re-election campaign. The senator had been responsive to Dad when he asked for support to rectify his military records. After I became a Reading Recovery Teacher Leader, I helped various candidates in their campaigns for office and invited many dignitaries to observe Reading Recovery behind the glass. During this time, I had fleeting thoughts of serving on the school board in some future time frame, but the idea sat dormant for years. Now I began to find the idea intriguing. I considered myself to be only a passionate teacher who was an advocate for the most under-served children. I was not well known; my family was not well known. I came from a lower-middle-income family. My answer to Nancy's question was, "I'll think about it."

As an educator of 35 years, I wondered what it would be like to sit on the other side of the table, to be one of the nine decision-makers who would impact the education of 87,000 students. Knowing that seventy percent (70%) of Metro students were living in poverty made the possibility of serving feel even more important as I weighed the decision.

I'd occasionally attended board meetings and watched some on television. Most members were businessmen and women who had little or no experience in schools and certainly didn't have the depth of knowledge educators bring to the table. From my perspective, in-depth discussions by board members concerning matters of instruction were non-existent. I sensed that the elected officials were mostly rubber-stampers. Some had children or grandchildren who had attended Metro Schools but no practical experience. A few were trying to step-ladder up to a higher office. Therefore, they approved most items with little to no discussion.

Nancy promised to endorse me if I chose to run and suggested that Jim Nordstrom would probably endorse me too, since he had offered to do the same for her. But was I up for this? I knew nothing about running for office. *How much money would it take? Where would I start?* A thousand questions ran through my head. I was an educator, not a politician. My political ambition was awakened by my passion to impact the lives of struggling elementary students. *Maybe I could help bring Reading Recovery back to Nashville again?*

Maybe we could reinstate an intervention that not only benefited struggling students but would also provide professional development to impact the entire school system. For 15 years I'd gone to school board members, politicians, government officials, city councilmen, business leaders, and church activist groups, seeking their help to expand Reading Recovery. I assumed they had the power to make things better, but they didn't. Maybe it was up to me. Maybe it was my work to do! The idea of running for office continued to incubate in my mind.

Dan loves Reading Recovery almost as much as I do. During the days of our early marriage, he wanted to talk about my work for hours on end. His interest was keen on how children who had given up on themselves could transform into successful, confident readers and writers. He had many questions, and we often talked into the night. Dan believed, as I did, that the underpinning of Reading Recovery was the way to live our lives and our marriage. Don't expect perfection. Accept approximations. Find the half-right in responses and praise that accuracy in order to stay engaged and to expand learning, confidence and love.

After much discussion with Dan, I summoned my courage and leaped. I went to the Davidson County Election Commission office, requested the paperwork to run for the office, and then went about collecting the required petition signatures in order to qualify to run for the seat. When I returned to file the petition, my feelings were a combination of excitement, fear, and anticipation as I thought about the campaign ahead of me.

I knew Jim Nordstrom because he was from a prominent family in Madison. As my school board representative, I'd met with him several times to talk about various issues concerning literacy in Metro Schools. I asked him if he would endorse me for his seat. Even though Nancy VanReece had assumed he would endorse me, his answer was "No." He didn't want to get involved. I realized at that moment that the road to election might be even more of a struggle than I had first anticipated.

I cast myself in front of anyone who would listen and advise me. I contacted the school board member who served before Jim. Sue Gallagher and I had become friends when I volunteered to work in two of her school board campaigns. We often had lunch or dinner together when she sought my opinion before critical votes on the board floor. She was also from a prominent family in Goodlettsville. When I told her I was considering a run for school board, she replied, "Well, I generally don't support teachers serving on the board, but you'd be different." I was appalled!

What? Would you say the same thing about a hospital corporation? Would you not "generally support" a physician to serve on a hospital corporation board? Why would you be reluctant to support an educator on the board of education?

It occurred to me that perhaps previous board members didn't want to take a chance on me because I was a mere teacher from an ordinary family with no political ties. I immediately felt the sting from the days of trying to gain employment with Metro Schools when Mr. Whitman thought I'd tried too hard - which he considered a lack of judgment. Rather than giving up and going elsewhere as I had done previously, I decided to give full rein to my passion. I didn't mind working hard when I wanted to accomplish something. I was determined to go for it.

My eyes were opening to people I'd previously respected. I later learned that Sue Gallagher had publicly endorsed my opponent, Chris Jameson, a coffee shop owner with no credentials in education and no children in school. He was a businessman like herself, endorsed by the Nashville Chamber of Commerce, who often sought candidates from the business industry to run for seats on the school board. For almost seven years, I'd considered Sue to be a friend of teachers, but her statement had confused me. I began to question if she truly valued educators. She seemed to treasure my opinions when she'd invited me to have lunch with her to discuss my views on school issues. But now I wondered if she had faith in retired educators' ability to make decisions that affected students' progress across Nashville.

A second opponent emerged. Mr. Lewis was a retired high school teacher and a previous judge. With two formidable opponents, I was a long shot. The two previous board members in the District 3 seat were from high-profile families; I was unknown. I leveraged every connection I'd made, including family, friends, teachers, and church members who could help finance and volunteer for my campaign.

Friends from church rallied around me and volunteered to help. Charles Davis from Unity of Music City church created my web page; Bea and Les Leff ran my campaign; Karen Elley made phone calls. My husband, Dan, and I did the lion's share of the work. I asserted myself with unknown business owners and was surprised that after a small conference, I was able to add more money to my campaign coffers. As I made connections in the community, I asked if I could place a campaign sign in yards, and Dan delivered them. The Metro Nashville Education Association endorsed me. By the time of the election, I'd raised $8,000 in cash. Chris, backed by the Nashville Chamber of Commerce and other groups with interests that didn't necessarily align with my campaign values, raised over $35,000. The only substantial money Mr. Lewis raised was from his endorsement from the Service Employees International Union, SEIU. Of the three candidates, I raised the least amount of money but that didn't deter me. In fact, it encouraged me to work harder.

With multiple candidates in the race, I only needed to command a plurality of the vote. I outworked both gentlemen and with less money, won the tight race, beating Chris by only 239 votes. With only 37% of the vote in a race with three candidates, I was elected by the people of Madison, Inglewood, and Goodlettsville to represent over 87,000 students. Perhaps my message resonated with the voters, or maybe it was the Holy Spirit's greater plan. Perhaps it was my drive that put me over the top. Perhaps learning from my many failures in life had brought me to this new, exciting place.

A friend, Belinda Cox, had been a long-term principal in Metro schools. She decided to retire when a previously elected superintendent gave her the choice of returning to the classroom or retirement. Not ready to leave her school, she appeared to be unhappy about being forced into retirement. Perhaps in retaliation, she ran for the board and became the superintendent's boss.

Belinda was a beautiful woman who dressed like a fashion model. She cared deeply for the children in her school, but once elected, she rarely spoke. Meeting after meeting, she sat quietly giving few rationales for her votes, but later explained that she was shy and didn't feel comfortable speaking in public. I took it personally! All these years I'd longed to see an educator on the board who would voice important opinions and change the trajectory of education for children in Nashville. I vowed to myself that I would never pass up an opportunity to speak at a board meeting. God gave me this platform, and I promised to never waste it. I ran on my expertise and experience in literacy instruction and acquisition. The district had implemented a hodgepodge of reading programming whose philosophies were not aligned. Essentially, the philosophies of some programs actually contradicted those of other literacy programs within the same school. No wonder teachers and students were confused.

As an elected school board member, I entered the field that had previously attempted to dominate my teaching for decades. As a teacher, I simply closed my door and did what I knew was best for my students, rather than follow the district curriculum. I had developed confidence in myself through extensive readings, post-graduate work, and learning to follow the needs of the students in front of me. I planned to use my voice to give our most disadvantaged children the best opportunities to learn to read by ensuring elementary teachers were provided quality professional development opportunities.

After I won the race, the Director of Schools, Dr. Jim Roberts, *finally* agreed to meet with me. At our first lunch meeting, he asked why I ran for office and what I hoped to accomplish. I shared my concern that I was appalled when he'd cut the positions of two new Reading Recovery Teacher Leaders. He responded that he had to cut the budget. I asked, "Did you have to cut our highest prepared reading instructors when our literacy rate in Metro Schools is dismal?"

Jill's swearing-in ceremony: Dan is holding the Bible, sister Betty, daughter Lori, brother Bobby, and his wife, Anne-Gayle are in attendance.

He saw my point. After that, Dr. Roberts always treated me with the utmost respect. I explained that I wanted to see alignment in our reading programs. Dr. Register knew my work history and seemed to realize my expertise in literacy acquisition. He listened quietly and then shared that his stepchild had participated in the intervention of Reading Recovery as a first grader, which had impacted his life and set him on a path to success. Aware of my experience with emergent readers and writers, Dr. Register became an ally and invited me to lead a literacy committee within the district; the goal was to write a comprehensive literacy plan for kindergarten through high school. Other Central Office administrators would assist to develop this plan.

Sadly, a stigma sometimes exists for some parents and administrators whose children need personalized attention in reading. Because Reading Recovery is known to be an intervention for the lowest-performing first-grade students, this can be considered a mark of shame for some. A few principals didn't want others to know their own children needed the intensive support of Reading Recovery. I wondered if Dr. Register had been embarrassed that his stepson had needed support? When I broached the subject, he was quick to say it was not his own child but his stepchild. It was interesting to begin to develop an even deeper understanding of educators' embarrassment around their own children's reading difficulties. Those who were unwilling to openly share their personal experiences could jeopardize the expansion of Reading Recovery.

A principal at an affluent school in East Nashville had a similar experience. She was embarrassed when her daughter qualified to receive Reading Recovery. After all, she was a teacher before becoming a principal, and she wondered what people would think about her having to seek support outside her personal expertise. A different principal didn't want her child to take advantage of Reading Recovery because she saw it as a failure of her own teaching skills. However, the child's father signed permission for his daughter to get the needed support while the principal continued to hide this information. These principals would never champion expanding Reading Recovery at principals' meetings due to their personal, latent embarrassment, even though their own children had greatly benefitted from the intervention. It was frustrating not to have the support of voices that could have been influential in the widespread expansion of Reading Recovery.

Dr. Alice Patterson had a different perspective than the aforementioned. Alice and I met at Vanderbilt University while we were working toward a doctorate in reading. Dr. Patterson is now a professor at Trevecca University. She asked me to provide Reading Recovery for her daughter, Leeanna. Although Alice had earned a doctorate in reading, she could see that she was not able to pinpoint the exact problems causing Leeanna to plateau in her literacy processing. Dr. Patterson was greatly appreciative that Reading Recovery existed in Metro Schools. She spoke at many board meetings to support the expansion of the intervention and advocated to make it available to more children. Leeanna graduated from Reading Recovery in first grade and just recently graduated from college.

I worked with a prominent family whose children attended a high-performing school in an affluent neighborhood. The Koopermans had twins. Their daughter, Maggie, had difficulty learning to read while her brother, Joe, excelled. Sherry Kooperman searched for solutions to help her daughter. That search led her to me, and I began teaching Maggie every morning before school. Sherry drove 30 minutes each morning through traffic to secure these lessons in an inner-city school and then drove back across town to take Maggie to her zoned school by 8:00. Maggie made excellent progress and caught up to the average of her class in less than 20 weeks. She, too, recently graduated from college. She and her family speak publicly for Reading Recovery every chance they get.

You know you've read a good book when you turn the last page
and feel a little as if you have lost a friend.[51]
~ Paul Sweeney

Chapter 38:

The Comprehensive Literacy Initiative

AFTER WINNING MY FIRST ELECTION, I embraced the opportunity to support literacy attainment for disenfranchised students. The esoteric work of building a comprehensive literacy plan for K-12 schools was an epic task. The administrative team and I delved into the intricacies of literacy with an earnest demeanor and calm detachment. Our first task was to define "reading." Definitions from many educational theorists were laid on the table for discussion. After much deliberation, we all agreed the district would follow a "Balanced Literacy Framework" embraced by cognitive psychologist, Dr. Marie Clay: "Reading is a meaning-getting, problem-solving activity, which increases in power and flexibility the more it is practiced."*

Jill reading to students

Once the definition of reading was embraced, our recommendation was to choose all future reading programs and interventions using Balanced Literacy as the North Star. If this were accomplished, we would not have a hodgepodge of reading programs across Nashville that conflicted in philosophies with one another. We anticipated that administrators and teachers would soon be able to commit the reading definition to memory. Providing outstanding professional development in Balanced Literacy would move our students closer to our goal of all students reading at grade level.

Knowing that Metro Nashville Public Schools had a large number of indigent, transient students, I was excited about how the plan would benefit those fragile learners. District support of our comprehensive literacy plan would provide consistency for children, even when their families might have to move frequently. Over

---

* Clay, M. M. (1993). *Becoming Literate.* Portsmouth, N. H. :Heinemann

3,000 homeless students are enrolled in Metro Schools. It was not uncommon for transient children to move three to four times during a single year. A system-wide comprehensive literacy plan would provide the cornerstone of support so students would be less likely to fall between the cracks if they faced homelessness or moved from school to school. The Comprehensive Literacy Committee developed the initiative in one academic school year and began implementation the following year.

The debate about the best way to teach reading and writing instruction has been raging for decades and is known as the "reading wars." In my own teaching, I used strategies from both sides of the "war" - whole language and phonics. A balanced approach is more likely to meet the needs of each individual child. For a year, executive directors, directors, coordinators, and I led a committee of 15 to create our Comprehensive Literacy Initiative, which included excellent first instruction, interventions, and trained volunteers for reading clinics. The overarching idea was to offer multiple layers of support for teachers and disenfranchised students who most needed literacy support:

EXCELLENT FIRST INSTRUCTION with Balanced Literacy called the Lipscomb Partnership: Dr. Tammy Lipsey from Metro Schools and Melanie Maxwell from Lipscomb University prepared a group of 42 literacy coaches from priority schools. In turn, the skilled coaches taught over 900 elementary, K-4 classroom teachers. Included in the Partnership were 12 English Language (EL) coaches. With the addition of the EL coaches, Tammy and Melanie's training impacted over 900 teachers that first year. The Literacy Partnership offered continuous, monthly professional development for coaches who received graduate credit for the amount of outside work expected through the Partnership. Educators met after school for three hours, twice a month to learn how to effectively support students' strategic processing in reading and writing. I knew this plan would work because I had seen the extraordinary progress of my students when I taught kindergarten and first grade. The question was, *Could we scale it to impact the entire district?*

The expectation was that each year more literacy coaches would be identified so that all 74 elementary schools would receive the yearlong Literacy Partnership training, followed by 33 middle schools and finally 25 high schools. With only two trainers, it was clear we would need to train and promote more leaders to fully implement a district with over 6,000 teachers. Each year a new cohort of 10-12 coaches began their learning process; the previous year's cohort continued their professional development to further enhance their skills teaching children to read and write.

We knew we had to focus on K-4 in the beginning. If students don't learn to read and write early, they will certainly have problems in third grade and beyond. The focus was to train coaches so they would be equipped to train classroom teachers. Prior to this time, there were no requirements or criteria for becoming a literacy coach; therefore, gains in literacy were minimal. Because of the work of the comprehensive literacy committee, coaches had clear expectations about their roles and responsibilities. Coaches committed to in-depth, long-term training that was required for them to become literacy experts. The literacy committee followed the board's strategic framework. The core value for literacy was: "We believe what research shows: Early reading success is a critical factor in a child's likelihood of graduation from high school and experiencing future life success."

The board had developed a clear path and conviction to ensure literacy attainment focusing on elementary schools. We knew that literacy is the cornerstone. Dr. Tammy Lipsey's mantra was, "All future learning rests on the shoulders of literacy." I knew this to be true in my work with children.

Our priority was to train coaches, but we were aware that just training coaches would not yield the desired outcome for all students. Therefore, we provide a layered approach.

The second layer was to provide research-based interventions to the neediest schools. We deployed the most intensive research-based interventions proven to be effective across North America to the children in our high-need schools.

-INTERVENTIONS: For those students who were not making progress, interventions were utilized to help K-3 students catch up. Reading Recovery was available for the lowest-performing first graders. The same Reading Recovery teachers offered K-3 group interventions each day. Reading difficulties do not differentiate by socio-economics. As previously mentioned, children of college professors, principals, and even the Director of Schools sometimes need intensive intervention. My experience demonstrated that Reading Recovery is the richest source of teacher development available. Educators testified that Reading Recovery was the most valuable training they had received during their many years in Metro Schools.

Julia Green Elementary is located in the affluent Green Hills area. Members of the Parent Teacher Organization observed a Reading Recovery lesson behind the glass and asked, "Why don't we have access to this powerful intervention?" Parents immediately began raising money to provide the Reading Recovery intervention at one of the most affluent schools in Nashville.

-READING CLINICS: The third layer was to provide minimally trained pre-service teachers to work with elementary students to supplement the work of the classroom and interventionists. Dr. Tammy Lipsey's dissertation led to the inclusion of training volunteers to work with elementary literacy students. Dr. Lipsey recruited, trained, and placed pre-service teachers, community members, and high school students at 21 out of the 76 elementary schools. Dr. Lipsey was the brains behind the Comprehensive Literacy Initiative. She had developed much of her knowledge through Reading Recovery and served as the Site Coordinator in Metro Schools. Tammy is a brilliant educational scholar whose contributions to the field of literacy education are inspiring, successful, and should be replicated widely. The Tennessee Commissioner of Education in Tennessee often called on her for advice during Jim Roberts' administration.

Nashville is referred to as the "Athens of the South" not only because of the replica of the Parthenon in Centennial Park, but because the city boasts six universities encompassed within the Metropolitan area: Vanderbilt, Trevecca, Lipscomb, Cumberland, Tennessee State University, and Fisk. The universities are a great place to solicit volunteers and mentors for disenfranchised students. True to Tennessee's history as the Volunteer State, Tammy recruited 200-300 volunteers each year.

The Comprehensive Literacy Committee articulated our commitment to equity. Rather than giving each student the same resources, our goal was to provide what each individual student needed. Some students need more support. It is our job as educators and board members to provide the necessary resources so that each student can become a successful reader and writer.

You do not need to know precisely what is happening, or exactly where it is all going. What you need is to recognize the possibilities and challenges offered by the present moment, and to embrace them with courage, faith, and hope.[52]
~ Thomas Merton

Chapter 39:

Lies, Mistrust, Betrayal

AFTER I WON MY ELECTION, teachers, friends, and family celebrated with me; however, I was curious that no board member reached out with a welcoming conversation. Through my 35-year teaching career, I'd watched candidates win elections, then quit before their term expired. *Why was this? Was it because there was some sorority-type mentality already established on the board that was difficult to penetrate?* I didn't expect an immediate connection, but I naively expected some innate affiliation. The person I connected with was another newly elected board member, attorney, and mom, Amy Frogge; other relationships were surface-level only. We were pleasant to each other, but no real friendships developed.

Amy's and my paths began to cross during our five-month campaigns. We were both long shots surfacing from obscurity. Perhaps it was that obscurity that magnetized our first encounters. Amy has a warm, wise demeanor and a passion for community schools to support children after school hours. Realizing the alignment of most of our philosophies over time galvanized our relationship.

Amy is a fierce advocate for schools. Prior to her work on the board, she served as a PTO president where she planted a school garden and supported literacy development and whole-child education. During our entire eight years together on the board, we never had a cross word or a hint of dissension. Amy was not only a colleague; she became a lifelong friend.

During my eight years on the board, I witnessed lies, mistrust, betrayal, and lack of professionalism within the MNPS administration, and with search firms. I worked with four superintendents in Metro Public Nashville Schools (MNPS) and participated in three national searches.

Dr. Jim Roberts had been a kind, supportive director who supported our Comprehensive Literacy Plan which included Reading Recovery. When Dr. Roberts retired, a previous interim director took the reins for another year while two sepa-

LIES, MISTRUST, AND BETRAYAL   *199*

rate searches took place. As expected from an interim, very little progress was made during that time, but the ship was steady.

Because the board was often in turmoil, a national search firm convinced board members that it would be difficult to attract a good director. In 2014, the firm narrowed the search to three candidates. At least two were mired in controversy. *Had the search firm set us up for bringing inferior candidates due to their perception of our "dysfunctional" board?* Meanwhile, the superintendent at the nearby affluent county applied for the position. Rumor had it that Dr. Michael Henderson applied for the position to maneuver an extended contract with a pay raise from his current board. Word on the street was that Dr. Henderson was not really committed to work in Nashville. Hearing these rumors, I asked Dr. Henderson if he was serious about the Nashville job. He assured me that his intentions were authentic while promising that he would accept the superintendent position if it were offered to him.

Weeks later the board offered Dr. Henderson the position of Director of MNPS, but the rumors were substantiated. He declined the position. I believe Dr. Henderson deceived the board and the Nashville taxpayers to benefit himself. His shenanigans worked; his board offered him a pay raise and a renewed contract. It appeared Nashville taxpayers and the Metro School Board had been exploited.

Board members were exhausted and disillusioned from the ordeal and decided to take a couple of months off prior to beginning a new search. The few months turned into six. Board members began to think that the Board Chair, Dr. Cathy Cowan, was dragging her feet. Because some board members began to publically prod and demand information about the starting date for the next search, Dr. Cowan finally set a date to commence the second search - this time with a new national search firm.

P. H. ASSOCIATES WAS CHOSEN BY A SEARCH COMMITTEE Created by the Board Chair. The CEO of the search firm was Mr. Pat Hughes. He also painted a bleak picture of the ability of the "dysfunctional Metro Nashville School Board" to attract a superb Director of Schools. Even so, a highly qualified candidate, Dr. Carol Johnson, brought her name forward for consideration. Several prominent Nashvillians remembered Dr. Johnson from 2001 when she had been offered the job which would have made her the first African American to hold the office of Director of Schools in Nashville. Because the board was split in its support, Dr. Carol Johnson rejected the offer; however, she went on to become Superintendent of Memphis Public Schools and then Boston Public Schools. Dr. Johnson's work around the country had been exemplary. Through the years she'd worked on various committees with many Nashville administrators. After hearing that Carol had submitted her application, I was relieved that we would not have to settle for a slate of mostly inferior candidates as previously experienced by the first search firm.

Dr. Carol Johnson's name had been on the list of candidates for weeks before the final recommendations were publicly disclosed. When the final tabulation of candidates was unveiled, Carol's name had been deleted. When Amy Frogge asked Mr. Hughes why Carol's name had been omitted, he said Carol had withdrawn her application. Dr. Johnson confirmed that this was not the case. According to Dr. Johnson , Pat Hughes had contacted her to indicate that P. H. Associates would be submitting six names to the Board of Education. Her name would not be included.

"Your name will not be forwarded because all six candidates are far more experienced and superior. We have checked with all the individual board members and you do not have the votes to be elected. Would you like to withdraw your name at this point?"

Although Dr. Johnson was surprised to hear Mr. Hughes suggest she withdraw her name from the applicant pool, she was thrilled to hear that so many high-quality candidates had submitted their applications for the position. Carol loved Metro schools and only wanted the highest qualified candidate to lead the district.

"No," she responded to Mr. Hughes,

"I have a long history with Metro Schools, and under no circumstances will I withdraw my name from the pool. I've come this far; let's see what the board decides."

Nevertheless, Pat Hughes replaced Carol's name with a candidate who had only attained an undergraduate degree. He didn't even have a master's degree! I couldn't help wondering . . . *Did the search company have an obligation to place one of their least qualified candidates? Did board members interfere with the search?* We may never know the reason, but one influential board member made the statement privately that he didn't want to see another "old" person (like Jim Roberts) leading the district. Age discrimination is illegal. Had Carol's name remained on the list, she would have surely been chosen because her credentials and experience were far superior to all other candidates. The press contacted her to inquire why she withdrew her name from the pool. Again, Dr. Johnson confirmed that she had applied and had not withdrawn from the applicant pool. In subsequent interviews, when asked why none of the finalists were female, the search firm indicated that all the female candidates had withdrawn because they were either no longer interested or were pregnant. Neither was true. This experience raised ethical questions about the board's process and the veracity of the search firm itself. Other insiders appeared to be complicit in the covert, manipulated process. I concluded that I was dealing with bad actors in a rigged contest. It appeared that egos had taken over the process - circumventing an ethical search to benefit the children of Nashville.

The chair of the board wields a lot of power. It appeared that the search firm, together with members of the search committee, successfully discriminated against a highly qualified woman due to gender and age. I believe they thought they must delete Carol's name from the list before the candidate list was revealed to the public because the school board would have certainly voted for the most qualified candidate. It would have been a slam-dunk for a candidate as qualified and passionate as Dr. Carol Johnson.

After working with the two national search firms, I would recommend to any future board member to be cautious using national search firms. They seem to have ulterior motives and sometimes advocate for less-qualified candidates they are trying desperately to place. I question whether their loyalties are with the school district that's paying them or the candidates they are attempting to place. Again, I was reminded of the previous practice of teachers' unions to support members even when there was strong evidence of lack of skill or accomplishment.

Clearly, the most accomplished, experienced candidate had been omitted from this search process. The slate of finalists included two African-American men and one Caucasian man who only had an undergraduate degree. None of the candidates had the vast knowledge and superlatives of Dr. Carol Johnson. Evidence supported that Mr. Hughes had lied!

ONE CANDIDATE WAS DR. JOSEPH, a young upcoming leader. His only experience as a superintendent had been a two-year stint in a school district with only six schools and a total of 3,500 students. Compared to Metro Nashville Schools with more than 129 schools and over 86,000 students, that was an enormous gulf to bridge. However, Dr. Joseph had previously worked as the Director of Teaching and Learning in one of the top 25 largest school districts in the nation with 208 schools and centers with more than 130,000 students. Even though Dr. Joseph's previous employment as a superintendent had been minimal, his work as an upper-level administrator in a large school district seemed to fill that chasm. I was pleased to learn that his previous district had the largest Reading Recovery site in North America. At his interview, Dr. Joseph sang the praises of Reading Recovery, so I was partial to him right away. He said all the right things during the interviews. Not only did he talk about his support for Reading Recovery, but he also mentioned an educational theorist I admired, Lev Vygotsky[53] (1896-1934).

Vygotsky was a Russian psychologist considered a pioneer of learning in social contexts. He was the first to examine how social interactions influence cognitive growth. Vygotsky advocated for a model of literacy whereby the teacher supports students' near-attempts as the child takes on more responsibility for the learning. Accepting near-attempts at half-right answers was near and dear to my heart. That's what I'd yearned for as a young child, and that was the way I'd taught my students. Dr. Joseph was singing my song. I genuinely believed that we had found the right person for the job!

As we neared the final hours in the decision-making process, the board was informed by a friend of Dr. Joseph that Dr. Joseph had another possible job offer on the table from a district in North Carolina. Even though Dr. Joseph's experience as a superintendent was limited, I was in favor of moving expediently to approve his contract due to his support for Reading Recovery and literacy. To my knowledge, the enigmatic North Carolina contract was never confirmed; however, due to fear of losing this candidate, we moved in haste to offer him a contract. He was elected by a unanimous vote. I and other board members were thrilled with our selection; we trusted him to practice all the leadership skills he'd proclaimed during his interviews. Because of the rush, our attorney later confessed, the contract had been approved even though it was heavily slanted in the director's favor.

Dr. Joseph was bright, cool, hip, and knew how to text. Our previous director didn't text, and that didn't go unnoticed. When Dr. Joseph called me on the telephone, our conversations often lasted two hours. On our first retreat, he gave board members three books published by the Arbinger Institute. The books expressed how to work together effectively and were filled with heart-touching stories that described servant leadership. I felt these books described the leader we'd hired. The board began to work together cordially; we bonded for the first time in my four years of service.

Arbinger Institute books are based on the psychology of human behavior and motivation. I consumed the books and embraced each concept. During a lunch with the director, I apologized that it had taken me so long to read all three books. Dr. Joseph chuckled as he admitted he had not read all three himself. I was surprised to hear him say this.

From the first week of Dr. Joseph's arrival in Nashville, some employees began to have reservations about the new administration. I thought their apprehension was simply due to change, so I disregarded the complaints but shared with Dr. Joseph that I was hearing voices of disquiet and potential upheaval from the ranks of administrators, teachers, and secretaries. Following board policy, I took all griev-ances to the director without revealing their origination; he assured me they were inaccurate. We both laughed off the complaints.

But when the director incorporated a gag rule, I began to wonder if I needed to take concerns from teachers and staff more seriously. At a retreat, Dr. Joseph told board members that in order to keep his message clear and clean, he wanted the board to receive our information directly from him - not principals, administrators, teachers, or workers. Dr. Joseph told his staff that all communication with the Metro School Board about administrative matters was the job of the director. Administra-tors, principals, and educators continued to talk with me but were fearful and asked if we could meet privately off-campus or exchange emails through private accounts rather than the district email. Employees voiced fear that the administration could be monitoring their email accounts. All of a sudden, my relationships with staff went undercover.

I'd been an educator in Metro Schools for 25 years and a representative of the board for over four years. The gag rule seemed fishy to me. Nashville may be a fairly large metropolitan city, but it is more like a small town. We know each other and share information, as is the norm in smaller communities. Because I'd been a long-term educator in the district, teachers and principals knew and trusted me. Ad-ministrators, principals, and educators needed to talk with Dr. Joseph's supervisors, but they feared for their jobs if it were known they'd communicated with a board member. Teachers continued to keep me informed of the issues they faced as a result of Dr. Joseph's leadership. As I listened to staff concerns, I became aware of Dr. Jo-seph's mixed messages to the board. My experience was that Dr. Joseph was giving the board one message, but a different message was communicated to staff. It would have taken me longer to discover this if I had not answered the call of administrators to meet with them in private.

Board members have only one employee - the Director of Schools. The board is responsible for selecting the superintendent, assessing performance, and ensuring effective organizational planning through the board's vision, mission, and policies. Therefore, Dr. Joseph had no power over board members to dictate our ability or inability to communicate with our constituencies; however, he could prohibit his employees from communicating with board members. After the gag rule was dis-cussed at a board retreat, board members agreed it was problematic. We had to be able to listen to the people who had elected us to office. By spring, Dr. Joseph and his chief of staff assured board members that the gag rule would be lifted; however, the rectification letter did not go out to staff until six months later. With the gag rule in place for a full year, the board operated without educators' and administrators' input for the first year of Dr. Joseph's tenure.

Although funding to train 40 new Reading Recovery teachers had board approval, Dr. Joseph froze the hiring of the last nine positions that were not filled when he began his tenure with Metro Schools. His rationale was that he had to ensure all classroom positions were filled before interventionists were hired. I understood and agreed that our first priority was the classroom. I later heard that the unfilled positions were in middle and high school - not elementary.

A reporter called asking why Dr. Joseph was not adhering to the budget. I shared Dr. Joseph's rationale and then called him to convey that a reporter had inquired about his deviation from the budget. Dr. Joseph assured me that the nine positions were not lost but would be carried over for the next fiscal year. I believed that Dr. Joseph was just being cautious and wanted to do a good job.

Teachers and employees continued to inform me of various problems, all the while begging me not to mention their names for fear of insubordination charges, being fired, or some other type of retaliation. Metro Schools had experienced a culture problem for at least a decade but I had never before seen the level of fear administrators and educators now exhibited. I didn't understand it. The Joseph I knew was kind, supportive, and honest. *What was going on? Why were employees so upset?* I had not seen this level of distrust during my 35 years as a teacher or four years as a board member. I continued to follow board policy and meticulously took all complaints to Dr. Joseph, who assured me there was some confusion. Perhaps a member of his staff had made a mistake, but he would straighten it out. I listened, watched, and waited, still supportive of him.

I thoroughly enjoyed having lunch with Dr. Joseph. Sometimes our conversations fringed into theology, so I invited him to attend my church at Unity of Music City in the neighborhood where he resided. Dr. Joseph arrived right on time for the 11 o'clock service. He left as soon as it was over so I didn't get an opportunity to introduce him to my friends. As part of the Praise and Worship Team at church, I welcomed and applauded him from the pulpit. I even sang a song dedicated to him for his work in our school district. I was so proud that Dr. Joseph was my director.

Deb Moore, Jill, Sherri Gentry, and Tim Sharp
singing at church

A competent leader can get efficient service from poor troops, on the contrary,
an incompetent leader can demoralize the best of troops.[54]
~ John J. Pershing

Chapter 40:

When Leadership Fails

DURING MY FIRST FEW YEARS ON THE BOARD, I worked with Dr. Jim Roberts to address the culture problem in Metro Schools. Educators and service staff had not been happy. Many experienced low morale. They didn't feel respected by the administration. Teachers had not had a pay raise in several years; longevity pay was practically non-existent due to the direction from the Tennessee Department of Education. Dr. Roberts and I didn't agree on every issue, but he listened and took steps to rectify most of my concerns.

Now, with Dr. Joseph's gag rule slowly to be lifted, the climate was increasingly and intensively growing worse. When I spoke to Dr. Joseph about the climate/culture issue, he disregarded my concerns, saying that Metro had always had a culture problem. He ignored my perspective that school and district climates were deteriorating at a faster clip than during previous administrations.

As soon as the board hired Dr. Joseph, he immediately began assembling his team. Early on, he brought a cadre of over 20 administrators from out of state, often replacing highly-respected, long-term Nashville administrators. Dr. Joseph explained that the incoming administrators made more money in their previous jobs; therefore, to entice them to leave their positions and move to Nashville, he had to pay over Metro's salary scale, even if they had less experience than local long-term administrators. When the Metro Schools' Director of Human Resources pushed back on the high salaries, Dr. Joseph threatened repercussions if she didn't conform to his wishes. Shortly after that encounter, she resigned.

Paying out-of-state employees above the salary scale upset Nashville's principals and administrators, and further exacerbated the cultural issues that had plagued Metro Schools for years. Dr. Joseph told board members that he was bringing the best in the country to Nashville, but it didn't take long to realize that many of his picks had less experience, qualifications, and expertise than Nashville's personnel.

As long-term employees saw the inferior caliber of many of the out-of-town adminis-trators, culture and climate problems worsened. Many administrators and principals began to notice a dichotomy of "them" versus "us." Problems only grew worse.

Dr. Joseph's previous mentor, Mo Carrasco came to Nashville at the invita-tion of the Director of Schools. Carrasco was given an executive officer position in leadership development. Although sexual innuendos began immediately, within 18 months, Carrasco officially was accused of sexual harassment by a long-time Nash-ville female executive officer. Board member Amy Frogge reported the accusation to Dr. Joseph early on. Dr. Joseph's appointed leader in the human resource office threatened the investigator of the case, Sam Lake, with consequences if he didn't make it all go away. Sam was told that if he didn't get this right, Dr. Joseph would fire him.

Phil Williams is the chief investigative reporter for NewsChannel 5's nation-ally award-winning investigative team. His report on this issue follows:[56]

In November 2017, a Metro Nashville Public Schools employee filed a sexual harassment complaint against a longtime Joseph friend, Mo Carrasco. The adminis-trator had previously worked with Joseph at two districts in Maryland.

Four months earlier, school board member Amy Frogge had informed Joseph that there were allegations from an unnamed victim against Carrasco. But instead of directing MNPS Human Resources to investigate, as required by district policy, the director went directly to his friend.

That was confirmed in an email from Carrasco to human resources. Joseph claims he did not order an investigation because MNPS does not investigate anony-mous complaints. (A news release, however, later said the district did accept anony-mous complaints.)

After Carrasco resigned from MNPS, he met with NewsChannel 5. His pub-lic statement that was given in an exclusive television interview follows.[55]

People need to know the truth. This district has been living too many lies. Dr. Joseph is someone I trained as a first-year principal. I mentored him for a long time. He was my daughter's principal. I nominated him for Principal of the Year.

This [MNPS] is one of the few districts where I've ever worked where the num-ber of vacancies goes up instead of down. People are leaving. People are not happy. And we keep saying to people that everything is great and we're making progress. We are not making progress.

NewsChannel 5 Investigates asked, "So why are people leaving?"

Carrasco answered: "There is a climate of mistrust. Privately, many veteran educators will tell you the same thing."

Carrasco went on to explain that part of that mistrust came from Dr. Joseph's failure to tap into the knowledge that already existed in Metro Nashville Schools - opting instead to bring in a slew of outside consultants to tell teachers how to teach.

"I made a statement one day to some of the executive staff that we have too many contracts, too many consultants in the district. They are running into each other, and I don't think that was taken very well."

Joseph raised eyebrows when he came to the district pushing through hundreds of thousands of dollars for consulting contracts. Among them was a contract with Gallup's StrengthsFinder program that was supposed to help district employees reach their full potential. Carrasco commented on that contract in his interview:

"We haven't even talked about how to turn those talents into strengths - and that was supposed to be the training - strength finding."

NewsChannel 5 Investigates asked, "What has the district received from all that money that's been spent?"

Carrasco responded, "Your guess is as good as mine."

Joseph also faced criticism for bringing in so many people, like Carrasco, from the outside - instead of seriously considering people who were already here. Carrasco commented on that practice.

"We are not transparent with people. We hire people and we put you through an interview process and we have you compete, but those decisions - 90 percent of the time - have already been made."

And Carrasco said he watched from the inside as that hiring practice became a continuing pattern.

"Sometimes I feel bad because sometimes those interviews are not the real thing. I feel bad because some people think they have a chance. Sometimes they do, but most of the time they don't. Those decisions are already pre-made."

When asked if he had ever been forced to hire someone he did not want to hire, Carrasco responded that he had, and he declined to name the person he was forced to hire, but he said there was a longtime Metro high school principal who he thought would have been a perfect fit for a new job.

"And I was given a resume by somebody above me and said this is the person you need to hire. I said this person doesn't have enough experience, and I was told this is the person you need to hire."

~~

The case involving Carrasco was only one of many sexual harassment cases filed against the district under Dr. Joseph's leadership. Some names have been changed. According to NewsChannel 5,

[A] middle school employee reported that principal [Steve Baker] had tried to coerce him into sexual acts. HR manager [Sam Lake] attempted to put [Baker] on administrative leave so the allegations could be investigated, but Joseph's number two HR person, Sharon Pertiller, intervened to keep Baker on the job.

MNPS claimed that [Lake] was using the wrong form.

Still, the files show that [Baker] returned to his school and retaliated against the victim.

Assistant principal [Henry Jackson] then filed a complaint, saying he was facing retaliation for reporting the victim's allegations to higher-ups. Joseph's team still did not put [Baker] on leave.

The district's own files show that an HR investigation uncovered substantial evidence against [Baker], including information that he tried to enlist employees in making up lies about the victim, allegations that he had hired a man he met in an adult bookstore that he frequented, and a claim by the school's bookkeeper of financial improprieties that needed to be audited.

HR, which reports directly to Joseph, decided to give [Baker] "management training."

[A] science teacher . . . filed a separate sexual harassment complaint against [Baker]. Again, Joseph's HR department did not place the principal on administrative leave.

When NewsChannel 5 Investigates began digging through those HR investigations, Joseph did nothing to review his HR department's handling of the cases.

Instead, in a memo to the school board, he expressed concern that NewsChannel 5 "will report on information that was 'alleged'" and promised to work to get state law changed so that the district could keep its sexual harassment files secret in the future.

After the first story aired, school board members said Joseph continued to tell them there was nothing to the allegations and they should ignore the NewsChannel 5 report.

It took pressure from board members to convince him to place [Baker] on administrative leave two days later. The principal decided to retire.

Three of [Baker's] victims later filed a lawsuit that alleged that Joseph's administration had a "policy and practice of ignoring complaints of sexual harassment, as well as interfering with investigations of harassment."

So far, MNPS has paid $350,000 to settle those lawsuits.

[Henry Jackson], who says he personally warned Joseph about [Baker's] behavior, has now filed a separate lawsuit for unlawful retaliation.

The alleged victim in the Mo Carrasco case has filed a $1.2 million lawsuit *against the district.*

Former HR manager [Sam Lake] has filed a separate lawsuit, alleging that Joseph's team began retaliating after he uncovered damning evidence against Carrasco and after he attempted to put [Steve Baker] on administrative leave. Metro has denied the allegations.

Under pressure from the sexual harassment scandal, Joseph convinced the board to give a $100,000 contract to Nashville law firm Bone McAllester to review his district's HR practices.

It is unclear how much MNPS has spent so far in defending those lawsuits. [56]

~~

Sam Lake eventually resigned due to retaliation and sued the district. Lawyers ultimately settled out of court. Sam walked away with almost $425,000 in his pocket. When he left Nashville schools, Sam was hired by a larger school district to fill a prestigious role in their human resource office.

After a principal's meeting which was attended by over 149 principals and administrators, I received calls that Dr. Joseph had played a short segment of a rap song at a meeting. Dr. Joseph told administrators under his supervision that during contentious board meetings, he thumbed through a Rolodex of songs in his head and chose "Blow the Whistle"[57] to focus on during meetings. Curious principals, unfamiliar with the song, began to google the lyrics in an attempt to understand the director's message. They found misogynistic, lewd, vulgar, expletive-filled language used throughout the rap song. The director projected the album cover of Too $hort flanked by two women biting and kissing the rapper's ear as Dr. Joseph played a few bars of the song. Although this meeting occurred at the Martin Professional Development Center, there was nothing professional about his conduct. Dr. Joseph appeared to have such excessive pride and self-confidence that I wondered if he thought he was above reproach.

I wished that I hadn't known this! I didn't want to take on this battle, yet how could I sit by idly and say nothing? Having grown up as a child with little or no control over the circumstances of my life when my father wielded his power in a harmful way, I could not stand by and allow Dr. Joseph to continue to exert that same type of behavior in such a potentially harmful way.

Even as a young teacher, I longed to work in Metro school and teach kids like me. Through some miraculous chain of events, I found myself as the Vice Chairman of the organization I admired. *I had to express my opinion!* I filed a Civil Service Complaint in the district's Federal Program's Office saying that Dr. Joseph's use of a brief clip from the song, "Blow The Whistle" in a public school setting was "highly offensive, reprehensible and inexcusable." This was my attempt to repurify and re-sanctify education in the capital city of Tennessee. Phil Williams at NewChannel 5 covered the story. Some names have been changed in order to provide consistency with the story as it is revealed within this book.

A rap song has now become a powerful symbol of the discord playing out among the leadership of Metro Nashville Public Schools.

It's a song that Schools Director Dr. Shawn Joseph says sometimes plays in his head during difficult meetings of the Metro School Board, and it's now triggered an official complaint by one board member.

"I could not understand how this misogynistic song could be appropriate in ANY educational environment," school board member Jill Speering said in [her] complaint sent to the district's civil rights coordinator. "What kind of example does this set for principals, teachers, and students?"

In recent weeks, Joseph's relationship with the Metro School Board has turned more contentious as he's faced questions about the district's spending from Speering and fellow board member Amy Frogge.

During one discussion, Joseph appeared to be rolling his eyes, although he later claimed in a tweet that "sometimes you need to look towards where your strength comes."

Attorney Jamie Hollin represents "more than five" principals who were in a meeting last Thursday for all the district's principals. That's when Joseph brought up the song "Blow the Whistle" by rapper Too Short. "He said, according to my clients, 'Here is what I am thinking about during school board meetings,'" Hollin told NewsChannel 5 Investigates.

According to Hollin and other principals who spoke to NewsChannel 5, Joseph told the group that, when dealing with a difficult board, he sometimes hears the song in his head. Joseph played the following lyrics: "I go on and on. Can't understand how I last so long. I must have superpowers. Rap two hundred twenty-five thousand hours." A school district spokesperson said that's where Joseph cut off the song to avoid any explicit lyrics.

*But some see the song's title, "Blow the Whistle," as a reference to street lingo for a sex act. "What's my favorite word? B****! Why they gotta say it like short? B****! You know they can't play on my court. Can't hang with the big dogs, stay on the porch."*

Reverend Enoch Fuzz, a community activist who has recently been critical of some of Joseph's budgetary decisions, said [that] playing of the rap song "seems to be out of a frustration."

Fuzz recently came to the defense of the two dissident school board members

after one of Joseph's fraternity brothers accused Speering and Frogge of engaging in
what he called a public lynching. When Frogge confronted Joseph, he denied that he
thought the two are racists. Still, he declined to rebuke a fellow fraternity member. "If
a member chooses to come and speak," Joseph said, "he has the right to say and do
what he feels is on his heart to say."

The [schools'] director also went on a radio show and compared himself to the
nation's first African-American president. "They beat up the last president I knew,
Barack Obama," Joseph said. "So, you know, it's expected. It's alright. I'm going to try
to keep cool like he is."

Reverend Fuzz said, "I don't like people trying to use me, based on racial pref-
erences." He added that he believes Joseph's use of the rap video reflects an unfortu-
nate tendency to demonize his critics, rather than fully engaging with them.

"I think I'd like to ask Dr. Joseph to help people understand what he's talking
about," Fuzz added. "Don't get mad. It's just business." He added that he thinks Joseph
and the school board could benefit from some expert mediation.

NewsChannel 5 Investigates repeatedly asked Dr. Joseph's office whether he
believed this was an appropriate statement to be aimed at board members who are
his bosses. A spokesperson repeatedly insisted that no objectionable lyrics were ever
played. In the end, she said: "We never want an employee to feel uncomfortable, and
we will carefully consider full lyrics in the future."[57]

~~

PLAYING "BLOW THE WHISTLE" AT THE PRINCIPALS' MEETING was a
breach of institutional norms administrators and principals had previously taken for
granted. Out of eight women on a nine-member board, I was the only one who spoke
publicly against this unprofessional behavior. The silence of the women on the board
was deafening! In my opinion, this song is the antithesis of what we should be doing in education. Even as a child, I took action when my dad's reprehensible behavior prevailed. As I healed from childhood trauma, I'd learned to respect myself for
standing up for my mother. I made no apologies for taking a stance for professionalism in education, but some members of the community chastised me for doing so.

Dr. Joseph's friends dismissed his behavior. It appeared to me that the director had whipped up racial tension into a destructive crescendo. Even though the
MNPS Board Chair denied permission for the Metro Council's Minority Caucus
members to speak at the school board's budget meeting, five city councilwomen hi-
jacked the meeting to disparage me publicly about my Civil Service complaint. They
supported Joseph's use of the song at the principals' meeting and said I was out of
line by filing a Civil Service complaint. They said I didn't understand black culture,

and it was their responsibility to halt their work for the city government to come to the board to "straighten me out."

I respectfully sat through their condemnation and yelling when I could have easily left the boardroom. Although I was fuming on the inside as they made their sophomaniac presentation, I tried desperately not to show it. I endured misery for the sake of appearances - something I will never do again. The whole experience was mean-spirited. Its underlying bigotry did not escape my awareness.

How dare they barge in on the business of the school board to do Dr. Joseph's bidding! I suspected it was all orchestrated by the director, but I had no evidence at the time. I began to perceive Dr. Joseph's regime as tragedy exacerbated by ineptitude. The cat was out of the bag. We had been duped! Dr. Joseph was not who he'd presented himself to be.

This experience brought me back to the days of my youth when my father would grow angry because I wouldn't follow his dictates. I felt myself being thrown against the wall as I bounced back with power and determination to continue the fight. I was empowered with courage and fortitude, knowing I was fighting for our employees and children in the same way I had fought for my mother. I stood up to a man towering over me who tried to quiet my voice. I would not back down - no matter the consequences. As a board member, I could not allow this misguided director to damage the district, teachers, and students I loved, even if I had to stand up to him alone. I had suffered ridicule, rejection, and insults often enough to recognize them without buckling. I knew I was strong enough to handle the pain while keeping my heart open.

When Dr. Joseph first came to Nashville, I was told by a high-ranking MNPS administrator that Dr. Joseph told her that if others didn't support his work, he would "throw the race card!" Such a thing had never occurred to me. It's something I'd never seen or experienced in all my years of working closely with leaders and professionals of all races and ethnicities, so I was surprised and taken aback to hear that this potentially divisive and harmful strategy had been premeditated by Dr. Joseph. He appeared to use race as a platform to engender his followers' rage, attempting to circumvent the negative nightly news airing on TV.

All board meetings are aired on television. At one of the next public participation meetings, Dr. Joseph's fraternity brothers filled the boardroom to criticize Amy Frogge and me. They insinuated we were "racists." No one had ever referred to Amy or me in that manner until Dr. Joseph became angry at us for bringing to the board floor concerns that could not be settled in personal conversations with him. I was exhausted by all the racially-motivated innuendos. The bi-monthly fracas left me mentally exhausted for as long as two days after many board meetings.

Many in the black community rallied around Dr. Joseph, refusing to acknowledge controversies surrounding him or his unprofessionalism. I sat in disbelief, knowing that more than half of the complainants who had come directly to me to share their deep concerns about Dr. Joseph's policies and degradations were themselves African-Americans.

I'm uncomfortable approaching the subject of race. A white woman criticizing a black man can be easily misunderstood and mischaracterized, especially if she is a supervisor of the man. *Wasn't it time to stop separating people by race? Wasn't it time to join together to support our employees and teachers?* It was clearly the time for servant leadership. It was time to focus on teachers and administrators to help them feel supported and respected. Doing so would impact students' progress. When educators are trusted and supported, student outcomes improve. When employees feel stressed and defeated, they cannot offer the level of support needed for children to become active, motivated, joyful learners! My experience and beliefs on this matter are confirmed by a study by Neene Banerjee from Valdosta State University and three professors from the University of North Carolina-Charlotte, who concluded, "It's no surprise that teacher job satisfaction affects their performance. . . . [S]tudents' reading scores are higher when they are taught by educators reporting high job satisfaction levels. . . . . "[58]

First and foremost, my job as a retired educator and now a school board member was to ensure student achievement and success. How could our teachers and administrators focus on children when such chaos and agitation reigned?

Meanwhile, I had been nominated to go to Parris Island for a week to represent the school board. I accepted the invitation, excited to get away from Nashville for a short reprieve.

Chapter 41:

Parris Island

DURING THE SCHOOL BOARD TURMOIL, I was reminded of my brother in the Marine Corps. With an unwavering proclivity for grit and rigor, Marines fight with resilience and honor. Had Bobby and I developed those qualities and perseverance through our many brawls with Dad?

For hundreds of years, Marines have fought honorably to defend this nation and our way of life. The Marine Corps is an organization built around success and the opportunity for growth and advancement. These men and women are fiercely proud of their traditions and how they mold and create those who fight to defend our country. Not everyone makes it through the rigorous training. Their motto is The Few, The Proud, The Marines![60]

Michael Steele, a high school principal in Metro Schools, and a previous Marine, called to ask if he could submit my name and his recommendation for me to attend the Marine Corps Educators' workshop, which would take place in January 2019 at Parris Island, South Carolina. Although most of the educators were high school teachers, administrators, and counselors, board members were welcomed. I knew my brother had received his recruit training at Parris Island when he joined the Marine Corps on his 18th birthday. The thought of walking that hallowed ground intrigued me. I was only 10 when Bobby left home, but I still had vivid memories of the stories he shared about his experiences in basic training. One, in particular, stands out in my memory.

While Bobby was in basic training in 1958, Mother sent him three boxes of homemade cookies before she realized that it was not allowed. Within the week, Bobby called on the telephone and asked Mom, "Please don't send any more cookies!" His Drill Instructor (DI) had made him eat all of the cookies at once in front of the other recruits. Mama cried for two days!

Bobby loved the Marine Corps. He was proud he had served in that branch of the armed forces. Even today, he often wears a Marine Corps cap or shirt and talks about how joining the Marine Corps was one of the best decisions of his life.

Although I didn't know what to expect during my time at Parris Island, the thought of escaping the school board turmoil and Tennessee's harsh winter sounded refreshing to me. Being on an island on the east coast with 10 hours of sunlight and 60-degree temperatures sounded like a vacation. *Boy, was I wrong!*

My first red flag appeared when I learned that two staff sergeants were going to pick me up on Monday morning at my home at 4:50 and accompany me to the Nashville airport. When I was first told about that crack-of-dawn hour, I suggested, "Can't I meet you there? I don't get up that early." The response was, "No, ma'am."

Once at the airport, I met high school educators from surrounding Middle Tennessee school districts before we boarded the plane for Atlanta. After two flights culminating in South Carolina, we prepared for a long bus ride. We finally arrived at Parris Island after dark. I was exhausted and ready to get settled into the hotel. I had no idea what I was about to encounter.

The Drill Instructor (DI) stepped on the bus and started yelling,

"Sit up straight. Put your feet on the deck. Look at me. You can say two things; 'Sir, Yes Sir,' and 'Sir, No Sir.' Do you understand?"

We must not have given the proper response, because he continued screaming while the veins popped out from his neck. "You can say two things, 'Sir, Yes sir,' and 'Sir, No sir.' Do you understand?"

His commands continued, "When you get off this bus, stand on one of the yellow footprints. Do you understand? Now go, go, go! Faster! Faster! You better not be the last one off this bus!"

I thought, *What have I gotten myself into?* And then I thought about Bobby. This must have been the way he was treated as a recruit. But I hadn't expected to be treated like a recruit, only told about the experience. My previous hypothesis was laid to rest!

Everything was confusing and frustrating. I felt shell-shocked. Once we were on the yellow footprints, the DI continued to shout orders. "When I say 'go,' run forward as fast as you can. Do you understand? GO!" We ran for about 15 seconds, and then he yelled "S t o p!"

Once we made our way back to the yellow footprints through a series of stop-and-go orders, the DI taught us how to do an About Face, Right Face, Left Face. He did not instruct with the sensitivity of a first-grade teacher, but with the blood-curdling force of my fifth-grade teacher, Mrs. Spurlock.

It was "Run . . . . Stop . . . . Go . . . . Stop" for the next five minutes.

Finally, we were commanded to march into the administration building together, where we were issued military jackets and backpacks. By 10:00 p.m. we were taken to our hotel; it was midnight before I got to sleep. How did my brother at 18 years of age take 13 weeks of this abuse? It was clear. Marine recruits had to learn to adapt quickly.

I thought about my brother almost every moment over the next five days. Walking in the shoes of a recruit was important so educators could intelligently answer and counsel students who might consider this option for the future. The Marines wanted educators to know how this branch of the service is different. Many teachers have not been in the military, so this type of experience is important in order to guide students to available opportunities. All fees, travel, lodging, and food were paid by the Marines. They reminded us that educators reinforce the same values and ideologies as the Marines. Honor, courage, and commitment are goals and values that both organizations share.

At breakfast each day, various dignitaries shared information about their recruitment efforts. The Marines don't want to recruit the lowest 10% from our classes in Metro Schools; they want the top 10%. A recruit can go into any field they desire as part of the educational benefits of the service. They can become doctors, nurses, attorneys, etc.

After eating a leisurely breakfast in the hotel lobby, we loaded the buses again for our first full day at Parris Island. Our group of 60 was divided into two platoons. We stood on the yellow footprints in order to learn how to stand in formation. It reminded me of teaching kindergarten students on their first day in school. Since my students didn't understand the concept of getting in a "line," I put a long piece of masking tape on the floor and instructed them to stand on the tape. They understood this, and now they knew what I meant when I said we needed to line up to leave the room. Kindergarten was basic, and now I began to comprehend the idea of "basic training" in the military.

Once we were in formation, the DI continued shouting commands. We responded to each directive by yelling "Sir, Yes Sir" or "Sir, No Sir." We counted off and remembered our number. If we failed to yell out our number at the appropriate time, the entire platoon did jumping jacks. Every time we gathered, the count off began to ensure everyone was present. We nudged those slow to respond. We were becoming a team! We weren't punished if someone was missing because no one ever missed. However, once a teacher from West Tennessee forgot her water bottle. The rest of us had to stand in formation with our water bottles in our right hands held high above our heads until the teacher returned with her mug. Team building is one of the most important concepts. After all, in the field, Marines have to rely on each other and work together as a unit. Their very lives depend on it!

This branch of the service accepts only those who are super intelligent, mentally prepared, physically fit, and able to think critically. The Marine Corps is a proud organization. Only the best-of-the-best are accepted and successfully complete the 70-day intensive training. Discipline and spirit are the hallmarks of a Marine. The DI shouted to us, "You will treat Marines with the utmost respect. We have earned our place, and we will accept nothing less from you."

These words brought me back to my father. *Was this the way he thought?* He was trained to demand respect, and he expected it from every person in his life - even from his young children. After decades with my father and years with Dr. Joseph, I was determined that I would expect to be treated with the utmost respect. I had earned it, and I would accept nothing less. I had earned my place in the education field, and I would accept nothing less than respect from Dr. Joseph and his followers!

The Code of Ethics is very strong in the Marine Corps. You must give 100% of yourself at all times. You must obey orders quickly, willingly, and without question. You never take what doesn't belong to you, and you are always honest! Again, I thought of my father when he laid down the law to his children, "When I say jump, I expect you to ask 'How high?' on your way up." My dad loved the military. He just didn't understand that young children should not be treated like 18-year-old men. Even though Dad wasn't a Marine, he was a proud officer in the U.S. Army.

During this week, I had the opportunity to witness the graduation of the rookie soldiers. This was an emotional experience for me, not only as the sister of a brother I dearly loved, but also as a patriot of this nation. Watching thousands of young men and women march with precision in straight formation, with every step perfectly synchronized, was an awesome sight. The national anthem always stirs my eyes to tears, but when the band played the Marine Hymn, I surrendered to my emotions. No words were spoken, but I could hear my brother's voice in my ear singing the lyrics to the 10-year-old me.

I found an old letter Bobby had written to Mother dated May 22, 1958, *Today is graduation day. After the commencement exercise, we were finally called "Marines" and allowed base liberty. I experienced freedom for the first time since arriving on the island, and the only time in 13 weeks we were allowed to walk by ourselves without marching in a platoon. Everyone went out to get a milkshake and look around for an entire afternoon before we boarded the bus for Infantry Training.*

Bobby at graduation
from Parris Island

Chapter 42:

From the Battlefield

I HAD ONLY BEGUN TO SEE how far Dr. Joseph would go to punish others. I continued to notice how the events of my youth bled into my current life. My father's narcissistic personality seemed to be reincarnated into Dr. Joseph. For years, Dad and I had been locked in conflict, and now I found myself fighting with the Director of Schools who seemed to think I worked for him when in reality I was one of *his* supervisors. It was my job to hold him accountable to the children and taxpayers in Nashville. Not only did this fact seem to escape his purview, but it also appeared to make him angry.

Dr. Joseph went on the radio and talked about me without mentioning my name. My friends kept me apprised of his comments. I tried to overlook all I could. Because I lacked trust in the director, I voted to lower the threshold for district spending by 75% (from $100K to $25K). The director's spending had gotten so out of control that the board explored hiring permanent internal auditors to monitor future spending in the district. This necessary expenditure would have likely cost the district another $200K a year, at a time when teachers and staff were underpaid and overworked.

Dr. Joseph's obsessive will to win whipped up into a vindictive crescendo. The more I did to hold Dr. Joseph accountable, the more he seemed to pursue ways to hurt me as he attempted to denigrate my reputation. I began to realize that no future could include us both. One of us would have to go, and it wouldn't be me. Unfortunately, I'd made a fatal mistake by trusting Dr. Joseph to lead our district with character and a servant's heart. He had demonstrated retaliation toward employees, and now he seemed to focus on me.

Dr. Joseph knew my love of literacy and the respect I held for the extraordinary work of the Literacy Director, Dr. Tammy Lipsey. Both he and his chief academic officer had praised Tammy for bringing up literacy achievement scores through the Comprehensive Literacy Plan. Tammy didn't have a staff. She was an office of one. Even in that capacity, she was able to conduct monthly training for all 74 literacy coaches, recruit and train volunteers for the 36 Reading Clinics and respond personally to principal and administrative requests to offer professional development at local schools. In just two years, literacy scores dramatically increased under Tammy's leadership.

Because Dr. Joseph's friends had displaced most long-term administrators in high positions, there was little historical knowledge about how the district had been managed, resulting in many needless mistakes. Dr. Joseph and his team often talked about building the plane as they flew it. This resulted in chaos throughout the district. Many staff meetings were late or canceled at the last moment.

Perhaps it was those last-minute decisions made by Dr. Joseph's team that caused the no-bid contracts to be established. No-bid contracts, possibly to avoid competitive bidding, came to my awareness as early as the first month Dr. Joseph arrived in Nashville. A piggyback contract is a procurement tool used by the district to acquire the same or lower prices from an existing contract. Piggybacks are permissible by law if using existing contracts within the state. Dr. Joseph and his team entered into piggyback contracts from out-of-state, thus breaking state law. Generally, a larger district such as Nashville can land a better price from vendors, but by utilizing piggyback contracts from smaller districts, most likely we did not get the best prices. As a board member, I wondered why Joseph was avoiding the established protocol for contracts? Under his administration, piggyback contracts became commonplace. Phil Williams from NewsChannel 5 reports:

"Joseph pushed his team to sign two no-bid contracts -- totaling $1.8 million -- with Performance Matters, a Maryland company with which he had previously done business. He had previously appeared in a promotional video for the company.

Emails show Joseph began discussing a potential deal with Performance Matters two weeks before he officially started his position as Director of Schools. Performance Matters suggested "piggybacking" on a recently awarded Shelby County contract to avoid bidding. One of those contracts - $1 million for software used to track student achievement - was awarded no bids, piggybacking on an out-of-state contract. That is prohibited under state law. Joseph blamed a procurement official for the error.

MNPS also signed a separate $500,000 contract with another company to write the questions for the student assessment software. But, after signing those contracts for $1.5 million, Joseph's team did not require schools to use the software. MNPS claims it has no usage statistics, but admits usage was likely low.

The second contract - $845,651 for software used to track professional devel-

opment training for teachers - was awarded to Performance Matters, piggybacking on a Shelby County contract. Emails show the district could have continued to use its existing system for a much lower price.

MNPS admits it spent millions of dollars using piggyback contracts with favored vendors without checking to see whether they could get a better price – a practice that Metro Finance Director Talia Lomax-O'Neal said does not represent best practices.

In another deal, Discovery Education -- a Maryland company with ties to Joseph and his team -- was given the inside track for an $11.4 million contract for science and technology curriculum. The person who headed that program says MNPS worked with that company for months to develop a plan, used that plan to develop a Request for Proposals, then put the contract out for bids, giving competitors just four weeks to develop a counter-proposal. MNPS says that was not illegal.

A Metro audit also confirmed other consultants were hired without following bidding or contracting procedures, including a man with no formal education training who was given contracts for $105,000 to advise schools on standardized testing.

He had previously worked with Joseph in [another state]."[56]

As Vice-Chair of the board and a long-time teacher and administrator of Reading Recovery®, I heard from administrators, principals, and teachers weekly about employees' concerns that Dr. Joseph was breaking the law for such things as questionable contracts, sexual harassment cases, election meddling, and failure to report teacher misconduct cases. As an elected board member, it was my job to channel complaints. Originally, I'd taken my concerns directly to Dr. Joseph. When Dr. Joseph began to see that I wasn't buying his responses about constituent and employee concerns, he began to talk about expanding Reading Recovery to special education, something I'd asked him to consider earlier. On one of those long phone calls, Dr. Joseph informed me he was going to talk with the Special Education Executive Director to tell her of his interest to expand Reading Recovery for special education students for the following school year. Although I hoped those comments were sincere, the information proved to be inaccurate; Dr. Joseph was just baiting me in an attempt to reel me back in.

In May of 2016 during the second round of Dr. Joseph's interviews for the Nashville job, he stated, "I'm a believer in Reading Recovery. We have over 100 Reading Recovery teachers in my previous school district. They are thriving. They are making an impact in our neediest schools."[62]

Dr. Joseph continued to acknowledge the power of the Reading Recovery intervention a year later in May of 2017 at the board's budget presentation to Metro Council: "Those [literacy] deficits actually increase over time if we don't take care of those reading needs early in their process . . . . We're also going to continue our investment in Reading Recovery, which is one of America's most well-researched reading interventions . . . . If you have not had an opportunity to see Reading Recovery in action, we will strongly recommend that you come visit one of our schools and see the magic those teachers do with that one-on-one highly intensive reading program."[63]

Following up on Dr. Joseph's invitation to witness Reading Recovery in action, at his request I drafted a letter that he signed and sent to Metro council members in October of 2017, which stated:

"The goal of Reading Recovery is to dramatically reduce the number of first-grade students who have extreme difficulty learning to read and write. One hundred percent of Reading Recovery students make progress; however, 67% can read at grade level within 12-20 weeks of instruction which totals only 30-50 hours of instruction."

In the spring of 2017, the board was informed of a significant decrease in student enrollment. The board wasn't provided data explaining why students were leaving, but my constituent feedback indicated that parents and students were unhappy with the director's leadership. Not only were students leaving the district, but great teachers and administrators also left to find high-profile jobs in other parts of the country.

Not only were white administrators leaving, but some of our most prominent leaders of color also left. Among those were the Tennessee Teacher of the Year, Cicely Woodard, and her husband Dr. Ron Woodard. Ron had served as a highly effective principal at a turnaround high school. Years before Dr. Joseph came to Nashville, Dr. Woodard had been chosen to transform a chronically low-performing school in a high-poverty neighborhood. Through Dr. Woodard's leadership, dramatic, significant gains were achieved within two years. Dr. Woodard was hopeful his turnaround success at Maplewood High School would help ignite a path for his advancement in the district. Neither Dr. Joseph nor his administration seemed to be interested in promoting local administrators like Dr. Woodard. It appeared to me that Dr. Joseph was more interested in bringing his friends and acquaintances from outside the state rather than promoting employees from within. Dr. Woodard had been hopeful that a fellow African-American leader would recognize his qualifications and vie to keep him in Nashville, but Dr. Joseph's administration gave him no hope of a higher position. As a result, Dr. Woodard left MNPS and accepted a position as Assistant Superintendent of Murray County Schools. I considered the loss of Dr. Woodard and his wife a travesty, but Dr. Joseph appeared unfazed.

In March of 2018, Amy Frogge and I called for an audit of Dr. Joseph's spending after the board was informed of a $7.5 million shortfall due to decreased student attendance and persistent problems that continued to come to my attention. Channel5 News reported: *For the first time in 15 years, Metro Nashville Public School's enrollment numbers have dropped. District officials thought they would add more than 1,500 students in 2017- instead, the district lost 500 students.*[64]

The loss of school enrollment occurred while Nashville experienced a population boom with an average of 83 people moving to the city each day from 2017-2018.[65]

Because of the shortfall, Dr. Joseph froze all school budgets in March of 2018, putting the onus of responsibility to balance the budget on the shoulders of schools and children - while he continued to hold tight to his need for a Metro School bus driver to chauffeur him around the city. Dr. Joseph contended that he needed the driver to work effectively as Director of Schools (DOS). He was able to read emails and return telephone calls while an employee drove him to various appointments and lunches. However, he utilized a driver even when other Metro schools' employees were riding in the same vehicle. It's my understanding that no other MNPS Director of Schools had ever required a valet except when a previous superintendent, Dr. Garcia, broke his leg and was unable to drive for a few months.

News media continued to report issues. According to their reports, the district sent a memo to employees stating, "This freeze will include all school purchases that fall into the budget category of non-staff expenses (software, supplies, transportation, field trips, IT purchases, equipment, etc.)."[66]

Answering phone calls from principals filled my day. Essential items like paper became an issue. After a high school principal's request for paper was denied, parents got involved and delivered cases of paper to the school. It became a newsworthy topic! A parent reported to NewsChannel 5 that she'd spent about $120 on paper. She exclaimed, "Parents shouldn't have to shell out hundreds of dollars for paper, ever."[67]

Principals were concerned that field trips planned early in the year to celebrate the completion of the year would have to be forfeited and their unused fund balance returned to the central office. A district spokesman later apologized for the confusion and announced the withdrawal of some of the stringent requirements.[67]

I could feel it in my bones; something was up. Perhaps it was the still, quiet voice within that prompted me to action. I had seen the Director of Schools retaliate against employees. With concern, I invited Reading Recovery teachers to come to the budget committee meeting, afraid that Dr. Joseph would use our most fragile children as pawns for retaliation against me.

Activism is something we are all responsible for. It is not something we turn over to a group of people. It's either in our daily lives or it's not.[68]

~ Glennon Doyle

Chapter 43:

Retaliation

T HE REDBUDS WERE BLOOMING IN EARLY APRIL. It was a frigid afternoon - one that chilled me to the bone - one that demonstrated the type of leader I'd helped to hire.

Dr. Joseph bragged about himself. Although he likened himself to Jesus, the Gladiator from the 2000 action/adventure film, and Barack Obama, I thought of him more like President Donald Trump. He often touted his honesty in private conversations with me and in public. This struck me as odd. I'd never met an honest person who bragged about his integrity - quite the opposite. An honest person lives their virtue. Their attributes are apparent through their words and deeds. There is no need to be boastful.

The budget process in MNPS is a long, cumbersome process that can take over six months. After months of meetings and listening to countless hours of feedback from 126 taxpayers, Dr. Shawn Joseph revised his proposed budget at the final committee meeting only one day before the budget was to be presented to Metro Nashville Mayor David Briley. During the previous months, at least 15 parents, classroom teachers, and principals had spoken on the effectiveness of Reading Recovery, delineating stories about how the intervention had changed the trajectory of their children's lives. On April 16th, 2018 Dr. Joseph made the following statements:

"If you haven't figured it out, if I say I'm going to do something, I'm going to do it. I'm pretty driven about that, and I'm proud of the integrity I've lived by for the past 22 years. People can say a lot of things about me, but they never will say I'm not a man of my word. It's important. It's a code that I have lived by for a very long time. That's why people either love me or they hate me because I will be raw and real all the time because that is very important . . . ."[69]

He then discussed recommendations made by his transition team two years ago about the need for excellent "first" instruction, but apparently he had waited until the eleventh hour of the budget process to bring in the new focus.

Just one month after I'd called for an audit of Dr. Joseph's spending, the arrow of his revenge struck my heart as he announced his new budget would omit 85 Reading Recovery positions, virtually eliminating this very important intervention tool and professional development opportunity within Nashville Schools.

Dr. Joseph inexplicably prefaced his announcement to cut the 85 teachers' positions by saying, "What we know about Reading Recovery as a program is that it's one of the most-researched - one of the best reading intervention programs out there in the country. Hands down! . . . If you get certified as a Reading Recovery teacher, you are skilled. You know how to teach a kid to read. No question. Hands down! You can do it!"[69]

On April 16th, 2018 - at the latest possible moment in the MNPS budget process - Dr. Joseph convinced the board that Reading Recovery teachers would be better utilized in the classroom rather than doing what they were trained to do - provide individualized, intensive intervention for students who need the most support. Riveted, I stood in the consequences of his deception. Dr. Joseph presented no plans to replace the intervention support for the most fragile learners across the district. With this eleventh hour dismantling of Reading Recovery, there were no opportunities for constituent feedback. The pistons of frustration grinded in my head.

Dr. Joseph's rationale for eradicating Reading Recovery was the lack of return on investment of the lowest-performing, first-grade students. It reminded me of the principal who'd said she didn't want to spend her money on *those* kids.

Dr. Joseph specified that his desire was to align the budget to the district's priorities - even though he acknowledged that literacy was the number one priority. The results of his recently completed internal and external program evaluations of Reading Recovery concluded that although students had made fast and efficient progress to close the gap in first grade, gains diminished in second and third grades after the intervention was completed. I argued that Reading Recovery was designed to bring the lowest-performing readers to the average of their class with approximately 50 hours of instruction. This intervention had met that goal, yet Dr. Joseph seemed to believe that 50 hours of intensive intervention for the most fragile first-grade students should be sufficient to propel the lowest-performing students' efficiency through third grade. No program can promise such gains unless quality instruction in second and third grades is assured. If student gains were diminishing over time, it was incumbent on the administration to problem-solve issues that contributed to the loss of academic gains after students completed the intervention. It was unlikely that graduates of Reading Recovery had received high-quality instruction after the completion of the intervention.

Because Dr. Joseph's decision was made in the dark of night, only hours before the budget was presented to the mayor, there was no attempt to solve the problem. This appeared to be another example of Dr. Joseph's penchant for punishment. He was taking his vengeance to a new level. Evidence was clear that he had retaliated against his employees; now he was attacking and bullying one who had hired him, had the authority to evaluate his performance, and vote on his contracts.

Dr. Joseph said he had chosen to look at programs with the biggest budget, but as I researched the line items, I could see that pre-k was more expensive. According to the MNPS Fiscal Year 2018-19 Budget that was approved by Metro Council in June of 2018, the pre-k budget was $7 million with only 55 positions compared to the loss of Reading Recovery's 85 positions costing $6 million.

The focus of pre-k is to give support to underserved four-year-old children in order for them to begin kindergarten on grade level. Like Reading Recovery, it is also an intervention. Interestingly, an earlier Vanderbilt study on pre-kindergarten concluded that pre-k successfully closed the gap for the majority of children while in progress, but additional support was needed in subsequent years in order to maintain those early acceleration patterns.[70] The results of the findings of the Vanderbilt study on pre-k and the Hanover brief on Reading Recovery appeared to be very similar. *So why did Dr. Joseph choose to ax the intervention he had touted with such enthusiasm?*

There had never been a discussion on the board floor or in committee about scrapping pre-k although we had discussed the findings of the Vanderbilt study. Teachers in pre-k serve approximately 15 students a year. Reading Recovery offered intensive, high-quality individualized instruction in first grade for half of the day and group instruction for students during the remainder of the day, which totaled an average of 50-70 students over the course of the year.

Dr. Joseph had called Reading Recovery teachers the "leaders of literacy in our district." He argued that these highly-skilled educators were needed back in the classroom where they could reach more students. It was a counterfeit argument, full of vigor and venom. First-grade teachers in priority schools serve approximately 20 students. In many cases Reading Recovery teachers more than tripled that number. Classroom teachers can not offer the same intensive, individualized, 30-minute, daily instruction.

When I first moved to Ohio to learn this new intervention, I'd wanted to make an impact in children's lives, but little did I know the far-reaching effects that year would have on Metro teachers and me. Over my 15 years as a Reading Recovery Teacher Leader and eight years as a Metro School Board member, we trained over

228 teachers in the year-long graduate program. Each one of these teachers led a life of consequence. Just over the course of one school year, Reading Recovery teachers impacted the achievement and self-concepts of over 3,780 young students.

I reminded Dr. Joseph and the Research and Evaluation team at MNPS about an earlier internal study of Reading Recovery that was authorized and completed under a previous Director of Schools. In 1997, an internal research study concluded that in just two years Reading Recovery had saved the district over $330,000 in retention savings alone. More first-grade students were promoted to second grade after the implementation of the short-term intervention as compared to those retained before Reading Recovery was in place. Dr. Joseph made no comment.

From the board floor, I asked the 50 Reading Recovery teachers in attendance if they would accept a classroom position proposed by Dr. Joseph. After all, if these "leaders of literacy" in our district were not willing participants in his new plan, not only would it fail, but we could potentially lose some of our most highly qualified teachers.

Not one teacher raised her hand.

Dr. Joseph sold the board on his last-minute transgression by saying that Reading Recovery was not working effectively based partly on an external research brief.[69] Oddly, the Hanover brief focused on the first two years of implementation which had occurred four years prior. In 2014-15, both of the trainers were fresh out of their training year, and all 24 teachers had not earned their certifications until the end of the school year in May. During 2015-16, only 50% of the teachers had completed the work for their certifications. Therefore, by choosing the first two cohorts of students, 75% of the teachers were novices and had not yet gained their certifications until the end of the year. Yet that was the data that Dr. Joseph hung his hat on -- a small number of students and 75% of teachers-in-training who were actively working on *becoming* a certified Reading Recovery teacher. The writers of the brief appear to have disregarded the 2016-17 cohort when the trainers had more experience and many more teachers had gained their certifications.

A quote from the Hanover brief about student success indicated that even though the Reading Recovery students were trained by teachers who were in training themselves, the students *outperformed* students who did not participate in the intervention. The quote follows: "[First grade] participants in and after the 2014-15 spring semester tended to outperform non-participants in Grade 1 with less consistent results in later grade levels." [71]

In other words, the intervention worked! The majority of the lowest-performing students in first grade closed the gap and performed above their counterparts.

Without strong second and third-grade classroom instruction there were less consistent results in later grades after the intervention was completed.

However, Hanover's research clearly didn't appear to meet the qualifications to be considered a high-quality study. In reality, it was a brief covering a review of limited sources. The authors of the report pointed this out in their own publication caveat: "The publisher and authors have used their best efforts in preparing this brief. The publisher and authors make no representations or warranties concerning the accuracy or completeness of the contents of this brief and specifically disclaim any implied warranties of fitness for a particular purpose."[71]

Nevertheless, the board moved forward and voted in favor of Dr. Joseph's new budget, essentially eliminating the most powerful support for struggling readers in Nashville. After the vote to remove Reading Recovery, a fellow board member told me that Dr. Joseph and his key staff were seen high-fiving each other in celebration.

Any type of research, as well as local research, can be designed with an outcome in mind. *Were administrators in Research and Development told the director wanted a negative report on Reading Recovery?* I will never know the answer to that question, but I remember Dr. Joseph's friend, Mo Carrasco, Executive Officer of Leadership Development, telling the media, "People need to know the truth. This district has been living too many lies. We are not transparent with people . . . ."[55]

Sometimes ethics go out the window when administrators feel compelled to follow the demands of their superiors rather than their own integrity. I continue to wonder how many employees negotiated their own moral code in order to follow the clandestine leaderships' requests of them.

Unfortunately, neither the Metro Schools Research and Development Office nor Dr. Joseph seemed to value high-quality research. What Works Clearinghouse (WWC) is an initiative of the U.S. Department of Education's Institute of Education Sciences and a trusted source of information for school decision-makers. It specifies:

For more than a decade, the WWC has been a central and trusted source of scientific evidence on education programs, products, practices, and policies. We review the research, determine which studies meet rigorous standards and summarize the findings. We focus on high-quality research to answer the question "[W]hat works in education?"[72]

Reading Recovery received the highest possible rating for general reading achievement of all beginning reading programs reviewed by the What Works Clearinghouse . . . . Recently, a federally funded independent evaluation found large gains for the lowest-performing students, as 3,675 teachers were trained in 1,321 schools across a 5-year scale-up grant.[73]

In one of the largest controlled studies ever conducted in the field of education, the growth rate for students who participated in Reading Recovery was 131% of the national average rate for first-grade students.[73]

The Consortium for Policy Research in Education from the University of Delaware concluded:

The rigorous independent evaluation of investing in Reading Recovery revealed that students who participated in Reading Recovery significantly outperformed students in the control group on measures of overall reading, reading comprehension, and decoding. These effects were similarly large for English language learners and students attending rural schools . . . .[74]

"Equity" does not mean providing the same resources to every child; equity means providing every child with the resources needed to be successful readers and writers. Some children need more than others to be successful. In 2016-17, MNPS Reading Recovery served 83% minorities, 54% who spoke a language other than English at home, and 77% who received free or reduced lunch. By passing this last-minute budget, far fewer of the most vulnerable students would have opportunities to work with a highly-trained teacher who knew how to support accelerated reading growth using authentic texts. After Reading Recovery was lost in MNPS, the most disenfranchised students received scripted programs with few opportunities for differentiation or expert support for their specific needs.

Although Dr. Joseph boasted about his honesty, openness, and transparency, I believe he worked behind closed doors to attempt to catch me off guard with his surprise budget. After a three-hour budget committee meeting, only three board members voted against the proposed budget. Joseph's new budget passed, allowing politics and retaliation to end rich literacy opportunities for struggling students. The majority of students impacted were students of color. The vote only took seconds to wipe out 15 years of Reading Recovery and 85 teaching positions - all reduced to a single, catastrophic moment.

Dr. Joseph apparently was confident the board would pass his alternative budget. He eliminated the positions of four Teacher Leaders and one director *before* the budget committee meeting even began. His chief academic officer met with the Reading Recovery Teacher Leaders 15 minutes before the meeting began on April 16th to alert them of their displacements. Thirty minutes before the budget meeting started, Dr. Monique Felder informed the Director of Literacy Interventions, Dr. Tammy Lipsey, that her position would be eliminated. *How could Dr. Joseph have been so confident that his budget would pass if he had not already gained the support of at least five board members?* When voting members promise support before the discussion takes place on the floor, it curtails open dialogue, debate, and aborts the process of true democracy.

In my six years serving on the board, the spring of 2018 was the first time I voted against a budget; that year the process had been flawed. The budget was filled with errors around "Chiefs" pay and Dr. Joseph's salary and benefits. I pointed out these discrepancies, but errors persisted. I'm not sure if the administration was attempting to hide money or if it was just one more oversight by an inexperienced and incompetent administration.

When Dr. Joseph sold the board on his proposal to delete Reading Recovery from the budget, he promised teachers they would be able to maintain the Reading Recovery certifications they'd worked so hard to achieve. He promised Reading Recovery would remain in MNPS and that any principal who wanted to employ a Reading Recovery teacher would be able to pursue those opportunities. I wish his word had been as reliable as he'd proclaimed! The incongruency of his words and acts was unfathomable. *Was he making false promises as a way to convince the board to proceed with his budget or, once again, was he lacking sufficient knowledge to make accurate statements?*

Dr. Joseph's assurances to Reading Recovery teachers proved to be untrue. When they later met with Dr. Joseph and his team, it was evident to them that Dr. Joseph and his administration had no plan of action to realize his false promises. Once again, he was building the plane while flying it. Teachers soon realized that Dr. Joseph and his administration either had a gross misunderstanding of what was needed for teachers to maintain their Reading Recovery certifications or it was all a farce. Unfortunately, six uninformed, hoodwinked board members trusted Dr. Joseph's erroneous statements and passed a budget that essentially terminated the intervention that had provided the "leaders of literacy" in MNPS.

Within months, three of the four Reading Recovery teacher trainers left MNPS and found prominent positions in other states. The other retired. Eighty-five Reading Recovery teachers began to pursue other opportunities for their expert literacy knowledge. Within three years, 64/80 (80%) of the highest trained reading teachers in the district left Metro Schools and secured positions in surrounding districts or other states. Taxpayer money had been utilized to benefit surrounding districts and other states rather than the children in Nashville.

The teachers were angry with Dr. Joseph and his administration. I knew how they felt. The anguish the teachers felt was obvious and heart-wrenching, although the worst travesty was the loss of expert literacy opportunities for children. Without Reading Recovery teachers, the most fragile learners would have few, if any, opportunities for rich literacy experiences to help them build confidence and accelerate their learning to become proficient readers and writers within 30-50 hours of instruction.

This was personal to me. I'd dedicated my career to helping children learn to read, but now I felt I was falling backward in time as thoughts of my childhood loomed over me. I'd worked diligently for the past six years to help build a comprehensive literacy program and support the training of teachers and interventionists who helped students stay on track with reading achievement. With this vote, it was all wiped away.

The success of Reading Recovery had inspired my life for 25 years, pulsing like a heartbeat behind everything I did. Sometimes there are no straight lines between effort and reward or even between right and wrong.[75] This experience was grueling. As Vice-Chair of the Metro Nashville Board of Education, I had an unobstructed view, allowing me to observe the machinations of power, politics, and panic.

Earlier as a teacher and later as a board member, I invited dignitaries to observe a Reading Recovery lesson and witness the power of the intervention in order to demonstrate that all children are capable of learning to read. One newly-elected board member who represented an affluent part of the district declined my invitation, suggesting that one of her schools was so impressed with Reading Recovery that they paid for it out of their PTO budget. On that occasion, Alice assured me she would never vote against Reading Recovery because of the support her teachers and principals had demonstrated for the intervention; however, her previous words carried no weight in the vote against Reading Recovery. The pain of more lies, mistrust, and betrayal flowed over me.

One board member couldn't comprehend that a retired teacher could be so passionate about an intervention without some kind of personal, monetary gain. She searched records, made national calls, and asked questions trying to determine my motives. Of course, she found nothing.

Living the life of a school board member was like living in an alternate reality. Board members didn't seem to respect me for my years of experience and knowledge. They didn't seem to respect Amy Frogge when she talked about legal issues, given her work and credentials as an attorney. *What kind of universe were we living in?*

Not only was I a subject of retaliation, but also at least five employees of color filed a lawsuit against Dr. Joseph for sexual harassment and retaliation. By the end of February 2020, the district had paid nearly $2 million[76] to settle these lawsuits out of court. Still, Dr. Joseph continued to enjoy the adulation of his community without any seeming scrutiny of his behavior.

Despite the commendations Dr. Joseph continued to receive from his most ardent supporters, on-going controversies were reported weekly and sometimes daily by NewsChannel 5 Investigates. The main topics included: sexual harassment lawsuits, MNPS morale crisis, pay disparities, questionable contracts, misleading statements to the school board, MNPS discipliine crisis, the Director's election meddling, failure to report teacher misconduct, use of a school bus driver, and lack of transparency. The complete summary is listed in the appendix of this book.[56]

Dr. Joseph could see the writing on the wall. As he began to consider an extention on his contract, members of the public and high-ranking elected officials contacted me to inquire about the projected timeline for Metro Schools to terminate his contract and release him from his failed leadership.

Chapter 44:

Beyond the Reach of Reason

GROWING UP WITH A FATHER WHO SLAPPED HIS CHILDREN, slugged his wife, and set mouse traps to catch his toddlers' fingers, I chafed against authority figures controlling others through punitive measures. Now I was confronted with another authority figure who had a penchant for punishment, except he had no authority over me. As a board member, I had the authority and the responsibility to stand up for what's right and attempt to hold Dr. Joseph accountable for his indiscretions and vindictive behavior. Time and again the actions of this director of schools brought to mind the actions of my father - especially his tendency to condemn others while refusing to take responsibility for his own mistakes. Dr. Joseph's administration had been a "dotted by legal and ethical issues."[78]

It was clear from the news, newly-filed lawsuits, and those lawsuits already settled out of court that Dr. Joseph had disregarded a whole host of basic institutional norms expected of a leader, thus delegitimizing his ability to lead with integrity. As a school board member and one who had advocated for him to lead the district, it was my job to delineate his problematic tenure in my bi-yearly evaluation of his performance. Our students, parents, schools, educators, and workers deserved better![77]

Even with nightly news reports, Dr. Joseph's friends continued to support him. The adulation without scrutiny was startling to me. Joseph's leadership for almost three years served to separate people rather than unite our city. He used race to divert attention from his questionable contracts, impropriety, and demeaning leadership, and to criticize three board members who were doing their jobs. Like my father, Dr. Joseph was beyond the reach of reason. I believe he attempted to disparage me in order to circumvent the negative attention that surrounded him. Dr. Joseph seemed to think that board members worked for him; he failed to understand he was our employee.

Every educational decision I'd made was rooted in how to help students others devalued. It was not uncommon for a frustrated teacher to give up on a particular child after she'd tried everything, and the student was still not making progress. However, once the child entered Reading Recovery and began to make noticeable progress in the classroom, the teacher was inquisitive to learn how this seemingly miraculous event had occurred. She wanted to know more! "What did you do? How did you do it? I want to learn this!" When a teacher, parent or principal thinks a student can't learn, it becomes a self-fulfilling prophecy. My self-determined goal was to banish the myth; Reading Recovery had been an effective tool as I worked to dispel that notion. During my 35-year teaching career, I had first-hand experience working with low-performing students. Teaching fragile students was personal to me; it spoke to the reality I'd lived as a child.

I continued to hold myself steady despite denigrating comments Dr. Joseph made in public. Although he didn't mention my name, it was clear to anyone who had been paying attention that he was referring to me. Things around me were imploding. In his nefarious attempts to hurt me, he hurt the children he had purported to help - the low-performing students. I'd taught in inner-city schools staffed by several nationalities and races. They were my friends and colleagues, equal in every aspect; the color of our skin was never an issue. I saw their teaching skills, their open hearts, and their desire to positively impact the children in front of them.

When Dr. Joseph first arrived in Nashville, he told a high ranking administrator of color that if things didn't work out for him, he would just "throw the race card." The administrator told me she was shocked that he was already talking about this divisive strategy during his early days in Nashville. This experience taught me that race can be a powerful deterrent to otherwise logical thought processes.

This director's antics were all too familiar. I'd grown up in a home where my father was the authority figure and no one could question him without suffering his wrath. I found Dr. Joseph displayed those same characteristics. In my first marriage, I was quiet and obedient like my mother, but through time I learned to trust myself to say and do what must be done. I would not abandon my ethics by supporting Dr. Joseph, even if it meant losing Reading Recovery, the intervention I knew worked for the most disenfranchised children. His apparent attempt to smear my name could not deter me or sabotage my passion for truth and justice.

My grueling agenda for the welfare of fragile children had been assiduously maintained for over three decades. My entire childhood trauma had been marshaled in service to improving education for children, but now I found myself flummoxed by the sudden removal of Reading Recovery with nothing to take its place. I was finished with the tyrant who had led us astray with his seemingly kind exterior demeanor - simply a veil for his unprofessional behavior. There was nothing left to feed my denial of his transgressions or to continue to support him. Dr. Joseph had shown his true colors; he had to go.

I decided to join the movement of teachers, parents, and administrators working to bring the tenure of this autocrat at the helm of our schools to a close. I stood up to my father when he bullied my mother. I had been a voice for the voiceless children, parents, and teachers who begged for an avenue to support their children in literacy achievement. I would not stop now. Dr. Joseph's attempts to hurt me only empowered me to metabolize his chaos into finding a new direction for the district. I tried my best not to let Dr. Joseph's austere leadership affect my personal life; however, by October 2018, I was in the hospital undergoing a Coronary Artery Bypass Grafting (CABG) - triple bypass, open-heart surgery. Although it took a year to fully recover, I returned to my seat on the board floor two months later. I wafted through the door, pale as an egg, but glad to be there. My colleagues greeted me enthusiastically as they welcomed me back for the public meeting. Dr. Joseph never even acknowledged my existence.

A group of parents from all over the district had formed a grass-roots effort to call for new leadership. During my absence, they had organized protests outside the boardroom, as well as held up signs at board meetings. When the community saw me back in my seat, a parent representing the group contacted me to help them spread the word. A total of three board members were now calling for Joseph to resign; the community needed teachers to speak out. Employees were rightfully fearful, as Dr. Joseph had demonstrated his proclivity for retaliation both through his decision to terminate Reading Recovery and also the sexual harassment and retaliation lawsuits that prevailed. Even as I continued to recover, I was drawn to take action to help the cause, so I sent a private text to 20 - 30 people in my contact list inviting teachers across the district to participate in a protest outside the boardroom. If they feared retribution, I invited them to wear a Mardi Gras mask to conceal their identity. My invitation for them to consider wearing masks was simply my attempt to garner their participation while also protecting them against the known retaliatory nature of our director of schools.

My private text was leaked to Dr. Joseph, which in turn, went viral. I never expected teachers to wear masks to the board meeting, only to the protests that were occurring outside the board room. A fellow board member called me to share that there was a Metro ordinance that forbids masks, hoods, or other devices while on public property. As soon as I learned this, I called several parents in the group and asked them to spread the word about this ordinance. As a result, no one wore a mask.

The protest was canceled. Nevertheless, the drama continued.

It hadn't occurred to any of the organizers or me that wearing Mardi Gras masks could be compared to white hoods and capes worn by the Ku Klux Klan, but somehow, given the racial environment Dr. Joseph had perpetuated, a fellow board member drew this conclusion and made the comparison from the board floor in my absence. Acquaintances and educators saw this as a mean-spirited stretch. Teachers and employees knew I had their best interests at heart. They saw through any comments that portrayed me negatively. They knew I was attempting to support them to express their voices without losing their jobs. Somehow Dr. Joseph received a copy of my private text and helped spread a false narrative about me as a racist. A pernicious seed had been planted; a misperception of me as racist was being purposefully spread throughout Nashville.

An editor of the *Tennessean* wrote a scathing article[79] disseminated through Twitter condemning me for my text. Although I had previously enjoyed a professional relationship with him, he never picked up the phone to call me for my side of the story. The unflattering narrative seemed to only gain traction. The press hammered on it for weeks. I appeared on three local television channels explaining that our group and I thought of masks as a way for teachers to be able to participate in protests while remaining anonymous. Fear of retribution was serious for educators. They wanted protection from Dr. Joseph's wrath. But none of the actual truth seemed to matter now. I wanted to at least appear to be unflappable, but I was stirred by distorted rumors and innuendo as I continued to heal from open-heart surgery.

The supercilious minority caucus consisting of mostly African-American women, demanded an apology from me, referencing my private text to hide the identity of teachers from a retaliating director of schools. Advisors closest to my campaign suggested that I hold steady and let it pass. I refused to crumble. I had entered a level of exposure I had never known as a teacher or administrator. I didn't know how the saga would unfold, but I was determined to stand firm in the truth and not allow those who accused me of being a racist to steamroll my reputation. It seemed that all my focus and expertise in helping children learn to read and write had been disregarded because of one private text taken out of context and misquoted even though I had rectified my mistake by calling off the protest.

I'd dedicated my life, my career, to developing the expertise necessary to equip me to advocate for all children, but now I was being attacked for all the wrong reasons. I was astonished to see how anyone, including councilwomen and state representatives, treated me only as a threat to Dr. Joseph's power, inciting mistrust and lies about race. I grew weary of being seen by some as very different from the person

I was. NewsChannel 5 shared additional stories nightly about the superintendent's mismanagement of funds and more lawsuits, giving taxpayers more reasons to want Dr. Joseph to leave Nashville.[56]

In her speech to accept her party's nomination for Vice President in August of 2020, Kamala Harris quoted Joe Biden when she stated, "We stand with our allies and we stand up to our adversaries." The late John Lewis said, "If you see something that is not right, not fair, not just, you have a moral obligation to do something about it." For 35 years, I'd stood up for children who didn't have an advocate in their corner in the same way I'd stood up for my mother when Dad was physically abusive. I had spent years working to fulfill my moral obligation, and now I had to continue to stand up to my adversaries.

The Metro Nashville Council's minority caucus continued to disparage me on behalf of Dr. Joseph. At-Large Councilwoman Elina Griffin sponsored a resolution to demand that I retract and apologize for my suggestion that teachers wear masks to a protest outside the boardroom to express their disapproval of the director of schools. I tried not to let the criticism disturb me. Councilman Ed Kindall, an African-American friend who had previously served on the school board for over two decades, knew me through my work as an educator. Mr. Kindall spoke in my defense and reminded Council members that I had been one of Dr. Joseph's biggest supporters when he had been unanimously elected as Metro's top school administrator. Mr. Kindall told his colleagues that he believed I'd supported teachers wearing masks based on my knowledge that teachers feared losing their jobs if they protested.

Councilwoman Griffin abandoned her resolution after the education committee voted earlier in the day to indefinitely defer it, signaling a lack of support from the full Council. Later that evening, the Metro Council voted not to intervene in ongoing Nashville school board tensions by calling for me to apologize to Dr. Joseph.[80]

The entire escapade was meant to embarrass me; however, I'm an adult, and no one has the power to embarrass or make me do anything. On the day of the Council meeting, I stayed away from the radio and TV. I clung to my spiritual essence and rested in the assurance that I was right to stand up for teachers. When the tweets began to roll in that the motion from the Council chamber had been defeated, tears welled up in my eyes as I burst into a boo-ha cry. The tears flowed for about five minutes as I wrapped my arms around myself and watched my tears transform into rhapsodic laughter. For the next six hours, I was in and out of laughter and crying - tears of joy, relief, and release. I had been peaceful all day before the meeting and was surprised to experience such unfettered emotion waiting to be released. My childhood experiences had given me plenty of opportunities to stand up to bullies. I am eternally grateful to Councilman Ed Kindall and all of the supportive Council members and community advocates for their help during this trying experience.

The *Tennessee Tribune*,[81] a local newspaper which reports news affecting the black communities of Nashville and Middle Tennessee, often criticized Amy Frogge, Fran Bush, and me for doing our jobs as school board members. They published articles demeaning us while palliating the allegations against Dr. Joseph. They continued the narrative of comparing my private text referencing Mardi Gras masks to the horrific and hate-motivated actions of the KKK. The stretch was unimaginable! Amy, Fran, and I remained unassailable while the *Tribune* continued to spread malice. Interestingly enough, cracks about the masks continued on Twitter until 2020 when the COVID-19 world pandemic made the use of masks commonplace. Finally, my mask comment seemed to be a moot topic.

Teachers and employees of various races and ethnic groups came to my aid privately, still fearful of speaking out, each of them harmonizing their voices to remind me of their support and appreciation. I carried this choir with me everywhere I went, and its sweet chorus still plays in my ear today!

Community activists protest by peacefully holding up signs during a Metro Nashville Board of Education meeting.

Local dignitaries continued to call board members inquiring about the level of board support for Dr. Joseph. Would there be an offer for an extended contract? Individual board members responded unequivocally, "No!"

The board had previously commissioned a Human Resource audit.[82] The HR report by law firm Bone McAllester Norton PLLC warned that the district faced a morale crisis that threatened its ability to attract and retain employees. The lawyers noted that Dr. Joseph's chosen Human Resources Director, Ms. Pertiller, was seen by employees as "extremely divisive, dismissive and, in their belief, incompetent" and suggested that she be "terminated, transferred or retrained." Dr. Joseph refused to make that move. Due to his decision, another board member joined three board members to gain traction to dismiss the director. We had four votes. We needed five.

Censorship is the child of fear and the father of ignorance.[83]
~ Laurie Halse Anderson

Chapter 45:

Censorship

ALTHOUGH DR. JOSEPH MAY HAVE FLIRTED WITH THE IDEA of a new contract extension, he must have realized those efforts were futile and began to campaign for a buy-out of his present contract. As a result, Dr. Joseph departed from Metro Schools with over $377,000[84] despite a pending recommendation by the Tennessee Board of Education to suspend his teaching license for failure to report teacher misconduct cases. The MNPS Board Chair included in Joseph's separation agreement the use of taxpayer money to defend against the suspension of his license if he chose to continue to work within the state of Tennessee.

Board members Amy Frogge, Fran Bush, and I continued to question Joseph's contracts and the decisions of his administration. Bruised but unwilling to give up, I pointed to the evidence Phil Williams and others had uncovered to hold Dr. Joseph culpable for his decision-making. This was my job as a school board member.

As previously mentioned, when Dr. Joseph first came to the district, he instituted a gag order when he asked employees not to communicate with board members about school issues. On his way out, Dr. Joseph included a censorship clause in his separation agreement "that prohibited board members from saying anything about Dr. Joseph - even if it's true - that would subject him to public contempt, disgrace or ridicule."[84] My understanding was that if a future employer asked individual board members for an honest evaluation of his performance, we were not permitted to be truthful if our comments were detrimental. If board members breached this clause, we could face an individual lawsuit. Dr. Joseph's Severance Agreement package was approved when the motion passed with a 5 to 3 vote. Three board members voted against it. The severance agreement became effective on April 17, 2019. The terms of the agreement were as follows:

The Board will not make any disparaging or defamatory comments regarding Dr. Joseph and his performance as Director of Schools. This provision shall be effec-

tive for the Board collectively and binding upon each Board member individually. Dr. Joseph does not waive any right to institute litigation and seek damages against any Board member in his/her individual capacity who violates the terms and conditions of [sic]Article of the agreement.[85]

ATTORNEY DANIEL A. HORWITZ, a constitutional lawyer and nationally renowned impact litigator, contacted the three board members who voted against the separation agreement and offered to pursue the case to rectify the egregious subsection pertaining specifically to censorship. Horwitz is the recipient of the 2018 Harris Gilbert Award from the Tennessee Bar Association and has been recognized by the Bar as one of the top 40 young lawyers in the United States. The Nashville Post has repeatedly recognized him as one of the "Best of the Best" lawyers in Nashville."[86] Amy Frogge, Fran Bush, and I agreed to sue Dr. Joseph and Metro over their attempt to censor us.

Mr. Horwitz argued that elected officials have First Amendment rights and a professional obligation to speak truthfully about matters of public concern that affect their constituents. He argued that any effort to prevent dissenting school board members from expressing truthful criticism about the former director cannot withstand constitutional scrutiny. *WE WON THE LAWSUIT!*

On September 15, 2020, Daniel Horwitz wrote in his press release: *In an order issued earlier this afternoon, Davidson County Chancery Court Judge Ellen Hobbs Lyle ruled in favor of Plaintiffs Amy Frogge, Fran Bush, and Jill Speering, who earlier this year sued Metro and ex-MNPS Director Shawn Joseph over the legality of the School Board censorship clause contained in Joseph's severance agreement. In a Memorandum Order, Chancellor Lyle struck down the censorship clause as unconstitutional on multiple grounds and permanently enjoined its enforcement.*[87]

Among other things, the clause prohibited elected School Board members even from truthfully criticizing "Dr. Joseph and his performance as Director of Schools." Upon review of it, Chancellor Lyle ruled that the clause violated the Plaintiffs' First Amendment rights, unlawfully prohibited them from speaking honestly with their constituents, and violated established Tennessee public policy. As a result, the clause was invalidated as unenforceable. Metro and Joseph will additionally be required to pay the Plaintiffs' "reasonable costs and attorney's fees," which have been pledged to charity.[87]

"This is a landmark victory on behalf of both elected officials' free speech rights and citizens' right to hear from their elected representatives," said attorney Daniel Horwitz, who represented all three Plaintiffs. *Metro and Joseph should be ashamed of*

their efforts to gag elected officials and prevent them from speaking honestly with their constituents about issues of tremendous public importance, and their illegal attempt to do so should serve as a costly warning to other government officials to think twice before violating the First Amendment.[87]

Davidson County Chancery Court rules that Metro's School Board and ex-MNPS Director Shawn Joseph illegally colluded to prevent dissenting School Board members from criticizing him. The unconstitutional censorship provision is invalidated.[85]

The contract's egregious illegality was formally approved and ratified by ex-Metro Law Director current Metro Council attorney - Jon Cooper. It was literal malpractice – in the actionable tort sense – and it will cost Metro tens of thousands of dollars. The city should sue him.[85]

This is a tremendous . . . win for Amy Frogge, Fran Bush, and Jill Speering, who endured extensive, baseless attacks for standing up for the public's right to receive accurate information from their elected representatives.[85]

Speaking of Dr. Joseph's defense, Horwitz tweeted, Their essential claim - that they meant the opposite of what they wrote down - was among the most dishonest defenses I have ever seen in my entire life.[85]

To be unmistakably clear, Amy Frogge, Fran Bush, and Jill Speering are heroes for taking up this righteous fight on the public's behalf. The right to hear from your elected officials is sacrosanct, and everything depends on it.[85]

~~

DR. JOSEPH WAS GONE! The board selected Dr. Adrienne Battle as the interim director and later elected her unanimously as the first African-American female to serve as Director of Schools in Nashville. As I attempted to process my feelings about the personal attacks and move forward from this dark period in my life, my greatest concern was how long it would take MNPS to overcome the trauma this administration had created, affecting thousands of educators and children.

In the midst of the turmoil dealing with Joseph's antics, came another ruby from the rubble. Even though my fellow board members voted to take away the First Amendment rights of three of their colleagues, Daniel Horwitz swept down from heaven and handed those rights - right back to us.

Now it was time to decide whether I wanted to run for a third term on the school board or open the door for another candidate. I had won my first election with 37% of the popular vote and my second election with almost 60% of the vote. I knew it would be an easy win for another term, but I was tired. My service on the board had taken a toll on my health.

When the board voted on the severance package to bid Dr. Joseph farewell, I received many appreciative emails, texts, and Facebook messages. I not only read each of them, but I took them into my heart, and they helped me heal. I carried their chorus of support with me through my most difficult days.

Above all, don't lie to yourself. The man who lies to himself and listens to his own lie comes to a point that he cannot distinguish the truth within him, or around him, and so loses all respect for himself and for others. And having no respect he ceases to love.[91]
~ Fyodor Dostoevsky, The Brothers Karamazov

Chapter 46:

Arbinger Summit

ARBINGER INSTITUTE[93] offers a behavioral approach for the improvement of organizations by helping individuals change from an inward mindset to an outward mindset - thinking about others rather than just oneself. The progress of an organization is greatly impacted by its leaders and employees' individual mindsets. When Dr. Joseph first came to Nashville, he brought representatives from Arbinger to train MNPS School Board members in the principles of an outward mindset. Soon after, the majority of the board traveled to Salt Lake City, Utah to become trainers in the Arbinger methodology. I loved reading the Arbinger books, and I thoroughly enjoyed the training. I believed that we were on the right track until things went awry.

DR. JOSEPH HAS BEEN GONE FOR ALMOST TWO YEARS. During his departure, I have been contacted by school board members in other states inquiring about my experience with Dr. Joseph and his previous cabinet. One school board member shared that she had seen a presentation Dr. Joseph delivered at the 2019 Arbinger Summit[92] when he shared thoughts about his Nashville experience. I listened to the presentation online and was surprised to hear him take some responsibility for a few of his failed leadership practices in Nashville.

Dr. Joseph spoke about his initial, extraordinary interview in Nashville because the Arbinger principles were at the forefront of his mind. After he was unanimously elected to lead the district, he became a celebrity overnight and was hailed by the community. Everybody wanted to have their pictures taken with him. What happened after almost three years of his leadership? He stated, "It's something I really have to take responsibility for, because the fact is, no organization exceeds the capacity of its leader."

Listening to his presentation, I was surprised to hear him admit to leading collusion efforts against three board members, confirming my assumptions that he'd tried to turn his fraternity brothers, church members and community against Amy, Fran and me. Although he didn't admit to it, using race was a cowardly, disingenuous, yet effective way to disparage us. He admitted that his behavior, which he described as "pure craziness,"[92] was driven by his need for justification. He said that when talking to the community, he pleaded, "Oh my God, why don't you do something? Don't you see how they're treating me? They're awful! Don't you see how they're coming after me? I mean, you're not doing anything about it!"

Dr. Joseph said that he knew what he was doing, but he just couldn't help himself. He admitted to not speaking to three of his board members for a year, "I've got nine board members. Oh, if I don't have three, the only thing I have to do is keep five."[92] Even though many people openly discussed the folly of his administration, he tried to present the image of being in control and having a great year.

When Dr. Joseph was in Nashville, I questioned some of the grandiose statements he made about student achievement, so I counseled him to be impeccable with his word. In his closing remarks at the Arbinger Summit, he seemed to continue his pattern of embellishing the truth about students' achievement. The two statements that mostly concerned me were: "At the end of the day, when you look at where we ended in three years from where we started, reading scores dramatically increased . . . Every, every student grew in math performance faster than the state for the first time in the history of the district."

These statements sounded pretentious to me. I wanted to know if his statements were accurate, so I contacted district officials and asked them to research Dr. Joseph's claims. After the research was completed, district officials informed me that Metro Schools could not confirm the veracity of Dr. Joseph's statements. *Had he touted these flamboyant statements so long he believed them, or was it toxic positivity, the practice of acknowledging only the positive in a situation while intentionally ignoring the negative?*

I decided to stop wasting my time and energy on endeavors that evoked no joy in my life. Instead I planned a trip to study a country with a literacy rate of 99%.

Chapter 47:

Land of Promise

SHORTLY BEFORE THE COVID-19 PANDEMIC took the world hostage, my husband of 21 years and I boarded a 16-hour flight to the South Pacific. With Dan as my faithful companion, I traveled to New Zealand with a particular mission in mind - to closely observe and study the educational system there, and attempt to understand how the country has maintained a 99% adult literacy rate since 2010. We chose to travel toward the end of February mainly because New Zealand's school year begins that month, but it didn't hurt to know that our foray to the other side of the globe would put us there during New Zealand's summer season (December through February), offering us a welcome escape from Tennessee's harsh winter weather.

We arrived three weeks into the school year. I was ready to feed my insatiable desire for continuous literacy learning by observing students and teachers at work. I was accustomed to going out of state for literacy training since professional development activities in the state of Tennessee were sadly lacking. But to travel out of the country to further my decades-long, voracious pursuit of superlative literacy instruction, was a first!

As the wheels left the runway and the flight began to soar in a southwestern direction, I reflected on how I, a young girl from Madison, Tennessee, who dreaded going to school so much that I regularly lost my breakfast, became an educator who'd made the sometimes tedious process of learning, joyous for children. The young girl who repeated the fifth grade because she struggled to learn in the way that seemed to come easily to other children had now learned how to make learning easier for children like herself.

Traveling more than 7,000 miles to visit the birthplace of Reading Recovery® punctuated my lifelong career as an educator and a passionate advocate for literacy education. I'd personally used Reading Recovery to the advantage of hundreds of children with phenomenally successful results. The intervention that a prideful man with a penchant for cronyism over probity eventually turned into a weapon against me as his tool of revenge. I believe his opposition was in response to my efforts to reveal his unethical leadership practices.

Reading Recovery started in New Zealand in 1974 when Dr. Marie Clay from the University of Auckland collaborated with teachers to align educational theory with classroom practice. Through the years, I learned a lot about teaching reading and writing by studying books by Dr. Clay and many New Zealand teachers. I learned the importance of teaching process-writing through my graduate work that utilized activities and strategies that created joy in learning. I learned how to discover the half-right answer in students' mistakes and praise that accomplishment, rather than the traditional method of measuring mistakes in fractions of degrees. What could the American educational system learn from this small country that avoided expensive textbooks and costly purchases of standardized curricula in favor of children's literature and educational plans written by their own teachers?

Matakana Primary, Auckland, New Zealand

Vanderbilt University had previously helped fund trips to China for various board and staff members in order to study their educational programs. I questioned why our school district and our city would want to pattern our educational system after a country where children's suicide rates were so high.[89] After months of voicing my opposition, the funding for these trips was terminated.

Meanwhile, I'd been dreaming of touring New Zealand schools for over 25 years. With less than a year of service left on the board, I wanted a platform to share my experiences about a country that had successfully mastered the art of teaching children to read. With only six months left on the board, I, along with Dan, decided to do it now and do it right. After all, I'd waited a lifetime, it seemed, to visit this country. Our business class seats were comfortable; the food was great. Well rested, we exited the plane in Auckland to visit our first school, Parnell District School. Touring New Zealand schools reminded me of my days teaching holistically when the children bounced through the classroom door each morning with such enthusiasm and love for learning, one would believe they were actually at play!

At Parnell, students are organized into specific "Houses" of varying ages. Students meet each Friday in their respective houses for common purposes: to play games and to get to know one another. Upper-class students are taught to respect and care for the primary students, who long for their attention. It's typical in America for older students to stray away from younger, more immature students. Commonly practiced, the Kiwi philosophy is that older students can learn a great deal about empathy and patience by befriending younger children. Although this is the exception in America, in New Zealand it is encouraged and nurtured. Lifelong friendships are often developed through these structured opportunities.

In some schools, older students are matched with younger people for multi-age groups, like big brothers or sisters. The family unit feels integrated into the school system. Students are called to action through projects completed together. Embedded in their curriculum are weekly opportunities to work together, take care of others, and respect each other's ethnic, social, philosophical and cultural differences.

At Parnell school, the teacher plans for Friday activities by inviting parents and the principal to oversee and guide students in various learning games.

Each school is autonomous with its own governing board, which oversees and helps integrate it into the community. Most schools require uniforms, including hats, for the 45 minutes of recess enjoyed at least once a day, if not twice. After ample opportunities to exercise their large motor skills and meet their socialization needs, students settle down to learn. In class, they are focused and moti-vated after their brains have recharged with

Parents and volunteers are leading students in instructional games for Fun Friday activities.

fresh oxygen from recess. They bring snacks and lunch from home.

When visiting at lunchtime, Dan and I observed what appeared to be a huge picnic in the schoolyard. The lunch break is generous in time and flexibility. After lunch, students organize themselves for games, sports, climbing trees, and other creative ways to interact with their peers and have fun. At some schools, the pool is open after lunch on hot days. Learning to swim is part of the curriculum, including dedicated time for mastering particular strokes and life-saving skills. This was especially personal to me since my brother drowned when he was only five years old. In New Zealand, swimming instruction is offered to those students starting school for the first time, who are called "new entrants."

New entrant classes are similar to America's kindergarten. In New Zealand, all children must be enrolled in school by the age of six; however, five-year-olds have the option to begin primary school on their fifth birthdays. Unlike children in U.S. schools, five-year-olds don't have to wait until school resumes in the fall to begin school. Some schools allow new entrants to start school at any time throughout the school year; either on the child's fifth birthday or on another date that better suits the family.

As a previous kindergarten teacher, I found this to be extraordinary. I know the eagerness children and parents feel on the first day of school. I remember my own enthusiasm as a young child on the first day of school. But to have your own special day to enter the world of public education – on your birthday; what an exciting way to focus on the individual child's uniqueness! This is remarkable, and it actually sets the stage for the philosophy that prevails in New Zealand. According to one school's website, *Te Whariki Primary is underpinned by a vision for children who are competent and confident learners and communicators, healthy in mind, body, and spirit, secure in their sense of belonging and in the knowledge that they make a valued contribution to society.** Oh, if I'd only had the opportunity to attend New Zealand schools when I was young!

When I taught students to write stories, I expected them to choose their own topics. I offered guidance in the process if needed. Likewise, in New Zealand, students are free to make decisions about how to best utilize their recess. They choose activities such as soccer, baseball, and climbing trees or they make up their own games and enlist others to participate. The planning and thinking processes are as important as the activity.

The country embraces student-centered learning. Rather than focusing instruction on the basic skills level of the group, teachers in New Zealand learn to personalize planning and teaching to meet the needs of each individual student. I learned this individualized approach in Reading Recovery training. I found that basing instruction on the individual needs and interests of students to be refreshing, given the vast contrast to American schools, where high-stakes assessments drive the practices.

In May of 2021, my 12-year-old granddaughter, Georgianna, announced, "Now that the achievement tests are over, we don't have to work anymore. We'll just play for the last two weeks of school." Has our educational system really been reduced to the lowest common denominator, which is the state achievement test? In the State of Tennessee, we profess to offer child-centered education, yet we implement federal and state mandates in direct violation of age-appropriate curricula and learning. Personalized learning requires teachers to have in-depth knowledge of each student's strengths and needs. Such knowledge is not an outcome of achievement tests.

A few years ago, there was a push in New Zealand to require young prima-

---

*https://www.education.govt.nz/early-childhood/teaching-and-learning/te-whariki/

ry students to be tested on a national achievement exam. Primary teachers, grades k-4, and principals revolted because of their belief that children do not need to be subjected to that type of stress; therefore, teachers engaged in a national strike. The Education Ministry listened to educators' concerns and halted the movement. Young children do not take national achievement tests in New Zealand thanks to the advocacy of their wise teachers and administrators.

The New Zealand curriculum demonstrates respect for the individual child through genuine student-focused, age-appropriate activities complete with meaningful books that relate to their individual backgrounds, knowledge, and interests. Many of their books are written by New Zealand teachers. Students are offered choices as they select the books they want to read from a menu of high-quality, relevant children's literature.

Hands-on experiences are abundant. With fall approaching, intermediate students (similar to our middle school students) were assigned a real school problem to determine the dimensions needed to cover a frame for a greenhouse to prepare for winter. This task could have easily been completed by maintenance staff; however, students were given the opportunity to utilize their skills in literacy and math to complete the project.

Values and competencies are interwoven into all learning areas of the curriculum. Pure joy in learning is the foundation of the Ministry of Education. Curricula and time are designed to help students develop the ability to think critically, self-manage, set goals, overcome obstacles, and get along with others. These attributes are necessary to succeed as adults.

How do children learn to get along with one another if time isn't organized during the school day for students to interact? Administrators and teachers respect students' time. Opportunities for them to interact with their peers are purposefully planned to provide ample time for socialization. Because of their focus on socialization and their understanding that children learn a great deal from each other, multiage classrooms are utilized in many schools. Each day, teatime is integrated into the schedule. During the 30-45 minute teatime period, teachers come together to enjoy coffee/tea and biscuits, while children go outside for their snack and engage in free play. Students are expected to follow established guidelines, and their compliance is noteworthy.

As an educator for 35 years, I rarely found opportunities to interact with another teacher. Teaching is a full-time job. In elementary school, there is hardly enough time to visit the bathroom, much less time to interact with the teacher next door.

In contrast, teatime in New Zealand is not only helpful for students to slow down and relax as they go outside to refuel and enjoy their friends; teachers find it an important part of their day, as well. Teachers can decompress, breathe, reflect on the morning activities and interactions with students, grow philosophically, and share concerns with peers. Most importantly, when something goes wrong at school or needs to be accomplished, collaborative time is built into the schedule to handle it. I saw the inclusion of teatime to be reflective of the deep respect for students and teachers that is part of the philosophy, custom, and culture in New Zealand.

Often adults lament that kids don't have social skills, yet time in American schools is not organized in a way that allows opportunities for them to develop these skills with peers. School calendars rarely accommodate time for teachers to interact with each other or learn from their peers. There is no cost to reorganizing time, but it would require a change in philosophy away from high-stakes, testing-based accountability to authentic child-centered education. Connecting child to child, child to adult, and adult to adult only occurs when time is deliberately taken to foster those relationships.

New Zealand's vision for young people is to nurture them into confident, connected, actively involved, lifelong learners. Rich literacy experiences occur daily. Scripted curricula are rarely utilized. There is little teaching of skills in isolation without going back and plugging the skill directly into a meaningful context. Our world is built around meaning. Our brains are wired for meaning and connections - not isolation.

How many children would want to ride a bicycle if they had to learn all the parts of the bike before being permitted to climb on the bike and ride? The process of learning to ride a bike is messy. Students fall off; they climb back on. Their motivation drives them to continue developing the skills and coordination to balance the various aspects of riding the bike.

When my granddaughter, Georgianna, was four years old, she wanted to learn how to climb out of the shallow end of the pool from the side. It wasn't a skill I encouraged her to develop. The desire came from within her. She practiced and failed, practiced and failed, each time growing stronger until one day she was strong enough to pull herself out of the pool from the side. Accomplishing this skill gave her great pleasure and built her confidence.

Reading is much the same. Children are highly motivated to learn to read. One year when I was teaching kindergarten, at the end of the first day, I asked them, "So how was your first day of school?" One replied with sad eyes, "I thought I would learn to read today!" I took her words to heart and decided that would never happen again. How I love when my students teach me what they need! This interaction taught me that every student in kindergarten should go home the very first day with some piece of writing they can read to their parents and friends. I found a variety of ways to fulfill this goal. It could have simply been a written nursery rhyme students had already committed to memory. Teaching students to match finger-pointing to text in a one-to-one correspondence was an important skill. Children left with the confidence they were learning to read. Enthusiasm and motivation grew.

In New Zealand, the Ministry of Education allows students to delve into books with support, like training wheels, so children can access meaning and experience success as they learn to read from the first day of school forward. Introducing a just-right book on the child's cutting edge of learning, so it's not too easy and it's not too hard, motivates children to read and supports their efforts because the book was carefully chosen to be a good fit for their strategic processing of print. Maintaining this delicate balance takes skill and should be taught to all elementary teachers in America. These teacher skills *can't* be taught through a one-day professional development setting. Such skills take continuous professional development over time. In Tennessee, the emphasis is on rigor, meaning "challenging." The philosophy in New Zealand is to make learning natural, easy and exciting, as the teacher helps children build on what they already know. Children are met where they are performing academically. The teacher's job is to facilitate moving them from that place to higher skills and thinking processes while nurturing students' self-concepts. In America, the emphasis seems to be that every child has to be taught on grade level, no matter their reading level. Children are different. To teach them all using the same texts, the same teaching methods, and the same grade-level skills becomes painful and is unnatural for many students.

Ask most adults in America if they enjoyed elementary school, and they will tell you "no"; but if those same people were asked if they liked to learn, they would say, "yes!" Our public school system has created the loss of joy in learning. As long as there are achievement tests and schools are organized around the teaching of those tests, this scenario will remain unchanged. Throughout America and especially in Tennessee, our Department of Education adheres to a belief in teaching skills in isolation. Exposing students to letters, sounds, and words, then requiring them to read decodable texts that follow a particular phonetic pattern taught that day, does not provide an opportunity for rich, motivational learning. Children are expected to read sentences like "Pat the fat rat sat on a hat."[90] I don't know any child who could get excited about reading when rich language is stripped from their texts. Decodable texts focus heavily on phonics instruction but desperately lack in meaning and often sentence structure. No wonder many of our children do not like school and consequently do not develop a love of reading.

New Zealand teachers became experts in literacy because Dr. Marie Clay, a cognitive psychologist and educator at the University of Auckland, worked with teachers to help train them in research-based, high-quality, continuous professional development in literacy. There is no "sit and get," which is often utilized in school districts in Tennessee. Such training is boring, and most often teachers walk away having learned nothing new. Educators want high quality professional development that will affect their practice. In New Zealand, the expectation is that teachers will learn through professional development activities and then implement that knowledge within their classrooms - and it works!

New Zealanders abide by the philosophy that the educator's job is to inspire students to want to learn and enjoy the learning process. Because of the focus on healthy living and the pursuit of individuals' interests from an early age, homework is assigned only when absolutely necessary. Educators and administrators in New Zealand understand that loading young children with homework leads to stress; the unintended consequences can all too easily result in children who hate reading, writing, school, and even learning.

Because of the moderate climate on the North Island throughout the year, many students come to school barefoot. It's not a symbol of poverty, but of culture and climate. My grandson, Michael, would have loved going to school barefooted. He often got in trouble for not wearing his shoes at Hillsboro High School in Nashville. Although the administration was concerned for his safety, keeping his shoes on just seemed to go against his inner drive for comfort.

Collaboration rather than competition is the rule of the day in New Zealand. Teachers support teachers, and students support one another. Social-Emotional Learning (SEL) is interwoven throughout the day, throughout each interaction between teachers and students, principals and students, and principals and teachers. SEL is not relegated to the beginning of the year or taught as a subject. It is lived and experienced throughout the daily curriculum. Students learn social and emotional skills because they are immersed in an environment that promotes self-respect and respect for peers and teachers.

Self-respect, respect for others, respect for the environment, and respect for the indigenous people are evident across the North and South Islands of New Zealand. The traditions, language, and culture of the Maori are taught, shared, and valued throughout all tiers of education. I fell in love with the people, the culture, and the educational system in New Zealand. I wish our country could learn from the successes of their culture. Perhaps it's not too late for Tennessee and America to make the necessary changes to benefit future generations. Perhaps the United States will learn from New Zealand and turn toward policies and procedures that will ensure opportunities for students to develop a love of learning and a joy in reading - away from high stakes accountability.

I hope there will come a day when parents will demand less testing and more humane teaching. By focusing on students' strengths and talents, rather than the expectation that every student will endure scripted curricula, we can change our educational outcomes. Our youth will prosper through their love of learning, and our educators will savor teaching. I returned from New Zealand in March of 2020 and retired from the board in August. I know it's possible to provide better education in Tennessee and across America, but educators and parents need to be more demonstrative about their children's education.

The spiritual quest is a journey without distance. You travel from where you are right now to where you have always been. From ignorance to recognition.[94]
~ Anthony de Mello

Chapter 48:

A Journey Without Distance

I THINK IT WAS A DREAM, BUT I CAN'T BE SURE. It felt so real. My father came to me after his death. He was lodged in my heart wanting me to notice his presence. When I finally gave his spirit my attention, he sat down, looked at me in a way I'd never experienced, and took my hand. He looked different now. A clean man about 33 years old, soft features, full in the face, gorgeous blue eyes that twinkled when he spoke. I could feel the love radiating from him as he told me how sorry he was for the way he'd treated me and our family. I did not doubt his sincerity.

Although we live in mortal bodies, our souls live forever, as they're made in the image and likeness of God. We all have idiosyncrasies that lead us to make regrettable mistakes. Dad wanted my siblings and all our family to know he lamented the many mistakes he'd made; he asked for forgiveness.

I've come to a place in life where I recognize the gifts from my childhood. Because of my harsh youth with my dad, I had first-hand experience of the type of life many of my students endured. Because of this, I could see past their current achievement levels and capitalize on their potential.

Many years ago, I worked with a therapist who led me through deep meditations to help heal my psyche. Together, we imagined a father who loved me - a father I respected and adored! One whose lap my inner child could crawl upon and snuggle knowing I was loved and protected. I adore watching my husband, Dan, play with our grandchildren; their giggles and belly laughs touch my heart. All of my sons-in-law are loving fathers. My brother's kids hold him in the highest esteem. Every time I'm around a kind father and have opportunities to witness the love between a father and daughter, I heal even more. These rubies come to my awareness at unexpected times and bring me to tears.

Another therapist once suggested, "What if? What if before you were incarnated, God said, 'Jill has agreed to learn some powerful lessons this lifetime. In order to do the work and help children heal, someone needs to volunteer to be her father to treat her in a certain way in order to help her become a powerful educator during this lifetime. Who loves her enough to volunteer for this difficult job?' Your father stepped forward and said, 'I love her enough to play this role.'"

I couldn't embrace this philosophy until my dream awakened me to its possibility.

My dad had been the bane of my existence. As a child, I thought Dad's sole purpose was to brutalize and dehumanize me and my siblings. Chaos raged around me. Dad defined me before I had the maturity to define myself. So I worked hard to earn self-respect. It wasn't a given in my home. It took a spiritual commitment and years of therapy to be able to laugh with my siblings about my father's defects and oddities without feeling anger. Because of my childhood experiences with Dad, I'd been easily taken off course by his abuse. Fear paralyzed me. Through the grace of God, commitment and time healed me.

After I'd finally reached a level of peace about my dad, Dr. Joseph became a source of intermittent misery. Having developed the ability to assert myself during encounters with my dad, I would not allow this bully to disrespect me as a board member or the professional educator I'd become over the years. I was not afraid of him. Because he could not erupt fear in me, he seemed to work even harder to hurt me. Even as he and his friends scrutinized every utterance I made on the board floor to hold him accountable, I stood firm in the truth given the evidence against him. As he pleaded with his community to come to his aid against the "awful"[92] board members, they continued to support him, attempting to circumvent the nightly negative press on local news channels. I see that now.

When I voted for Dr. Joseph, I'd been so impressed with him that I imagined my work and spiritual life coalescing as I served with this director, but just the opposite happened. Dr. Joseph's transgressions created a slow burn in the pit of my belly. Like my father, Dr. Joseph lived in my head as I'd recounted his many infractions and the way I perceived he'd hurt our children, our community and Metro Schools. As time went on, I could go weeks without thinking of his infringements, and then they would resurface again.

It was clear Dr. Joseph had illegally colluded[85] to prevent dissenting school board members from criticizing him. But hearing him admit to leading collusion efforts against three board members in his Arbinger presentation was a novel experience. During the three years the elected board supervised him, I don't recall ever hearing him take responsibility for his mistakes.It seemed he either blamed others or tried to circumvent the bad press by putting negative attention on others. I'd heard rumors that he had led the community to attack Amy, Fran and me, but now his acts of collusion were out in the open![92]

When I worked with him for almost three years, I'd never seen him display humility. But now I glimpsed a bit of humility and interpreted his words to signify regret for a few of his many mistakes. He never admitted to his retaliation against a board member, but the evidence was clear in my head. At least he seemed to have started the process of self-examination. I commend him for that.

Bullies are scared people. They may lash out because they feel overwhelmed. Cowering to a bully never works. I had first-hand experience with my father and then later with Dr. Joseph. It's important for children and adults to never let a bully's aggression get to us personally - easier said than done. I stood up for my mother when my dad was on a rampage, and I stood up to Dr. Joseph when he presented misinformation, and when I perceived he'd let his key priorities take a back seat to his lust for retribution.

Despite the difficulties of the past two years working with Dr. Joseph and my open-heart surgery, I had faith in God and in my own utility. Even though my family wanted me to resign from the board, by the grace of God I was able to regain my health and complete my full term in office. There was more Spirit wanted me to accomplish.

What was the lesson I needed to learn? How could my soul transform these former negative experiences into peace?

Although I could focus on the rubble in my life, my spiritual teachers and inner guidance taught me to find the rubies. When I began to look, I discovered there were many. I found a ruby in my mom's inability to leave Dad and save her children from his wrath by earning a college education, so I could become an independent woman. Observing Mom yield to Dad's authority was agonizing; yet it inspired me to develop a voice for the underdog. From my fifth-grade teacher, I found determination and became relentless to learn how to teach the most vulnerable children to read. Although I'd failed Linda, my first-grade student at Kirkpatrick, when I recommended her for placement in Special Education, that failure made me more determined not to rely on Metro Schools to provide the training I so desperately needed to be successful. I sought outside avenues and advanced degrees; I traveled out of state and paid for my own professional development. I resolved to learn all I could to ensure the achievement of my most disadvantaged students. From Metro Schools, I was given the rubies Reading Recovery training which impacted countless children and educators across Tennessee.

Would I have become the Distinguished Educator of the Year in 2006 if my fifth-grade teacher had demonstrated respect and supported me along the way? Earning a master's degree, working toward a doctorate, and following my guidance on the next step along the path brought me the accolades of Master Teacher with Career Ladder III status, Middle Tennessee Exemplary Educator of the Year, and Vice-Chair of the Metropolitan Nashville Board of Education.

Who would I have been without these experiences? Had I not tried to save Mom from Dad's wrath, would I have been interested in serving on the Metro School Board and cast a dissenting vote against a rogue director? Did all these experiences mold me into who I am today? Would I have ever heard Dr. Kubler-Ross speak on death and dying if Mr. Whitman had hired me when I first applied to teach in Nashville? Were the hardships and failures of my past the substance for my future success? Had my difficulties and seeming failures in life actually catapulted my achievement? Did these experiences propel me to become a voice for the voiceless?

As I have written this book in my mind and now in print, I have come to realize that every experience I've had with my mother and father molded me into the person I am today. Had I not had those experiences in my youth, I could not have evolved into the educator I became.

Like a chick hatching from the egg, the entrapping shell from my childhood

required the emergence of a passion greatly needed to break through the shell to a life of vigor. More than likely, I would not have been drawn to work passionately with fragile learners, especially those at Kirkpatrick Elementary where 100% of impoverished children lived in the depravity of public housing. The events of my early life propelled me to pursue more advanced degrees in search of knowledge. As a result, I became a finely-tuned, ever-evolving educator.

The Koru fern image is the Maori symbol in New Zealand. 96   Image by Jon Radoff

Forgiveness is about unlocking myself from the prison cell of the memories that linger in my mind. The indigenous people of New Zealand are called Maori. The Koru is the Maori symbol which exemplifies new life, growth, strength, and peace.[95] It is an integral symbol in Maori art, carvings, and tattoos.

The Holy Spirit has been with me every step of the way along my life's journey. The path was always highlighted for me. Sometimes I struggled against it, but when I surrendered to the guidance of this nudge, this yearning, this still quiet voice, I found that there have been no mistakes in my life. Even when times looked dismal, there was a rainbow that eventually demonstrated the omnipotence of God's love - the miracles of madness. Living through the extreme pressures of life's hardships cultivated my brother into a brilliant ruby. My spectacular life has brought me the strength to hold firm to my convictions, to stand steady even when others condemned me for doing so, and the peace of knowing that if I had it all to do again, I wouldn't change a thing.

According to Albert Einstein, "There are only two ways to live my life. One is as though nothing is a miracle. The other is as though everything is a miracle."[1] I choose the latter. As I continue to find rubies in the rubble, my healing continues.

Epilogue

Life since 2021

As the sun peaks up from the horizon, its rays reflect in the clouds, creating a beautiful new day. Another 24 hours lie in front of me to cherish each moment of my existence. As I watch the river and sky pace slowly before me, I'm seduced to leave my office window to come outside, smell the morning, and twirl to the melodies of the songbirds.

I retired from the school board in August 2020. Within two months I'd finished the first draft of this book. It poured out of me like a fountain. I had so much to say and finally the time to say it. Then the editing began. That was the hardest part. There were days when I re-

Jill's view looking out the window from her home on the Cumberland River in Madison, Tennessee

lived the dark nights of my soul. I longed for someone to talk to who understood the pain of writing as I revealed my soul and vulnerability.

My entire life has been a race against time. Sometimes I felt like I ran around like a chicken with its head cut off. What I lacked in knowledge and skill, I overcame through determination and effort. The most difficult part was having a project unfinished for so long. As a teacher, I started the year in August and wrapped it up by the end of May. There was a beginning, a middle, and a clear end in sight. My book has been very different. As I wrote and talked with my siblings, I discovered more stories I wanted to incorporate. I asked my friends and family to read the manuscript. They were kind to read and ask questions, which prompted me to write more. Living in my manuscript around the clock, I couldn't even watch a TV program without hearing a phrase or a word I wanted to incorporate in my book. This experience became all-consuming for me. It took over my life until I finally had to limit myself on the number of hours I could work on it each day.

Meanwhile, life continued to move forward. My sister, Betty, was growing feeble. Her husband Tommy had died three years earlier. They had been married for 60 years. Betty was ready to go. Short of 82 years in age, Betty passed from this life in 2020 during the global pandemic. She was the same age as my father when he made his transition. As my sister lay dying in her daughter's home, my nieces and I reminisced about my mother's death 42 years earlier when we'd all gathered to say our goodbyes. I believe Betty and both my parents have been with me in spirit as my words have manifested in print.

Choosing education provided a balance beam for me to walk between home and school. My husband, Dan, and friend, Amy Frogge, were my anchors as I navigated the muddy waters of the school board. My daughters were my cheerleaders even as they voiced concerns about my health. Teachers and friends from church followed the news and lent a supportive ear as well as approving comments on social media platforms such as Facebook and Twitter. Even though I acquired popularity with certain populations, haters also found their way into my consciousness.

I'd dedicated my life to fostering a positive education for young children. I let my reputation stand for itself. I'd spent a portion of my life seeking approval, but I came to understand that some people love you for what you can do to improve their lives and then turn on you the next minute. People are fickle. I learned not to count on them for my self-worth. Relinquishing the outside world in order to cultivate my inner guidance has brought me peace and stillness.

The moment I have realized God sitting in the temple of every human body, the moment I stand in reverence before every human being and see God in him - that moment I am free from bondage, everything that binds vanishes, and I am free.[97]
~ Swami Vivekananda

Appendix

The following is a direct transcription from NewsChannel 5 on April 5th, 2019 by Phil Williams. Bracketed [] names have been changed in order to provide consistency with the story as it is revealed within this book. NewsChannel 5 reported: [56]

Metro Schools Director Dr. Shawn Joseph now finds himself facing a vote to potentially terminate his contract a year before its scheduled expiration.

Some Nashvillians have expressed confusion about the nature of the controversy surrounding the embattled school director. Some supporters have tried to characterize Joseph as the victim of racially motivated attacks. The director himself recently said, "The media has refused to delve deeply and thoughtfully into any of these issues." In fact, NewsChannel 5 Investigates has delved "deeply and thoughtfully" into various allegations against him, finding some not worthy of pursuing and discovering serious questions in other cases.

Below is a summary of the controversies:

Sexual harassment

In November 2017, a Metro Nashville Public Schools employee filed a sexual harassment complaint against longtime Joseph friend, Mo Carrasco. The administrator had previously worked with Joseph at two districts in Maryland.

Four months earlier, school board member Amy Frogge had informed Joseph that there were allegations from an unnamed victim against Carrasco. But instead of directing MNPS Human Resources to investigate, as required by district policy, the director went directly to his friend.

That was confirmed in an email from Carrasco to human resources.

Joseph claims he did not order an investigation because MNPS does not investigate anonymous complaints. (A news release, however, later said the district did accept anonymous complaints.)

A month later, a middle school employee reported that principal [Steve Baker] had tried to coerce him into sexual acts. HR manager [Sam Lake] attempted to put [Baker] on administrative leave so the allegations could be investigated, but Joseph's number two HR person, Sharon Pertiller, intervened to keep [Baker] on the job.

MNPS claimed that [Lake] was using the wrong form.

Still, the files show that [Baker] returned to his school and retaliated against the victim.

Assistant principal [Henry Jackson] then filed a complaint, saying he was facing retaliation for reporting the victim's allegations to higher-ups. Joseph's team still did not put [Baker] on leave.

The district's own files show that an HR investigation uncovered substantial evidence against [Baker], including information that he tried to enlist employees in making up lies about the victim, allegations that he had hired a man he met in an adult bookstore that he frequented, and a claim by the school's bookkeeper of financial improprieties that needed to be audited.

HR, which reports directly to Joseph, decided to give [Baker] "management training."

Science teacher Sonji Collins filed a separate sexual harassment complaint against [Baker]. Again, Joseph's HR department did not place the principal on administrative leave.

When NewsChannel 5 Investigates began digging through those HR investigations, Joseph did nothing to review his HR department's handling of the cases.

Instead, in a memo to the school board, he expressed concern that NewsChannel 5 "will report on information that was 'alleged'" and promised to work to get state law changed so that the district could keep its sexual harassment files secret in the future.

After the first story aired, school board members said Joseph continued to tell them there was nothing to the allegations and they should ignore the NewsChannel 5 report.

It took pressure from board members to convince him to place [Baker] on administrative leave two days later. The principal decided to retire.

Three of [Baker's] victims later filed a lawsuit that alleged that Joseph's administration had a "policy and practice of ignoring complaints of sexual harassment, as well as interfering with investigations of harassment."

So far, MNPS has paid $350,000 to settle those lawsuits.

[Henry Jackson], who says he personally warned Joseph about [Baker's] behavior, has now filed a separate lawsuit for unlawful retaliation.

The alleged victim in the Mo Carrasco case has filed a $1.2 million lawsuit against the district.

Former HR manager [Sam Lake] has filed a separate lawsuit, alleging that Joseph's team began retaliating after he uncovered damning evidence against Carrasco and after he attempted to put [Steve Baker] on administrative leave. Metro has denied the allegations.

Under pressure from the sexual harassment scandal, Joseph convinced the board to give a $100,000 contract to Nashville law firm Bone McAllester to review his district's HR practices.

It is unclear how much MNPS has spent so far in defending those lawsuits.

MNPS morale crisis

The HR report by Bone McAllester warned that the district now faces a morale crisis that threatens its ability to attract and retain employees.

Lawyers noted that MNPS employees viewed Pertiller as "extremely divisive, dismissive and, in their belief, incompetent." It suggested that she be terminated, transferred, or retrained.

The report describes a meeting between Joseph and a group of principals who asked to meet with him to discuss hiring and communications issues.

Joseph demanded that the principals "turn off their cell phones and other electronic devices," apparently so the meeting could not be recorded, the report says.

When they attempted to hand him a list of suggestions, Joseph "refused to accept the copy of the typewritten notes and asked that they all be destroyed at the end of the meeting" so they could not be disseminated.

"The stakeholders stated that this meeting was demoralizing and the Administration was dismissive to the stakeholders present, who have many years of experience in the system," the report says.

"In fact, it was expressed that the morale amongst these principals was as low as they could ever remember."

Some school board members have complained that Joseph never addressed allegations about his conduct or concerns about Pertiller.

At the most recent board meeting, the director said he has not done more to follow up on those specific allegations because the board has not provided him with "guidance on how we can best engage with the legal firm."

He has not publicly asked the board for such guidance.

Pay disparities

Joseph also hired friends or friends of his top staff, paying them above the district's approved pay scales.

Cumberland Elementary principal Carolyn Cobbs, who has a master's degree, gets paid a base salary of $120,000 a year. The official schedule shows her pay should top out at $108,103.

In fact, several longtime elementary principals with doctorate degrees are capped at $111,376.

A longtime MNPS administrator has filed a complaint and is threatening to sue the district.

Failing to fix those kinds of disparities, Bone McAllester warned, "would be unconscionable."

Joseph has not indicated that he has any plans to follow that recommendation.

Questionable contracts

Joseph pushed his team to sign two no-bid contracts -- totaling $1.8 million -- with Performance Matters, a Maryland company with which he had previously done business.

He had previously appeared in a promotional video for the company.

Emails show Joseph began discussing a potential deal with Performance Matters two weeks before he officially started his position as Director of Schools. Performance Matters suggested "piggybacking" on a recently awarded Shelby County contract to avoid bidding.

One of those contracts - $1 million for software used to track student achievement - was awarded no bid, piggybacking on an out-of-state contract. That is prohibited under state law. Joseph blamed a procurement official for the error.

MNPS also signed a separate $500,000 contract with another company to write the questions for the student assessment software.

But, after signing those contracts for $1.5 million, Joseph's team did not require schools to use the software. MNPS claims it has no usage statistics, but admits usage was likely low.

The second contract - $845,651 for software used to track professional development training for teachers - was awarded to Performance Matters, piggybacking on a Shelby County contract.

Emails show the district could have continued to use its existing system for a much lower price.

MNPS admits it spent millions of dollars using piggyback contracts with favored vendors without checking to see whether they could get a better price – a practice that Metro Finance Director Talia Lomax-O'Neal said does not represent best practices.

In another deal, Discovery Education -- a Maryland company with ties to Joseph and his team -- was given the inside track for an $11.4 million contract for science and technology curriculum. The person who headed that program says MNPS worked with that company for months to develop a plan, used that plan to develop a Request for Proposals, then put the contract out for bids, giving competitors just four weeks to develop a counter-proposal. MNPS says that was not illegal.

A Metro audit also confirmed other consultants were hired without following bidding or contracting procedures, including a man with no formal education training who was given contracts for $105,000 to advise schools on standardized testing.

He had previously worked with Joseph in Maryland.

Misleading statements to the school board

Joseph outright denied that his personal connections with Performance Matters played any role in awarding contracts. He told the school board that the company was utilized because Shelby County Schools "had been using it historically."

"It's not something that we brought in, that was, we brought it in because we knew Performance Matters and said, 'Hey, here is a contract,'" Joseph said. "They were using it in the state effectively."

That was false.

In fact, emails show Performance Matters first pitched the idea of using the Shelby County contract to avoid competitive bidding on June 13, 2016. That contract with Shelby County wasn't signed until June 30, 2016.

At the most recent board meeting, Joseph changed his story that "it's not something that we brought in ... because we knew Performance Matters."

"Any board would understand that a CEO who has a track record of success in getting results will bring with him or her knowledge of services that have been successful," Joseph said.

The director did not address the fact that his administration spent $1.5 million to implement Performance Matters' student assessment software without requiring schools to use it.

At that same June 2018 board meeting, current MNPS Purchasing Director Jeff Gossage told the board that it was his "understanding" that Joseph's administration had used a piggyback contract with Performance Matters for the professional development software because "we didn't have time to conduct a normal Request For Proposal (RFP) process."

That also was false.

Emails show that then-Purchasing Director Gary Appenfelder informed Joseph's team that there was plenty of time for competitive bidding. That suggestion was ignored.

Neither Joseph nor anyone on his team made any effort to correct the current purchasing director's suggestion that there had been no time for bidding.

MNPS discipline crisis

Teachers all across MNPS describe "chaos" in the schools as a result of policies put in place by Joseph to reduce suspensions, especially for African-American students.

They say Joseph implemented the policy change without giving them the resources they need to deal with troubled children.

"Students are in school and they are disruptive and running through the halls. They are using profanity and hurting other students," said elementary school guidance counselor Constance Wade.

"You reduce discipline because we cannot suspend students. But by the same token, you've kind of opened up Pandora's box because students aren't always feeling like they get consequences so they continue."

Middle school teacher Sonji Collins said, "It's like a domino effect."

"When one child sees that nothing is going to happen, then the rest of them will follow suit. 'Oh well, nothing is going to happen to me because nothing happened to my classmate.'"

Both women are African-American.

Joseph himself acknowledged the problem in a recent meeting with support workers.

"I do see and hear of the escalating behaviors," he said. "I think we are seeing more aggressive behaviors than ever before."

Joseph did not accept that his own policies might have anything to do with it.

Instead, he blamed Nashville's increasing cost of living for increasing stress on families.

Election meddling

In the fall of 2018, during in-service training for bus drivers, Joseph was captured on an audio recording, hinting that they should vote against vice mayor candidate Sheri Weiner.

Weiner, who was acting vice mayor and running for election to the seat, had voted against a proposed property tax increase that would have given more money to schools.

"There was a tie. There was a tie, right? And then who breaks the tie? Is it the vice mayor? Yeah, it's the vice mayor," the school director told the bus drivers.

At that point, several drivers exclaimed: "Oh!"

Joseph continued, "We don't have to say it. We don't have to say it. There was a tie. There was a tie. There was a tiebreaker. All you've got to do is do a Google search, and search it. You'll figure it out."

He added, "I'm just saying it's important for you all to know the facts -- and vote."

Tennessee's "Little Hatch Act" makes it illegal for educators to engage in political activity during work hours or on government property.

Teacher Misconduct

Tennessee State Board of Education staff recommended a one-year suspension of Joseph's state license for failure to report teacher misconduct cases to the state.

The State Board identified a dozen cases that Metro Schools failed to report.

State law puts the responsibility on the Director of Schools.

Joseph argued the expectation is unrealistic, especially in a school system with 11,000 employees. His attorney promised to wage an aggressive defense.

Use of school bus driver

Since he arrived in Nashville, Joseph has used school transportation employees to chauffeur him around town – including for doctor's appointments and early morning breakfasts on his way into work. The person usually assigned to that duty was a school bus driver.

The director has faced criticism for pulling a bus driver from the streets at a time that the district faces a bus driver shortage and children are often left waiting for an hour or more in the evenings for a bus to take them home.

After almost three years, Joseph finally committed to using the bus driver only when he is not needed to drive students.

Lack of transparency

Shortly after Joseph arrived in Nashville, there were questions about the qualifications of some of the people he had brought with him from Maryland.

In one case, Joseph put a woman in charge of overseeing other principals even though she had never worked a full year as a lead principal anywhere. Her previous principal job ended in controversy after six months.

Another woman, put in charge of teacher training, had been in sales just five years before and had no classroom experience.

NewsChannel 5 Investigates submitted written questions about the employees' qualifications, but an email later showed that Joseph directed his staff not to answer those questions.

"I don't want us to respond," Joseph wrote. "If he does a story, we will follow up with a very direct statement towards his conduct . . . period."[56]

Resources

Quote 1 **Page i, 257** https://www.goodreads.com/quotes/987(Accessed, 2/3/21)

Quote 2 **Page i** https://www.brainyquote.com/quotes/wallis_simpson_127252 (Accessed, 2/3/21)

Quote 3 **Page i, 71** https://www.goodreads.com/quotes/19914- (Accessed, 2/3/21)

Quote 4 **Page 2** https://www.pinterest.com/pin/351984527101633085/ (Accessed, 2/3/21)

Quote 5 **Page 2** https://en.wikipedia.org/wiki/The_Ugly_Duckling (Accessed, 2/3/21)

Quote 6 **Page 8** https://www.forbes.com/quotes/1706/ (Accessed, 12/17/20)

Quote 7 **Page 15** https://www.azquotes.com/quote/450735 (Accessed, 11/8/20)

Quote 8 **Page 18** https://en.wikipedia.org/wiki/Requiem_for_a_Nun (Accessed, 2/3/21)

Quote 9 **Page 21** https://www.azquotes.com/quote/856561 (Accessed, 2/11/21)

Quote 10 **Page 26** https://www.brainyquote.com/quotes/dwight_d_eisenhower_136897 (Accessed, 2/4/21)

Quote 11 **Page 32** http://www.yoddler.com/page=/Quote&q=229#page=/Quote&q=22 (Accessed 10/7/20)

Quote 12 **Page 34** https://quotefancy.com/quote/866449/Maya-Angelou (Accessed, 2/13/21)

Quote 13 **Page 39** https://www.brainyquote.com/authors/dale-archer-quotes (Accessed, 3/1/21)

Quote 14 **Page 45** https://www.passiton.com/inspirational-quotes/7814 (Accessed, 2/3/21)

Quote 15 **Page 51** https://www.pinterest.com/pin/16466354865390118 (Accessed, 3/1/21)

Quote 16 **Page 57** https://www.pinterest.com/pin/16466354865390118 (Accessed, 3/1/21)

Quote 17 **Page 63** https://quotefancy.com/quote/1015139 (Accessed, 3/1/21)

Quote 18 **Page 65** https://quotefancy.com/quote/1015139/Maurice-Sendak (Accessed, 2/5/21)

Quote 19 **Page 68** https://www.brainyquote.com/quotes/willie_nelson_456986 (Accessed, 2/8/21)

Quote 20 **Page 75** https://www.goodreads.com/quotes/9584288 (Accessed, 2/5/21)

Quote 21 **Page 75** https://www.goodreads.com/en/book/show/1486118 (Accessed,3/6/21)

Quote 22 **Page 76** https://www.brainyquote.com/quotes/truman_capote_103858 (Accessed,1/7/21)

Quote 23 **Page 79** https://www.goodreads.com/quotes/9622884 (Accessed,12/15/20)

Quote 24 **Page 80** https://www.quotemaster.org/qadcddf00ef8c4696d9232cc26f06fc08 (Accessed, 2/14/21)

Quote 25 **Page 83** https://en.wikipedia.org/wiki/Saint_Cecilia (Accessed, 2/5/21)

Quote 26 **Page 86** https://quotefancy.com/quote/1640244/Jane-Fulton-Alt- (Accessed, 3/4/21)

Quote 27 **Page 89** https://en.wikipedia.org/wiki/Kenneth_Jones (Accessed, 3/3/21)

Quote 28 **Page 90** https://www.brainyquote.com/quotes/rose_kennedy_134996 (Accessed, 2/6/21)

Quote 29 **Page 92** https://www.brainyquote.com/quotes/martin_buber_133855 (Accessed, 1/18/21)

Quote 30 **Page 99** https://www.brainyquote.com/quotes/rumi_597890 (Accessed, 3/1/21)

Quote 31 **Page 103** https://www.simonandschuster.com/books/On-Death-and-Dying/Elisabeth-Kubler-Ross/ 9781476775548 (Accessed, 2/19/21)

Quote 32 **Page 109** https://www.123stitch.com/item/Impression-Obsession-Loss-Immeasurable (Accessed, 2/19/21)

Quote 33 **Page 111** https://twitter.com/glennondoyle/status/1249408706871205891?lang=en (Accessed, 2/17/21)

Quote 34 **Page 116** https://dc.etsu.edu/cgi/viewcontent.cgi?article=4078&context=etd (Accessed, 2/17/21)

Quote 35 **Page 120** https://quotefancy.com/quote/1229740/S-I-Hayakawa- (Accessed, 3/5/21)

Quote 36 **Page 126** https://en.wikipedia.org/wiki/The_Very_Hungry_Caterpillar (Accessed, 3/5/21)

Quote 37 **Page 129** https://www.goodreads.com/quotes/915574 (Accessed, 3/5/21)

Quote 38 **Page 132** https://quotecatalog.com/quote/unknown- (Accessed, 3/5/21)

Source 39 **Page 133** https://www.newspapers.com/clip/82219601/jill-waddell-teacher/ (Accessed, 4/5/21)

Quote 40 **Page 134** https://www.heinemann.com/products/e00525.aspx (Accessed, 4/5/21)

Quote 41 **Page 1135** https://www.heinemann.com/products/e00461.aspx (Accessed, 4/5/21)

Source 42 **Page 136** https://scholarworks.wmich.edu/cgi/viewcontent.cgi?article=1717&context=reading_horizons (Accessed, 1/14/20)

Quote 43 **Page 143** https://www.pinterest.com/pin/656962664383842592/(Accessed, 2/17/21)

Quote 44 **Page 150** https://quoteinvestigator.com/2014/09/02/job-love/ (Accessed, 4/4/21)

Quote 45 **Page 153** https://www.goodreads.com/quotes/750708- (Accessed, 4/4/21)

Quote 46 **Page 157** https://www.bible.com/bible/116/PRO.31.8-9.NLT(Accessed, 1/8/21)

Quote 47 **Page 161** https://www.goodreads.com/quotes/236965-i-like-the-night-without-the-dark-we-d- (Accessed, 6/4/21)

Quote 48 **Page 174** https://www.brainyquote.com/quotes/kate_dicamillo_367106 (Accessed, 3/21/20)

Quote 49 **Page 180** https://www.highpoint.edu/blog/2014/05/general-colin-powell-addresses-hpus-class-of-2014/ (Accessed, 4/9/20)

Quote 50 **Page 188** https://www.goodreads.com/quotes/798495-the-pessimist-complains-about-the-wind-

Quote 51 **Page 194** https://www.brainyquote.com/quotes/paul_sweeney_104325 (Accessed, 3/14/21)

Quote 52 **Page 198** https://www.goodreads.com/quotes/243053-you-do-not-need-to-know-precisely-what-is-happening (Accessed, 11/6/20)

Quote 53 **Page 202** https://www.simplypsychology.org/vygotsky.html Accessed, 2/4/21)

Quote 54 **Page 205** https://www.unl.edu/general-john-j-pershing-display/ (Accessed, 2/4/21)

Quote 55 **Pages 206, 227** https://www.newschannel5.com/news/newschannel-5-investigates/former-mnps-administrator-people-need-to-know-the-truth- (Accessed, 3/30/21)

Quote 56 **Pages 206, 209, 220, 231, 236, 260** https://www.newschannel5.com/news/newschannel-5-investigates/what-you-need-to-know-about-shawn-josephs-controversies (Accessed, 2/26/21)

Quote 57 **Page 211** https://www.newschannel5.com/news/newschannel-5-investigates/school-directors-rap-song-sparks-new-controversy

Quote 58 **Page 213** https://www.edweek.org/teaching-learning/survey-teacher-job-satisfaction-hits-a-low-point/2012/03 (Accessed, 2/25/21)

Quote 59 **Page 214** https://www.goodreads.com/quotes/1324527-a-smooth-sea-never-made-a-skilled-sailor (Accessed, 1/15/21)

Quote 60 **Page 214** https://www.marinecorpstimes.com/news/your-marine-corps/2017/03/30/marines-are-once- (Accessed, 1/15/21)

Quote 61 **Page 218** https://www.nps.gov/frde/learn/photosmultimedia/quotations.htm (Accessed, 1/22/21)

Quote 62 **Page 220** https://www.youtube.com/watch?v=9pEVF7uOwxM&t=3635s (2nd round of interviews) May 10, 2016

Quote 63 **Page 221** https://www.youtube.com/watch?v=S6GNkxRyw4s"(Accessed, 6/15/21)

Quote 64 **Page 222** https://www.newschannel5.com/news/75-million-missing-from-mnps-budget (Accessed, 6/15/21)

Quote 65 **Page 222** https://www.tennessean.com/story/news/2019/04/18/nashville-population-growth-slows-2018/3498194002/ (Accessed, 6/15/21)

Quote 66 **Page 222** https://www.tennessean.com/story/news/education/2018/03/08/nashville-schools-placed-under-purchasing-freeze/406837002/ (Accessed, 6/15/21)

Quote 67 **Page 222** https://www.newschannel5.com/news/paper-outage-at-school-blamed-on-confusion-highlights-mnps-budget-shortfall (Accessed, 2/11/21)

Quote 68 **Page 223** https://www.pinterest.com/pin/694187730053145175/ (Accessed, 7/13/21)

Quote 69 **Page 224** https://www.youtube.com/watch?v=WFggsdCgQGQ (Accessed, 4/16/18)

Quote 70 **Page 225** https://news.vanderbilt.edu/2016/10/25/spending-more-on-pre-k-doesnt-guarantee-success-report/ (Assessed, 4/27/20)

Quote 71 **Page 226, 227** www.hanoverresearch.com (Accessed, 4/16/21)

Quote 72 **Page 227** *WWC* https://ies.ed.gov/ncee/wwc/WhatWeDo (Accessed, 4/27/20)

Quote 73 **Page 227, 228** https://readingrecovery.osu.edu/learn/Reading_Recovery_Overview.pdf (Accessed, 8/7/20)

Quote 74 **Page 228** https://www.cpre.org/reading-recovery-evaluation-four-year-i3-scale (Accessed, 8/7/20)

Quote 75 **Page 230** https://www.goodreads.com/quotes/9653803-there-s-no-straight-line-between-effort-and-reward (Accessed, 1/17/21)

Quote 76 **Page 230** https://www.newschannel5.com/news/newschannel-5-investigates/new-settlements-put-mnps-sexual-harassment-bills-near-2-million (Accessed, 3/14/21)

Quote 77 **Page 231, 232** https://www.goodreads.com/quotes/103315-the-wound-is-the-place-where-the-light-enters (Accessed, 3/14/21)

Quote 78 **Page 231** https://www.newschannel5.com/news/newschannel-5-investigates/metro-schools/shawn-joseph-ends-journey-dotted-with-legal-ethical-issues (Accessed, 3/14/21)

Quote 79 **Page 235** https://www.tennessean.com/get-access/?return=https%3A%2F%2Fwww.tennessean.com%2Fstory%2Fopinion%2F2019%2F01%2F08%2Fnashville-school-board-jill-speering-circus-atmosphere-shawn-joseph%2F2512728002%2F (Accessed, 3/15/21)

Quote 80 **Page 236** https://www.tennessean.com/story/news/2019/02/06/nashville-council-wont-intervene-school-board-member-masks-comment/2768394002/ (Accessed, 11/15/20)

Quote 81 **Page 237** https://tntribune.com/school-board-members-frogge-and-speering-big-on-policy-if-it-doesnt-apply-to-them/ (Accessed, 6/7/21)

Quote 82 **Page 237** https://www.newschannel5.com/news/newschannel-5-investigates/mnps-faces-morale-crisis-confidential-report-warns (Accessed, 3/4/21)

Quote 83 **Page 238** https://www.goodreads.com/quotes/471726-censorship-is-the-child-of-fear-and-the-father- (Accessed, 4/12/21)

Quote 84 **Page 238** https://www.newschannel5.com/news/newschannel-5-investigates/metro-schools/school-board-approves-shawn-josephs-364-000-severance-deal-non-disparagement-agreement (Accessed, 4/13/21)

Quote 85 **Page 239, 240** https://threadreaderapp.com/thread/1305974067573518338.html (Accessed, 4/14/21)

Quote 86 **Page 239** https://horwitz.law/attorneys/daniel-a-horwitz/ (Accessed, 4/14/21)

Quote 87 **Pages 239, 240** https://danielhorwitz.com/category/first-amendment/ (Accessed, 4/12/21)

Quote 88 **Page 244** https://www.goodreads.com/quotes/21690-there-are-far-far-better-things-ahead-than-any- (Accessed, 5/15/21)

Quote 89 **Page 245** https://www.scmp.com/news/china/society/article/2145372/child-suicide-covered-china-says-think-tank-it-calls-authorities (Accessed, 4/12/21)

Quote 90 **Page 250** https://en.wikipedia.org/wiki/Decodable_text (Accessed, 3/24/21)

Quote 91 **Page 242** https://www.goodreads.com/quotes/7759967-above-all-don-t-lie-to-yourself-the-man-who-lies (Accessed, 4/23/21)

Quote 92 **Page 242, 243, 254** https://www.facebook.com/arbingerinstitute/videos/833206530510706 (Accessed, 4/23/21)

Quote 93 **Page 242** https://arbinger.com/approach.html (Accessed, 4/23/21)

Quote 94 **Page 253** https://quotefancy.com/quote/1323292/Anthony-de-Mello-The-spiritual-quest-is-a-journey-without-distance-You-travel-from-where (Accessed, 2/6/21)

Quote 95 **Page 256** https://en.wikipedia.org/wiki/Koru (Accessed, 3/31/20)

Image 96 **Page 256** https://commons.wikimedia.org/wiki/File:Koru_Unfurling.JPG Koru_Unfurling.jpg Image by Radoff, Jon, Copyright © 2000,2001,2002 Free Software Foundation, Inc. (Accessed July 2021)

Quote 97 **Page 259** https://www.brainyquote.com/quotes/swami_vivekananda_213406 (Accessed, 4/9/21)

Quote 98 **Back Cover** https://www.google.com/search?q=ss.&aqs=chrome..69i57.1409j0j15&sourceid=chrome&ie=UTF-8 (Accessed, 5/23/21)

Acknowledgments

To MY PRECIOUS HUSBAND, DAN, who took up the slack at home with shopping, cooking and cleaning as I cloistered myself in my office - writing. You are precious! Thanks for your understanding and support. I look forward to getting back to you!

My life has transformed due to many people. To my brother, Bobby, I owe the greatest debt for making this book possible. My brother's contributions have been invaluable in the writing of this book. Bobby and his wife, Anne Gayle Farley Smith, shared many personal accounts of Bobby's adult life that touched my heart. She and Bobby read each of my early drafts. Their encouragement, questions, and suggestions prompted me to continue writing.

Deep appreciation to my dearest friend and sister, Phyllis O'Neill. From the beginning, she reminded me that I was not only writing my story, but in many ways, it was also hers.

My cousins have willingly answered questions and shared their own extended-family research with me. Much appreciation to Fran Stribling for sharing her knowledge of the Redman family, to Lyn Neal Walker and Vivian Valencourt for answering questions about the Neals.

Without John Ed Garrett's vision and support, this book would not have become a reality. In addition to his encouragement, he showed me the way to publication. His entire family has been instrumental in the production of this manuscript. Carol Blackmon, an outstanding educator, and master of Google Docs was always available when I needed help. She read my entire book to me orally so that I could listen with a different ear. Much appreciation to Nancy Adams Arnold for her exquisite cover design, layout design, and production.

Melanie Ladd, my dearest friend, was encouraging throughout the entire process. I greatly appreciated her suggestions and questions that spurred more revisions. Dr. Victoria Risko and her magnificent husband Dr. Marino Alvarez have mentored me through my years in education and on the board. Their expertise and leadership have made me a better teacher. Even while recuperating from surgery, Vicki took the time to offer valuable feedback on my manuscript.

Amy Frogge has been my closest companion through my work on the board and the writing of this memoir. Thank you for your wonderful editing suggestions.

Other editors and proofreaders include Dr. Kevin Stacy, Bea Leff, Ali Palumbo, Dr. Tammy Lipsey, Laurie O'Shea, and Emily Masters.

About the Author

Jill Speering*

A 35-year educator, Jill served on the Metro Nashville Public Schools Board for eight years when she met a tyrant like her father, and the forgiveness lessons continued.

In 1984, Speering earned the title of Master Teacher through the Tennessee Career Ladder program when she achieved the highest status - Career Ladder III. In 2006 she was named Exemplary Educator of the Year for Middle Tennessee. Speering has shared her vast literacy knowledge in school districts across the state. She has presented at local, state, national and international conferences. Speering is the author of an educational research case study, multiple magazine and newspaper articles. This is her first book.

Mother of two daughters, she is the grandmother of four children and great grandmother to one. Speering lives in Nashville, Tennessee with her husband, Dan.

You may reach Jill at:

jillspeering@gmail.com

https://twitter.com/jillspeering

Facebook.com/JillSpeeringNashville

---

*Photo by Gary Layda, used by permission from the Metro Nashville Board of Education.